Gao Village Revisited

Gao Village Revisited

The Life of Rural People in Contemporary China

Mobo C. F. Gao

The Chinese University Press

Gao Village Revisited:
The Life of Rural People in Contemporary China
By Mobo C. F. Gao

ISBN: 978-962-996-578-5 (hardcover)
       978-988-237-109-5 (paperback)

Published by The Chinese University Press
              The Chinese University of Hong Kong
              Sha Tin, N.T., Hong Kong
              Fax: +852 2603 7355
              Email: cup@cuhk.edu.hk
              Website: www.chineseupress.com

Printed in Hong Kong

Contents

Preface

This book is a sequel to *Gao Village* (1999, 2014) and is an update starting from 1997, when *Gao Village* left off. However, this book is very different from *Gao Village*, not only in terms of structure but also in content. The first Gao Village book, which "has put the village on the map" in the words of comments from a couple of readers, arranged the content in terms of themes such as education, health care, the Great Leap Forward, and the Cultural Revolution, whereas this book focuses on individual personalities. Thus, there is a chapter on the poorest in the village, a man named Gao Lati; a chapter on the richest person, Gao Wenshu; and two chapters on one of my brothers, Gao Changxian, and his wife, Gao Mingxia, when I discuss the Gao clan-run hotel business. The rationale for this arrangement is my belief that in the Mao era, Gao Village was vertically organized, whereas in the post-Mao era China, it is horizontally organized. Many Gao villagers do not live and work in the village anymore, but are scattered all over the country. The personal lives of Gao Changxian, Gao Mingxia, and Gao Wenshu reflect both what is happening in and outside Gao Village. These personal stories not only demonstrate, but are also related to, changes in other parts of China.

It is interesting and also relevant to mention, however briefly, two aspects of readers' responses to the first Gao Village book. The first aspect is that reviews of the English version of the book are more positive than comments from readers of the Chinese version. In China, formal reviews of *Gao Village* (which was later translated into Chinese and published by the Chinese University Press in 2014) were rarely seen as the book is unofficially banned, but the occasional comments on social media are passionately divided: those who like it, like it and those who don't, hate it. This leads to the second aspect of the responses: those of the left political persuasion have been more sympathetic with the book, whereas the anti-communist and anti-Mao readers tend to be condemning. In other words, readers take positions: Maurice Meisner (a Marxist scholar), for instance, commented in a personal communication to me that *Gao Village* was "the best village study in the field"; no Chinese liberals would ever be so generous. The fact that the Chinese "liberal" intelligentsia would publish commentaries in the influential *Nanfang Zhoumo* newspaper condemning the book without even having read it was not surprising.

Of course, many critiques of *Gao Village* are not political, at least not overtly or consciously. Some are critical of *Gao Village* due to their conceptual approach. The economic rationalist approach, especially the neoliberal kind, for instance, would not be inclined to accept my description of education and health care during the Cultural Revolution years as the "golden period" in Gao Village, because their approach dictates that only free market systems and private ownership of means of production can be the most efficient in allocating resources. The post-Mao Chinese political and intellectual elite who genuinely wanted to say farewell to the concept of revolution—and not to just the 1949 Revolution but any revolution, including the French Revolution—would be least likely to accept my description. They in fact go further, according to comments made on social media, and accuse me of defending the inhumane Cultural Revolution by ignoring my qualification that it was the "golden period" within the context of Gao Village and only in the areas of education and health care. Some Chinese commentators even engaged in personal attacks, to which I did not think it was worth responding.

However, writing *Gao Village Revisited* is in many ways my response to the concerned readers of the first Gao Village book. I have received requests from time to time from readers who would like to read an update of the village, including high school students and people who attended my talks on Gao Village, such as my talk in 2017 at the Hopkins-Nanjing Center for Chinese and American Studies. This book also addresses my rather negative portrayal of rural China from the late 1980s to the late 1990s, which was not a Maoist defense but a socio-economic concern for the rural Chinese who were at the very bottom of society; my concern for the future direction of rural China; my adopted methodology, which is not only "thickly descriptive" but also trans-disciplinary, a methodology that it is often claimed to have merit but is very difficult to practice, as scholars are by definition trained in a single discipline; and my aspiration for a conceptual approach to understand China that is not only "Chinese" but also global. More of this is expressed in the appendix.

Finally, I would like to take this opportunity to acknowledge my debt to those who have contributed to the final product of this book, while realizing the impossibility of including them all. First of all, I would like to thank my relatives and Gao villagers, Gao Changxian, Gao Mingxia, Gao Changwen, Gao Wenshu, Gao Lati, and all the others mentioned in the book, for their assistance and their hospitality. Second, I would like to thank the many Gao villagers who are not mentioned but with whom I spoke and who helped me with personal or village information. Thirdly, I thank Kathrin House who read and edited every chapter of the draft before I handed it in to the publisher. I would also like to express my gratitude to the reviewers of the book commissioned by the publisher, who took the trouble not only to read the draft but also made comments, all of which were valuable and enabled improvement of the final product. May I also thank Dr. Lian Jia, who read the draft from time to time and encouraged me along the way. Let me further thank the publisher, The Chinese University Press, for commissioning this book, not only in English but also a Chinese version that will follow. Finally, I thank the publisher's editors Roberta Raine and Rachel Pang for their painstaking and meticulous editing and rigorous comments, which have further improved the manuscript and helped to turn it into this book. They are the kind of editors that every publisher should have.

It goes without saying that any errors and mistakes are my own.

The Gao Family Tree

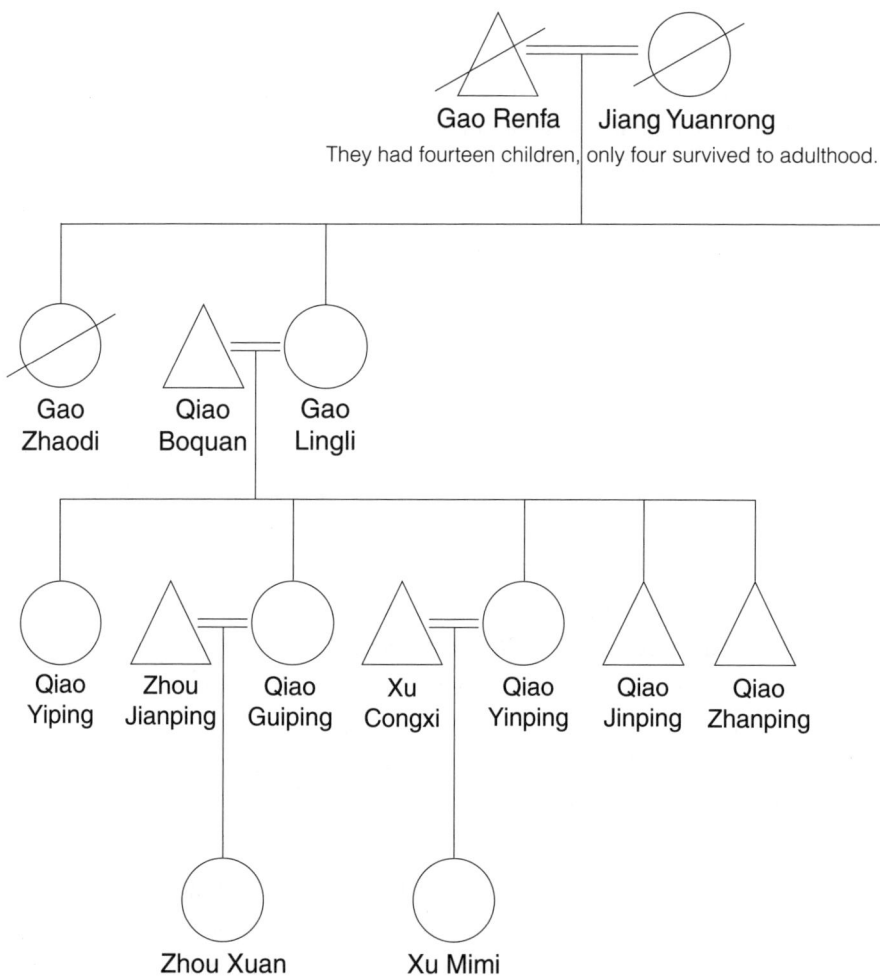

Gao Renfa | Jiang Yuanrong

They had fourteen children, only four survived to adulthood.

Gao Zhaodi

Qiao Boquan | Gao Lingli

Qiao Yiping

Zhou Jianping | Qiao Guiping

Xu Congxi | Qiao Yinping

Qiao Jinping

Qiao Zhanping

Zhou Xuan

Xu Mimi

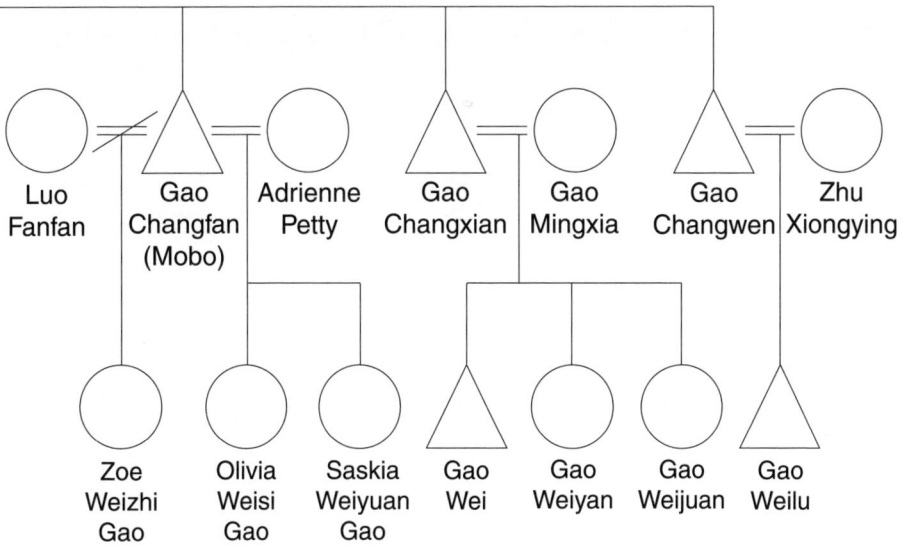

CHAPTER 1

Introduction: Why Gao Village?

A century from now, when historians are arguing about how China came from nowhere to become one of the most powerful economies in the world, they will assess the impact of culture, ideology, leadership and globalisation. But how will they weigh the dogged ambition of hundreds of millions of farmers who poured off China's fields to claim a different destiny?

"The Village and the Girl," *BBC News*, Carrie Gracie, 2015

China's recent dramatic and paradigm-shifting economic development has been hailed as a miracle in the news. At the same time, there has been no shortage of predictions that the Chinese political regime is going to collapse and that the Chinese economy is going to go bust (Chang 2001; Shambaugh 2015). There are, of course, optimists who tend to overestimate China's economic development and over-praise the Chinese regime's capacity for survival. Let me declare my interest up front: I do not wish for the collapse of China. The fact that I do not wish for China's fall has nothing to do with Chinese nationalism, a sentiment that some Westerners and some Chinese inside China assume that so-called overseas Chinese hold (Gao 2008b). Nobody should wish for the collapse of China, no matter how anti-Communist or anti-China they are, because the collapse of China would not only mean disaster and misery for millions and millions of ordinary Chinese, but also more problems for the world, including the affluent West.

To look for the reasons behind China's economic success, one should not always look at China's individual leaders. Of course, government policies are important, but there are other factors that are perhaps equally, if not more, significant. In the case of China, one is always tempted to look at the Chinese leadership in Beijing for answers, but the top leadership in China may well not be the main reason for China's economic success. For instance, it is hard to pin down exactly what former President Jiang Zemin or his successor President Hu Jintao did to boost China's economic development (Gao 2012). Former Premier Wen Jiabao was talked of in Chinese social media as an actor who always *zuo xiu* ("acts right"), pretending to be righteous, intellectual, and liberal.[1] The internal dynamics of the market economy with a strong state-owned enterprise (SOE) sector has its own logic and will develop in a certain direction without much wisdom from top leaders, or perhaps even despite their follies. One can argue that Deng Xiaoping was not, in fact, the father of modern China and its reform, as assumed by many in and outside China (Vogel 2011). As for the present leadership under President Xi Jinping and Premier Li Keqiang, the jury is still out.

I also think that Westerners in general have a skewed perception or impression of China because Western reporting of China, from which most understanding of China is derived, focuses on two things: elite politics and Chinese dissident opposition to the Chinese government, such as Liu Xiaobo (Gao 2012), or more recently the visually impaired lawyer Chen Guangcheng. Peter Hessler, an American who has lived and worked in China for 11 years, far away from the urban centers of the first-tier Chinese cities, and who became the "most influential popular writer on China for decades," observes that the dissidents who are opposed to the Chinese Communist Party (CCP) are "poorly

---

1   An example of Wen being politically "righteous" is his speech at the Royal Society in London in 2011, during which he condemned the CCP, the ruling party of which he was not only a main leader but also a huge beneficiary, by declaring that the Cultural Revolution had brought 10 years of *haojie* (holocaust or calamities) to the Chinese people.

connected and often dysfunctional" (Johnson 2015). Hessler's opinion on this may be seen by many as single-minded, but it is true, as Ian Johnson comments:

> Many readers realize intuitively that if China were a country primarily defined by the troubles reported in the media, it would be a basket case. Yet this does not match the rising power they know of from their shopping malls or workplaces. (Johnson 2015)

As a migrant from China, I am intensely concerned about China, not entirely because China is my place of origin, but because I have an extended family still living there and because my occupation of teaching and research is about China. This book demonstrates my concerns: my personal concern about my extended family and Gao villagers and the concern of a social scientist about the future of China. Hence, the title of this book has two parts: *Gao Village Revisited: The Life of Rural People in Contemporary China*.

The overall aim of the book is two-fold: First, it aims to provide an explanation of China's economic success, but an explanation from the grassroots, from the individuals who are not political dissidents but who took advantage of opportunities to make a better living. Second, it aims to offer a conjecture on the future direction of rural China. It is true that the post-Mao economic reforms have set up the platform for China's final economic takeoff, but there is no miracle, as it is often claimed. The post-Mao reforms provided the environment and channels, but the hard work, including the hard work done in the time of Mao, such as agricultural infrastructure and a comprehensive industrial base, was done from the bottom up. As for the future, China is not going to collapse that easily, not the way that you read in news headlines or comments from think tanks. How am I going to prove that and how will my proof be convincing? That is what I have set myself to do in this book. I want to do this by engaging with the non-elite Chinese individuals, whose concerns, feelings, and behavior are different in just about every way from myself, but the understanding and sympathy of which are not only required, but also essential.

Map 1. Location of Gao Village (drawn by Saskia Gao)

Different Regions, Different Chinas

As one of my politician friends from South Australia commented after a three-week visit to China, "China is a world of itself. It does not need help from others." However, others, mostly Westerners, always want to help, either to spread the Gospel to save the Chinese by bringing them to God or to civilize the Chinese by teaching them the value of human rights and democracy. It is this desire to help by Western politicians, academics, journalists, do-gooders or whoever, to transform the Chinese into their own image, that perpetuates their understanding and interpretations of China. But China has to be understood and interpreted on its own terms. For this very reason, I have been pondering a question for a long time as I travel between China and the West, as I do my fieldwork, and as I talk to the people who live in Gao Village. The question is: What are the ingredients for China's seeming economic success?

Once as I was walking in Panyu, an expanding suburb of Guangzhou, I saw a little girl crawling like a dog in and out of a garage door that was only slightly raised. Then I realized that a family was living in that tiny garage and the door was raised up only a little so that the family could have some privacy. The child seemed happy, and above the garage there was a beautifully painted three-story house. Each story had a balcony that was decorated with colorful flowerpots. The owners of the house lived upstairs and the garage was rented to this migrant worker family.

This scenario is not unusual in Guangdong Province. As assembly lines and sweatshops were set up all over Guangdong, initially by Hong Kong and Taiwan business people, and later by mainland Chinese themselves, land values skyrocketed. The local residents, who were farmers, had become wealthy overnight, simply because they happened to be there. They have built lavish houses on the basis of the increase in their land values and have become "de-ruralized." They might set up a shop or might not, but they have become wealthy enough not to have to farm anymore. If there is any more land left for farming, they will get migrant workers from inland China to do the work, and if they want more income, they simply rent some of their houses, like the little garage that I have just described.

This arrangement of renting out a garage shows the resourcefulness of both the tenants and the landlord. It is more than that, however. Why would a family want to live in a garage? Why would they migrate to Guangdong to live a life like that? This is what we mean when we say China is a world of its own, because there are so many layers of differences in China. There are first-tier cities, like Shanghai, Beijing, Shenzhen, and Guangzhou. There are second-tier cities like Nanjing, Jinan or Zhengzhou, and there are third-tier cities like Xi'an, Guiyang or Urumqi. There is a difference between Zhejiang, Jiangsu, and Guangdong provinces and Jiangxi, Henan, and Hunan provinces. There is also a difference between Shanxi and Shaanxi provinces, and a difference between Hebei and Ningxia. It is because of geography and history that these different areas have different industries, different levels of economic development, and even different lifestyles.

In addition, there are many differences between what is called urban and rural in China. People divided by different political and economic conditions have different educations, housing, mentalities, and lifestyles. Industry is more highly valued than agriculture; until very recently, rural industry was created to subsidize urban areas, state budgetary planning has typically been skewed in favor of the urban sector, and the rural sector has been left to take care of itself in issues like roads, health care, and education.

Furthermore, in any area, urban or rural, there are different classes of people. There are the rich and powerful, the self-made entrepreneurs, and the unemployed. There are global travelers who go all over the world on business-class flights, and there are beggars in the streets. There are tourists who visit the Sydney Opera House on one trip and shop at Harrods on another, and then there are people who struggle to find enough money to buy a bowl of noodles. There are those who go to Las Vegas or Macau to gamble hundreds of thousands of dollars away in the blink of an eye, and there are those who pull a rickshaw so that they can save enough money for their children's textbooks.

Is this fair? No. Do the Chinese complain? Yes. But most rural Chinese (who are the majority in China), like the Gao villagers that I know, try very hard to improve themselves, in different ways under different circumstances. It is this uneven development in different areas and the unfair circumstances of different people—and above all, their drive for self-improvement, just like the garage arrangement mentioned above—that gives China the vitality that sustains not only the country's unity but also its seemingly miraculous economic development.

The Resourcefulness of Rural Chinese

The Chinese government has been making use of the resources that have been developed as a result of Chinese traditional values such as hard work, placing importance on self-improvement and education, having a purpose in life, and a drive for commerce and accumulating wealth. It is for this reason that I am not pessimistic about China. I am particularly encouraged by the resourcefulness of the rural Chinese. They are the backbone of China and it is their resourcefulness and inner strength that makes the economy tick. Time and again I find this resourcefulness and inner strength among Gao villagers when I go back to undertake research. This book is about how that quality has played out in the transformation of China.

The following quote by Song Dong offers a good example of the resourcefulness of the rural Chinese. Song is an artist whose work has been exhibited in many countries including India, America, and Brazil. He recounts his mother saying:

> A piece of paper can first be used to practice calligraphy or write math exercises on, after which it can be used to make paper toys for children. Then the same piece of paper can be re-used to wrap things up. After that it can be further used to wipe a dirty table or furniture, after which it can be used again to wipe the mud floor. Finally the same piece of paper can be used as firewood. (Chen 2011, E21–22)

I believe that such resourcefulness is a crucial ingredient in the success of contemporary China. It is because of this invisible but widespread resourcefulness among rural Chinese people that I think the Chinese economy is not as fragile as it looks from the outside.

The Rural Chinese Are Looking After the Government

For all the injustice, inequality, and unfairness, for all the lack of equity, corruption, and abuse of power, and for all the misery and suffering, the majority of Chinese, including those at the bottom of society, seem happy, content, and full of purpose. Yes, there are *fangmin*, people who travel from poor rural areas to urban centers where the authorities are located to *shangfang*—i.e., to complain and ask for redress for perceived injustices. But the very fact that there are *fangmin* means that they believe there is still a sense of justice and that justice can be obtained. Yes, there are dissidents who complain, as well as the many angry voices you can hear on social media. Yes, there have been suicides at sweatshops like Foxconn, and there are strikes like the one that happened at a Honda factory. Nonetheless, most would agree that China still has one of the lowest crime rates in the world. Moreover, most crimes are committed by the poor against the poor, and by the disadvantaged against the more disadvantaged (Bakken 2000).

Why? That is one of the secrets of China's economic success: the resourcefulness and the struggle of the Chinese people to improve their lives, especially the rural Chinese, like the garage tenant family. They do not blame others for their hard lives and they do not think others owe them a living. They want to work hard to make it. It is hard now, but it will be better.

Everyone tries to do something to make a living. For example, a motorcyclist at the entrance to a busy road will wait to take you to the other side of town for RMB 3, less than US 50 cents. If you cannot afford a taxi, or if you do not want to take a taxi, or if you do not want to wait for a bus, why not get a ride? Or a person has set up a sewing machine on the pavement: do you want to mend a button? It's only RMB 0.5. Do you need your shoes repaired right now? There is a guy along the road who will do it for RMB 1. Do you want a pancake with an egg on top? You can buy it for RMB 5 and have it in a couple of minutes. These people, either from rural China or the urban unemployed (although it is more likely they are the former, because in most cities the unemployed have some minimum allowances, which exceed what can be earned by these street businesses), may make just enough to buy a bowl of noodles, but it is better than nothing.

The dynamics and vitality are just incredible and in many ways mind-boggling. You can get someone to clean your house for almost nothing, by Western standards. On many street corners in Shenzhen, I found cardboard notices announcing free collection of any rubbish, because almost everything can be recycled for some amount of money. In our flat in Shenzhen, there was a huge abandoned fish tank. I thought it would be almost impossible for us to dispose of it without some major operation involving trucks and so on. But one of these street peddlers came by, and like a miracle, everything disappeared without us doing anything. If you walk around the city, you will notice a lot of stickers on the pavements that are not much bigger than a small mobile phone. You might think they are rubbish thrown away by passers-by, but if you read them, you will find that they are advertisements, with the service and telephone number specified.

It is quite likely that the family I noticed living in that garage has been working hard and accumulating money, and in a few years, with help from other sources such as loans or gifts, they will build a three-story house back in their home town. If the estimated 200 to 400 million rural Chinese spread across China all live and work like this, you can see the enormous impact it would have on the country's economy. The Chinese government does not need to spend a cent to look after these poor and disadvantaged people. Instead, these people are looking after China, taking care of the Chinese government. They are also making commodities cheaper for people all over the world.

Through their resourcefulness, hard work, and struggle to create a better future for their children, these people not only help themselves survive, but also drive the Chinese economy forward, making China one of the world's major exporting countries, improving life for urban people, and allowing the elite more leisure time. Furthermore, they prop up the real-estate boom, which increases demand for concrete, steel, and everything else associated with building construction. The stories of the Gao villagers illustrate the continuing rise of the real-estate industry in rural China.

For some, these introductory remarks of mine about the resourcefulness of rural Chinese may sound too romantic. Others may find them too culturally deterministic, and for still others, my praise of the contribution made by the rural Chinese may be too un-Marxist. While these worries are not unwarranted, let me try to dispel some possible misunderstandings. First, while emphasizing rural people's hard work and resourcefulness, I am not saying they are the sole factor in China's economic success. The urban working class has also made great contributions in both the Mao and post-Mao eras. They are also resourceful and hardworking. Second, the rural Chinese are not peasantry anymore, and migrant workers are a large part of China's working class. Rural Chinese in this book are therefore not just the people who are physically dwelling in rural areas but also migrant workers who don't have urban resident status. Finally, economic policies designed by the post-Mao Chinese elite were successful not only because they were dependent on the foundations laid down during the Mao era, but also because of the work done by the people, the majority of whom are rural. Of course, entrepreneurship cannot be brought into full play unless a suitable macro-policy environment is provided. For instance, the family with the little girl in the garage would not have been there had the Chinese government still prohibited their travel. Policies have to be acted upon and have to be responded to by agents. How agents act upon a certain policy depends on what resources they can employ. Resourcefulness accumulated in a culture is one of the most important types of cultural capital, as the chapters on individual entrepreneurs will demonstrate.

Of course, hard work alone, like digging the earth harder with a spade, does not lead to higher yields or iron-ore finds. Economic takeoff requires trade, in which you export something you have, like labor, to get something you don't have, like a Boeing 737. To get higher yields or find iron ore, you need technology. But to pay for the trade and acquire that technology, you need to work hard and work resourcefully. It is this aspect of the ingredients of China's economic success that I am stressing.[2]

Wei Ran's Discovery

The story of Wei Ran and his discovery of rural China is a further illustration of what I mean about the quality of rural people. Wei Ran[3]

---

2   Here I thank the anonymous reviewers for leading me to address these issues.

3   蔚然 are the characters for this name.

was a typical urban "white collar" professional. What happened in 1991 changed his life. In that year he went to a rural village in Gansu Province, on a casual visit on behalf of his colleague. In order to treat him to a good meal, the poor villagers collected RMB 11 and bought one kilogram of pork to cook for him. Of the RMB 11, the biggest note was only 20 cents. Wei was so shocked by the villagers' poverty on the one hand and so moved by their generosity on the other that he wanted to know more about these people. Therefore, in 2006, he started his planned journey of visiting 10,000 of the poorest villages by bicycle. After more than four years, Wei had managed to visit a little more than 4,000 villages, written journal entries totaling more than 1,000 pages, taken more than 10,000 photos and published the first volume of *Grain Citizens: Will Rural China Disappear?*[4]

Wei finds that though China is supposed to have 800 million rural people, only less than ten percent of them actually work on the land. It is these people who work hard, day in and day out, to provide enough food for China's population of 1.3 billion people. What surprised Wei is that not only did these people not complain, but they told him that the government had been good and that if they didn't live well it was their own fault. For them the next generation is bound to be better off (Wei 2010).

Gao Village and Stories of Gao Villagers

This book is an update of my first book on Gao Village, entitled *Gao Village: Rural Life in Modern China* (hereinafter *Gao Village*), which first appeared in 1999 and was reprinted in paperback by Hawai'i University Press in 2007, after which a Chinese version was published

---

4   The Chinese title is:《糧民 —— 中國農村會消失嗎？》. Wei uses a pun here: the first character, 糧 ("grain"), has the same pronunciation as the word "good," to mean that the grain-producing people are good people who are law-abiding, good citizens (Wei 2010).

by The Chinese University Press in 2014. *Gao Village* is a cross-disciplinary study of Gao Village, where I was born and raised. It is a history of Gao Village from 1949 to 1997, but it is also about the politics, the economy, the sociology and anthropology of that village during that period. In *Gao Village*, chapters are structured in thematic topics so that each chapter deals with a specific topic, like education, health care, population, living standards, the Great Leap Forward, the Cultural Revolution, and so on. In addressing each topic, what happened in Gao Village is related to the big picture of China, so that what happened in Gao Village is contextualized and the two—the case of Gao Village and "China" in general—are correspondingly examined.

In this book, which updates life in Gao Village since 1997, some chapters are structured thematically, like the chapter on local governance and the reach of the state, and the chapter on change and continuity that attempts to discuss conflicting values held by Gao villagers. At the same time, a considerable amount of the text is about personal stories of several Gao villagers. For example, there is a chapter about the most successful entrepreneur in the village, Gao Wenshu, as well as a couple of chapters on my brother Gao Changxian, his wife Gao Mingxia, and our relatives in the hotel business in Guangdong. There is also a chapter on the real estate boom, and related to it, a rubbish collector, Gao Changqi. In addition, there is a chapter on the poorest villager, Gao Lati, to show how and why he is poor. These are preceded by a chapter that is a critical review of the overall situation in China and a brief survey of the village in terms of themes so as to give a general picture of Gao Village since 1997. There is also a chapter on one entrepreneur who is not a Gao villager but is a national figure, so as to enhance the general theme of how the resourcefulness of rural Chinese like Gao villagers has been a vital factor for China's economic success and how this relates Gao villagers to villagers in other parts of the central China provinces of Hunan, Hubei, Henan, Anhui, and Sichuan.

There are a number of reasons why this update of Gao Village is not entirely arranged in thematic chapters. First of all, Gao Village, since the post-Mao reform, is no longer a self-contained economic entity, as it used to be in the Mao era when there was a collective system. Now, the basic economic unit is the family. Secondly, there is not so much direct state political intervention in Gao Village as there used to be and there is no longer political movement or social structure reorganization. Thirdly, Gao villagers are more connected and linked with the outside world, with life and economic activities thousands of miles away. Most of this connection is carried on and best demonstrated by individual villagers. Finally, during the Mao era, more or less everyone in Gao Village was the same, doing the same kind of farm work, living the same kind of organized life in the commune, and having the same kind of living standard. Nowadays, however, there are huge differences among the villagers in terms of type of work, place of work, experience, and living standard.

There is now depoliticized politics, marketized personalities, and commercialized existence. Therefore, it is hard to pin down the thematic compartmentalization of the totality of Gao Village. Gao Village is disintegrated and life is personalized. For these reasons, individual personal stories offer a lot of insights and present very convincing explanations of what is happening. Their stories provide us with details that show the intricate ways that Gao Village is connected with the outside world, how the rural area links with the urban sector, and how the present leads to the future.

Research Questions and Methodology

Personal stories of Gao villagers in the book are told in order to answer some crucial research questions: What is Gao Village like in the big picture of China's rapid changes since 1997? Who has settled in urban centers and why? Who is farming and why? Will Gao Village disappear? How are individual personal stories related to this big picture of China's overall development? By answering these questions, the book hopefully will not only advance our knowledge of what is happening in contemporary rural China at a grassroots level, but also provide the likely future direction of central rural China.

Just as in *Gao Village*, methods employed in this second book on Gao Village research are mainly qualitative, i.e., done through informal interviews, with questions prepared but not confined to pre-designed questions. In the 18 years since 1997, the year when the first *Gao Village* book left off, I visited Gao Village on average once every two years. Sometimes I was also a participant, like a guest at someone's wedding. In Gao Village, I might bump into someone in the street and start talking. I would also drop around from household to household to talk to anyone who happened to be in the house. I also paid special visits to the more articulate members of the community, such as the Gao Village schoolteacher Gao Anyuan, the retired head teacher of Qinglin High School Gao Chaozhen, and a person from the neighboring Xu Village named Xu Xianchang. I have also kept contact with them through email or WeChat and have asked them about this or that from time to time, from a distance. My brothers Gao Changxian and Gao Changwen are permanent assistants because I always ask them questions, or raise an issue for them to inquire about or clarify, either face to face or by email or WeChat. I also visited two destinations of Gao Village migrants: I went to Panyu three times, and to Xiamen two times, and have talked to each of the individual personalities in the book three or more times, sometimes with specific questions prepared and sometimes not.

Qualitative information of this kind is aimed at producing what Geertz (1973) described as "thick description," concentrating on the details of local villagers while connecting them to wider social processes and issues. This description of personal stories provides a narrative that entails not only the live history of Gao Village, but also the politics, the sociology, the economy of the village, and its people. It is a description and analysis of the transformation of central rural China in the process of urbanization and industrialization. In a word, it follows the transformation process occurring in China as it unfolds before our very eyes.

In accordance with postmodernist and poststructuralist epistemology arguments, I agree that my representation of Gao Village is already an interpretation through my eyes—that is, I am positional. Further, along the lines of Clifford (1973), my representations of Gao Village are always texts. I have assumptions and rhetorical devices that may or may not be shared by others in the field. I cannot see how any research by anyone can avoid being positional. As Gadamer (1976) and Iser (1987) argue, understanding of anything is always from the position and point of view of the person who understands. Secondly, my research of Gao Village has not been an expedition in search of "the facts," but a conversation extended to the people with whom I am not only sympathetic, but also emotionally connected. This does not mean that we should, or that I have, abandoned all methodological rigor. First of all, I have to adhere to the language of observation and evidence that are conventional in the social sciences. For example, I can translate what has been recorded either by audio, visual, or written materials, but I cannot fabricate figures and make up speeches that have not taken place. The reader may ask: how do I know? Well, indeed. The reader needs to read more to either confirm or refute my view, and my colleagues in the field need to review and examine what I present here.

The methodological approach is inter/cross-disciplinary in that it dissects the political, socio-economic, and historical development of a small village, while referring to the big picture of the future direction of rural China. There is an issue of whether sound macro-implications can be drawn from a micro-study of one village. At a methodological level, it may be argued that no case study of a part (a village) can make any logically, valid, general claim of the whole (rural China). However, a case study can provide insights and empirical data that can be tested by other case studies, which in turn may be confirmed or refuted by other case studies.

The Chinese proverb *yiye zhiqiu*, meaning "one falling leaf is an indication of the coming of autumn," is instructive here, as I hope this book on Gao Village, like a leaf, will have large-scale significance, since Gao Village is located in the heart of Jiangxi Province, a largely agricultural area like Anhui, Henan, Sichuan, Hunan, and Hubei provinces.

In the field of China Studies, there are many examples of successful micro-studies that have proved to have macro-significance. For instance,

Robert Marks bases his work on the case study of Haifeng and Lufeng peasant revolutions (Marks 1984), Elizabeth Perry carried out a classic case study of the Huaibei region of northern China to understand Chinese peasant rebellions (Perry 1980), and Susan Naquin's case study improves greatly our understanding of Chinese religious uprisings (Naquin 1976). Along the same lines, this Gao Village book is a micro-study done where evidence is available and, as Little states, "it is impossible to understand the higher level [of rural China] without understanding the local level [of a village]" (Little 1989, 207). Even without macro-generalizations, a micro-study is of significance in the field, as both Skinner (1977) and Geertz (1968), for instance, would argue, and, as Little writes, "differentiation rather than generalization is most useful for social sciences" (Little 1989, 212).

On the other hand, I do hope readers can reach some macro-generalizations; and I believe they can. Just as the first book on Gao Village has proved that a village study can have macro implications, this study will enable us to see the big picture of generality in central, rural China. So let me conclude by answering the question posed at the beginning in the title of this chapter, "Why Gao Village?" This second book on Gao Village aims to update Gao Village since 1997 and to indicate part of the future direction of China.

CHAPTER 2

A Critical Overall View of China since the Late 1990s

Introduction

In this chapter an overall critical examination of China is outlined. For a country of this size there are always variations and exceptions to any generalizations. In this overall view, no attempt is made to be comprehensive. Topics and issues included here are what I think are relevant to the descriptions and discussions of Gao Village since 1997. Some readers might find that the pictures presented in this chapter are too negative. Indeed, the visual images of environmental problems presented here may be emotionally disturbing. The aim of this chapter is not to show how much progress China has made since 1997, but instead, it aims to show, as an introduction, the problems China faces now so as to contrast with what the reality is in Gao Village in later chapters. To generalize problems in contrast to what Gao Village is like aims to show exactly that generalizations are too general, though they are legitimate. In short, it is so designed that the problems often seen in the news headlines, repeated here, are balanced by on-the-ground reality in Gao Village as is narrated in other chapters.

Rapid Economic Development

The Chinese economy has continued growing at a fast rate since 1997, when the research of the first Gao Village book ended. In 2010, China overtook Japan as the world's second largest economy, Germany as the world's largest exporter of goods, and the US as the world's largest manufacturer, ending 110 years of US dominance (Wen 2011).[1] China is now the world's largest market for cars and the second largest producer and consumer of energy after the US. It consumes 60 percent of global iron ore and 52 percent of coking coal. It is also the world's biggest user of aluminum and copper, and the world's biggest producer and consumer of steel (Yeates 2011), with steel production having jumped from a mere 15 percent of global production in 2000 to 45 percent in 2011, in just a short span of ten years. With nearly three trillion dollars in foreign exchange reserves, China is the world's largest creditor and is now the major trading partner of Japan, South Korea, Brazil, and Chile and a range of other countries. By 2010, China had overtaken the United States as the main market for Saudi oil (Dyer et al. 2011). On top of all that, China has managed to bring several hundred millions of rural Chinese out of absolute poverty. A development of this scale, of this magnitude and at this speed[2] is unprecedented in human history. This development has been a shock to many and hardly understood by many more. "It's almost as if the continental plates of global politics are shifting beneath our feet," Orville Schell, Director of the Asia Society's Center on US-China Relations, is quoted as saying (Dreyfuss 2010).

It is almost beyond doubt that China's role in the world economy will continue to grow. The 12th Five Year Plan targets adopted by the Chinese government in March 2011 included 36 million low cost

---

1   China accounted for 19.8 percent of global manufacturing output in 2010, while the US accounted for 19.4 percent (Hartcher 2011).

2   It has to be pointed out that by the late 1970s, when the era of Mao was coming to an end, China had already developed to be the sixth largest industrial country in the world, from a base in 1949 when China's industry was only as big as that of Belgium (Meisner 1999).

housing units (equivalent to the entire stock of housing in the UK), a large rise in spending on health, education, and welfare, increases in wages by 13 percent per annum, a quintupling of what is already the world's largest high-speed railway network, an additional 36,000 kilometers of highway, US$300 billion on subways and the same amount on the electricity grid, substantial investment in renewable energy, and the construction of the second new airport terminal in Beijing in a decade, as well as new airports in 54 other cities (*The Economist* 2011a; Garnaut 2011).

China has 170 cities with a population of one million or more (Wade 2011). The proportion of China's 400 million households owning a car has gone from virtually zero to 12 percent between 2000 and 2010. The proportion of households owning microwaves has risen from 16 to 58 percent, while the number of computers owned per 100 households has risen from eight to 70 and mobile phones from 16 to 188 (Gittins 2011). Six million students graduated from universities in 2010, up from just one million in 1999 (*The Economist* 2011b). This sketch is only an indication of the rapid economic development in China.

Problems Ahead

However, doubts have been expressed about the sustainability of China's growth, and this was even admitted by former Chinese Premier Wen Jiabao, who described the economy in 2007 as "unstable, unbalanced, uncoordinated, and unsustainable" (*The Economist* 2011a). The Chinese development strategy has depended largely on high investment in infrastructure, as well as intensive and extensive development of manufacturing capacities, but has also depended on low consumption and extreme exploitation of cheap labor. This kind of strategy has led to the expansion of low-tech industries, a race to the bottom of profitability, dependence on exporting increasingly lower-priced manufactured goods, environmental degradation, and growing labor unrest. The Chinese authorities are now trying to change development strategies by moving low-tech and labor-intensive industries to inland areas, and by gearing GDP towards household consumption and the domestic market; but so far the success of such efforts is not visible, except in certain pockets like Chongqing. This kind of transformation is difficult and fraught with problems. To boost household consumption, wages have to be raised. Higher wages pose a threat to the country's export competitiveness. To reduce the household savings ratio, the Chinese government has had to spend enormously on healthcare, unemployment benefits, medical benefits, and pensions, but the expenditure required to boost social protection to this degree would inevitably challenge the interests of the capitalists (Zhu and Kotz 2010), something very hard to do in today's China since political interests and capitalist interests are more or less one and the same.

Aspirations are rising at a faster rate than wages, alongside increasing resentment at growing inequality. The rich have become fabulously wealthy and membership of the swankiest yacht clubs is burgeoning, as are sales of exclusive Western brands (Watts 2011; Hart-Landsberg 2011). "Mass incidents" have become increasingly frequent, rising from 10,000 in 1994 to 72,000 in 2004, and then to 180,000 in 2010 (Whitehouse 2011). There are increasing signs that the Chinese working class is about to stand up for itself (Li Mingqi 2011). Strikes by Honda workers in 2010 quickly led to more than 200 copycat strikes and protests (*The Economist* 2011b). There was a report of a workers' protest at a Hitachi plant in 2011 (Sacom 2010), and a workers' strike in Shanghai (Clem 2011). There was also news of workers demanding better pay and conditions at a Pepsi plant (*China Labour Bulletin* 2011).

Other problems that keep the Chinese leadership awake at night include inflation, an asset-price bubble—particularly in housing and commercial real estate—the escalation of debt held by local government investment bodies, a looming demographic bust, and rapid environmental degradation. The government is trying to rein in inflation and the asset-price bubble by tightening credit. Progress in addressing environmental problems is very slow, which inflicts huge damage not only on national health but also on the ecosystem, at a cost equivalent to 13.6 percent of GDP each year according to one estimate, outstripping the 10 percent growth in the economy (Evans-Pritchard 2011).

To conclude, economic development has certainly brought visible benefits to the people of China, including rural people, but also serious problems and costs, both of which are analyzed in *Gao Village*. In the remainder of this chapter, I outline some specific problems that China as a whole faces today, as a context for the chapters that follow.

China as an Assembly Line for the Global Market

For decades, much of China's rapid development was tied to the export of manufactured goods to the rest of the world. For instance, 37 percent of China's output in 2006 was exported to the global market (Koopman et al. 2008) but many of the factories that produce China's output are actually owned and managed by large US, Japanese, and other multinational companies. Therefore, a large proportion of the output is produced for the benefit of the multinational companies, the shareholders of which are largely in developed countries. For instance, according to Linden, Kraemer, and Dedrick (2007) as reported by Koopman et al. (2008), the Chinese export value per unit of a 30 GB video camera in 2006 was about US$150, but the value added attributable to producers in China was only US$4.

That the lion's share of this kind of production goes to foreign companies can also be seen in the chart below from the website of the Chinese General Customs Bureau (Wang 2015). The chart shows that within a eight year period from 2010 to 2017, in US dollar terms, foreign companies comprise about 40 percent of China's exports, with SOEs taking less than 20 percent of the total and other Chinese private or collectively-owned companies taking more than 40 percent.

Chart 1. Export percentage of various enterprises.

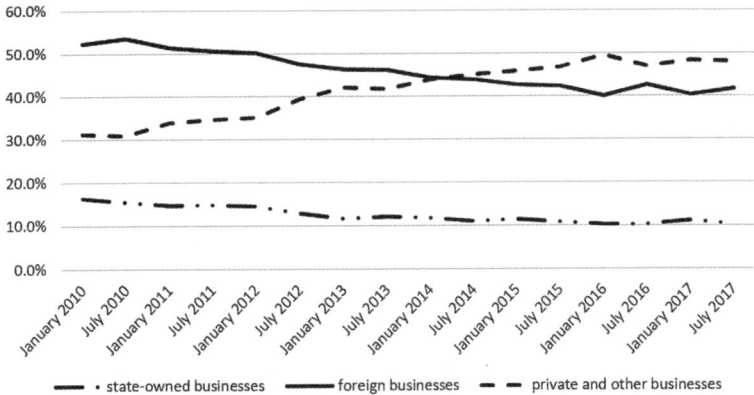

Source: Website of the Chinese General Customs Bureau.

In this arrangement, with China being the world's assembly line, the developed world enjoys the benefits of imported cheap goods from China, hence importing deflation, while China is importing pollution and environmental degradation. What is interesting is that apart from the big capitalists, nobody is thankful to China or the Chinese for this model of development. Both the working class and the progressive intelligentsia in Western countries are especially critical of China (Dreyfuss 2010).

Migrant Workers

According to the Chinese National Statistics Bureau, there were about 230 million migrant workers in 2011 and about the same number in 2016. Of these, 150 million are a new generation of migrant workers, most of whom left their home villages as soon as they finished their nine years of compulsory education (and some even earlier). Unlike their parents, these new migrant workers have never worked as farmers and they do not intend to go back to become farmers. They are more inclined to demand better pay and conditions. This difference is dramatized by the fact that in 2011, 12 migrant workers in the large Taiwan-run company Foxconn committed suicide by jumping from their dormitory buildings (Beckett 2012). Eighteen-year-old Tian Yu was one. She jumped and survived, but both her legs were paralyzed. "It is just too tiring to live," she said during an interview (Li and Zhang 2011).

Transnational companies come to China to make a profit by exploiting Chinese migrant workers and by dumping waste in Chinese rivers and on the land. Despite this, the Chinese are blamed for these companies not employing workers in their own countries and dumping cheap goods on their markets. In fact, the Chinese political and intellectual elite can only blame themselves. There was about a 20-year ideological consensus among the Chinese elite from the late 1970s (though that consensus has been broken since the late 1990s) that China was backward in technology and management and that it needed foreign technology, management, and capital to catch up with the perceived developed areas, such as Hong Kong, Singapore, Taiwan, Korea, Japan, the US, and Europe. Therefore, tax concessions, almost-free land with infrastructure, concessions on lower wages, and concessions in relation to minimal working and environmental conditions were made available to foreign companies. At the same time, the strict household registration system (*hukou*) that controlled movement from rural to urban China was relaxed, as large numbers of workers were required for these foreign companies. The wages were so low and the conditions were so terrible that even the urban unemployed would not think of accepting a job in these factories. The mainstream Chinese political and intellectual elite, amid an intellectual and emotional backlash against dogmatic egalitarianism and a society of scarcity in the Mao era, thought that adopting such a development model was a necessary sacrifice, first in the name of it being the "primary stage of socialism," and later being "socialism with Chinese characteristics." Some even thought that rural migrant workers deserved to be treated as working animals since they were of lower quality (Gao 2008a).

Working Conditions

So much of China's economic success has been dependent on the hundreds of millions of migrant workers from rural areas. These highly competent and well-educated young workers work under appalling conditions for wages that were stagnant for more than 20 years from the early 1980s, and were only raised in recent years. It is therefore quite clear that hundreds of millions of rural Chinese were not lifted out of poverty by the Chinese government. Instead, they slogged to lift themselves out of absolute poverty (Murphy 2002). The conditions under which these migrant workers work and the contributions they have made to the world are amply and accurately documented, for instance by Chan (2001), Solinger (1999), Pun (2005), Pun and Chan (2012), Yan (2008), Gao (1994, 1997 and 1998), and Chang (2008).

However, Western critics can be accused of being hypocritical at least if they only condemn Chinese policymakers and their cohorts. They really need to direct their criticism towards the multinational companies that benefit enormously from this development model. These big companies sometimes turn a blind eye to the kind of working conditions that they would not dare to think of in their home countries. For instance, scores of young workers in Suzhou, where the most advanced Apple iPhones are made, were reported in 2010 to have been poisoned by the chemical n-hexane (Branigan 2010). In response, Apple pointed out that its code of conduct set strict requirements for working and environmental practices.

> But the 2010 audit shows that manufacturers are routinely breaching the code. The majority—54%—broke the 60-hour weekly work limit more than half the time. Another 39% failed to meet occupational injury prevention requirements; 17% failed on chemical exposure standards; and 35% did not meet wage and benefits requirements, with 24 of the 102 factories audited paying less than minimum wage for regular hours. (Branigan 2010)

Another example is the suicides of young workers at Foxconn. Suicides did not happen in just one incident. Between January and May in 2010, a shocking 13 young workers attempted or committed suicide by jumping from tall buildings. The company was so panicked by these deaths that it installed nets around the lower parts of its workers' dormitory buildings. According to Chan and Pun (2010), there are at least three factors that are responsible for tragedies like these. First, *leading international brands* have adopted unethical purchasing practices, resulting in substandard conditions in their global electronics supply chains. Second, *management* has used abusive and illegal methods to raise worker efficiency, generating widespread grievances and resistance at the workplace level. Third, *local Chinese officials*, in collusion with enterprise management, systematically neglect workers' rights, resulting in widespread misery and deepened social inequalities.[3]

Rampant Labor-Rights Violations in ICTI-Certified Factories

According to SACOM (2011),

> Students and Scholars Against Corporate Misbehaviour (SACOM) has been monitoring the working conditions in the toy industry in China since 2005 and has sadly seen little real improvement in working conditions of the toy workers. In the summer of 2011, SACOM investigated three toy factories, namely Dongguan On Tai Toys Co. Ltd., Sturdy Products Factory, and Hung Hing Printing Group Ltd., which are suppliers to renowned global companies, including Disney, Mattel, Lego, McDonald's, Marks and Spencer, and Walmart. All three factories have been certified by the ICTI CARE for several years

---

3   Another example was reported by Sacom (2010).

already. However, after all the years of monitoring by the ICTI CARE,[4] they are still violating fundamental labor rights. The ICTI CARE, again, has proved itself to be just a cover-up scheme for big companies' exploitation of workers in China.

An example is the labor-rights abuses at On Tai, Sturdy Products and Hung Hing: The workers have to work excessive overtime—up to 140 overtime hours a month, about four times the legal limit; their wages are always paid in arrears; they are denied a copy of their labor contract; they are also denied social insurance benefits; and, of course, they are denied the right to freedom of association (Litzinger 2013).

Left-Behind Children

One reason why factories and companies can get away with such low pay and why migrant workers are willing to accept such low pay is that migrant workers are usually young. If and when they have children, they leave their children in their home villages. In other words, the employers only have to bear a partial responsibility of maintaining the labor force. The current state of affairs seems the best arrangement for both the

---

4   ICTI CARE is "the ethical supply chain program for the global toy industry. An independent, not-for-profit organization established in 2004," which claims to "work each day to improve working conditions at our factories by implementing the ICTI Code of Business Practices" (http://pastbackup.com/e/content/cat_page.asp?cat_id=285, accessed 2nd May 2018). ICTI CARE claims that it aims to "ensure safe and humane workplace environments for toy factory workers worldwide." Factories that pay a fee to the ICTI CARE and pass its audit are certified as decent factories with good labor practices. The charge is levied on the factory, but the global brands and retailers are required to pay 780 toy brands and companies worldwide, such as Mattel, Hasbro, Lego, Disney, Walmart, Toys R Us, and Marks & Spencer this arrangement, that all their toy suppliers must be certified by the ICTI CARE. The global toy brands and retailers join ICTI CARE because it is a free service and it is a good risk-sharing and responsibility-sharing mechanism. It helps in covering up the labor-rights violations (Sacom 2011).

Chinese state and transnational or Chinese businesses. Neither the state nor the business has to bear the full cost of maintaining a migrant worker. Children are left behind and there is no cost of maintaining a family and a migrant worker, as they will go back home if there is no work or if the worker is sick or injured or too old to work; therefore, there is no cost for social security.[5] What underpins the possibility of this convenient arrangement is the legacy of the Mao era: collective ownership of land and equal distribution of land on a per capita basis. While this development advantage is obvious for the Chinese state, the personal and emotional cost of the migrant workers is only sometimes revealed, but very often invisible. One of the emotional and personal costs is the *liushou ertong* ("left-behind children") themselves, children left at home in rural villages to be looked after by grandparents or relatives while their parents work far away in urban areas (Ye and Pan 2008). If they are lucky, these children may see their parents once a year during the Chinese New Year (Spring Festival) holiday.

There are many reasons why these children are left at home. One is the discriminatory policy against rural people. In a city like Shanghai for instance, the resident population is actually shrinking and many schools are being shut down. However, the Shanghai city authorities and the Shanghai residents for a long time have resisted accepting children of migrant workers. They would rather close down the schools. It is true that there are practical issues, such as who is paying to run the school if the migrant workers cannot pay, which they cannot. There is also fear. Since there are so many migrant workers everywhere, realistically no education system in any city could cope once the floodgates are opened. Another reason why children are left behind in villages is that the parents really don't have the time or energy to look after them. Normally the parents work 12–14 hours a day, six and sometimes seven

---

5   The Chinese government of course realizes that this arrangement is not sustainable in the longer term and therefore has started to work out a social security system, even for migrant workers and rural people.

days a week. The migrant workers themselves are often cramped in dormitories, sharing common toilet and washing facilities. How can they have children with them?

Other aspects of politics also work against migrant workers. Why would the state agents care about the children of these beasts of burden since matters of this kind are not a performance index for their official career? They care more about how the streets look when their supervisor is driven past, and they care more about whether there is an accident or incident that will draw negative attention from the media, so instead of assisting migrant workers in the education of their children, urban authorities in various cities constantly bulldoze very rudimentary schools set up by migrant workers themselves. Those schools are accused of being illegal, because they are deemed to be lower quality, unsafe or untidy.

According to Liu Sha (2012), China is home to 58 million left-behind children; 70 percent of whom are cared for by their grandparents and five percent of whom live on their own. According to a survey by the All China Women's Federation of more than 7,000 people in five major metropolises including Shenzhen, Beijing, and Guangzhou, over half of the respondents said that they were raised by their grandparents. "I was a left-behind child and suffered the loneliness of living without my parents, but now my daughter is enduring the same experience," Wei Chulin, a 30-year-old migrant worker in Shenzhen originally from Maoming, Guangdong Province, told the *Global Times*.

One of the most shocking cases emerged last year, when a 12-year-old girl named Xiaoli (a pseudonym) from Guxian Township in Yanshi, Henan Province, was found to be four months pregnant. Xiaoli's sole guardian was her 65-year-old grandmother. Xiaoli had been sexually abused by a man surnamed Li, who molested Xiaoli repeatedly, threatening to throw her into a river if she ever told anyone of the abuse. In East China's Anhui Province, 43 students aged under 13 from four different counties were reportedly sexually abused by their teachers last year. Most victims were children of migrant workers. The All-China Women's Federation and the People's Procuratorate in southern China's Guangdong Province conducted joint research on children living in parentless homes and found that 2,506 children under 18 had been sexually abused over the last three years, with more than half of the victims under 14, reported by the official *Guangzhou Daily*, as in Liu Sha (2012).

The Beast of Burden and Child Labor

For about 20 years migrants from rural areas were treated as necessary nuisances at best and unwanted trouble at worst by many urban authorities. They were initially called *mangliu* ("blind floaters") by the urban and official media. Migrants had to carry identity cards with them all the time and be ready to be questioned and searched at any time. If any of them were found without identity cards or work permits, they could be arrested and put into a detention center. Only in 2004, when the death of Sun Zhigang ignited a debate in the media that drew the attention of the Beijing authorities, was the practice of jailing migrant workers in a detention center put to a stop.[6] It is reasonable to speculate that Sun was certainly not the first victim of such a system, but it just happened that Sun was a university educated migrant and his friends were articulate enough to draw media attention. It also so happened in 2004 that there were so many Chinese who were connected on social media.

---

6   A young man called Sun Zhigang was one day walking in the street when he was stopped by the local police in Guangzhou. It happened that Sun was not carrying his ID papers with him and he was arrested and taken to one of the detention centers. In spite of his protest and explanation, he was not released and he was literally beaten to death. Sun's death was posted on the internet and the news spread like wildfire. Eventually the conventional media reported it as well and it caused an uproar all over China. The outrage was so intense that Beijing immediately issued a decree to abolish all detention centers. This is known as the famous Sun Zhigang Incident in contemporary Chinese history.

There has been improvement in some aspects of labor conditions but also not much change in others. One serious problem is the existence of child labor, which is officially illegal in China. There was recently a report, for instance, of 40 children aged between 12 and 14 who were rescued from an electronics factor in Shenzhen.

Dozens of children were found working in an electronics factory in Shenzhen's Longgang district in the latest child labour scandal to hit the city. At least 40 children, aged from 12 to 14 and all from the remote county of Mianning in Sichuan province, worked for three months at the Megatrend Electronics factory. They worked 13 hours a day for about five yuan an hour. (SCMP, 2011)

Faced with a shortage of labor in the Pearl River Delta, the factory, which makes Bluetooth adapters, recruited the children through a labor agency. All the children had fake identity cards showing they were 16 or older. The factory paid them RMB 7.10 an hour, from which the agency takes RMB 2.10 as commission. Critics said that child labor has been a daily fact of life in Guangdong for years and that the government turned a blind eye. "We heard that many small factories in Guangdong—especially toy and clothes producers—still used child laborers until last year," said Debby Chan Sze-wan, from Hong Kong-based Students and Scholars against Corporate Misbehaviour. In April 2008, local media revealed that thousands of children from Sichuan's remote Liangshan County were sold to Guangdong factories over the previous five years. The children were abused and forced to work 12 hours a day, almost every day, under slave-like conditions. Most of the children were from ethnic minorities and aged between 9 and 15. A dealer in child workers was quoted as saying that children who were abducted or bought in Sichuan were sold in cities in Guangdong, including Dongguan, Shenzhen, Guangzhou, Huizhou, and Jiangmen. In 2007, four companies—Lekit Stationery, a Taiwan-invested firm in Dongguan; Yue Wing Cheong Light Products, which makes bags and other products in Shenzhen; Eagle Leather Products, based in Hong Kong; and Mainland Headwear—were accused of using child labor and of labor abuse by the Brussels-based International Trade Union Confederation (White 2011).

Corruption and Inequality

Piketty, Li, and Zucman (2017) did a macro study of inequality in China and their conclusions include that "China's inequality levels used to be close to Nordic countries and are now approaching US levels" and that "wealth inequality used to be lower in China than everywhere else, and it is now intermediate between Europe and the USA." Their study states that in China, "The top 10 percent income share rose from 27 percent to 41 percent of national income between 1978 and 2015, while the bottom 50 percent share dropped from 27 percent to 15 percent." In most developed countries, the share of public property in national wealth used to be around 15–25 percent in the 1960s-1970s, and is now close to zero percent, their study says. It has even recently become negative for the United States, Britain, Japan, and Italy (meaning public debt exceeds public assets) and is just barely positive for Germany and France. This means the West has essentially moved away from a model of public ownership of the economy to a more fully privatized market model.

In China, however, the share of public property is still in the 30 percent range. "To put it differently: China has ceased to be communist, but is not entirely capitalist; it should rather be viewed as a 'mixed economy' with a strong public ownership component," Piketty et al. concludes. The Picketty et al. study does not address specifically the inequality between the urban and rural sector. While discrimination against the rural sector and appalling working conditions on the factory floor impact on Gao villagers directly, corruption at a higher level of politics and the finance sector don't have much visible impact on them, unlike in the late 1980s and early 1990s when local corruption was not only rampant but also explicit and overt. Two crucial developments since the beginning of the 21st century have helped reduce conditions for local corruption in rural China. One development was the abolition of all and any agricultural taxes. The other development was the reduction of pressure on family planning.

However, corruption at high levels erodes the seeming legitimacy of the Party and the state machine, and all of the Chinese leadership knows that. The current Chinese leadership under Xi Jinping has taken the crackdown on corruption very seriously, the fact of which sends chills down the spines of some state agents. According to Moore (2013), the *Economic Observer* newspaper obtained a Chinese Central Commission for Discipline Inspection report that suggested that nearly 10,000 luxury homes had been sold by officials in Guangzhou and Shanghai in 2012 alone. It also claimed that US$1 trillion, equivalent to 40 percent of Britain's annual gross domestic product, had been smuggled out of China illegally in 2012.

There are numerous reports on the increasingly worrying and deteriorating corruption by Chinese officials, army officers and the so-called "princelings" (sons and daughters of high-ranking government officials and army officers). Poyang County, where Gao Village is located, is one of the poorest counties in China and for that reason the county is not even open for foreigners to visit.[7] Despite being such a poor county, where agriculture is the main source of income and where the central government had to subsidize its agriculture, and for which the total financial income was only RMB 410 million in 2010, a department head of the county's Finance Bureau, Li Huabo, was able to embezzle RMB 94 million of state agriculture subsidies without being noticed from 2006–2011. Li Huabo's wrongdoings were only discovered when he called from Canada to "apologize" for taking so much money, thinking that he was free outside of China. In 2015, Li was listed as one of the 100 criminals publicized for international notification and wanted for arrest by the Chinese police (*Jiangxi ribao* 2015).[8]

7　In the late 1990s when a BBC documentary director wanted to make a film about Gao Village, his request for a permission to visit Gao Village was refused.

8　The latest news about him in May 2015 was that he was arrested by the Chinese authorities with the help of the Singaporean government. See creaders.net 2015.

The Gap between the Rich and the Poor

Photo 1. People on social media were angered by this image of female soldiers in Lanzhou carrying Louis Vuitton and Gucci products (Fauna 2011).

The Chinese government officially still claims that China is a socialist country, but they qualify this by saying it has "Chinese characteristics." Therefore, it is embarrassing for China to be known as one of the most unequal and unfair countries in the world. In the book *Unequal China*, (Guo and Sun 2012), it was reported that in May 2010, the Gini co-efficient had reached 0.48 in China, overtaking the recognized warning level of 0.4. Chen Jia writes in the *China Daily* that China's wealth divide has gone past the warning level (Chen 2010).[9] According to a Chinese official statement in 2013, China's Gini coefficient was 0.474 in 2012, down from a high of 0.491 in 2008. To put this in context, a reading of 0.5 would make China among the most unequal societies.

Photo 1, above, caused an outrage online that a solider would travel with such luxury items. The case of how much the CEO of Ping'an Insurance earns a year is another example of the gap between the rich and the poor. It was revealed in 2008 that Ma Mingzhe, the CEO of Ping'an Insurance, earned a yearly income of RMB 66,160,000. In that year, the average income of a worker in rural China was RMB 4,140 (Liu Feng 2008).

Nothing happens in human society that does not involve the guiding of values or an intellectual narrative. Going from one of the most economically equal societies in the Mao era to one of the most unequal societies in the world did not happen because the Chinese suddenly became greedy. The enormous increase of the gap between the rich and poor is a consequence of designed policies and the promotion of certain values. Since the late 1970s the main value in China has been development, or in the words of Deng Xiaoping, *fazhan shi ying daoli* ("development is the core value"). Therefore, it does not matter how you get there so long as you get there (white or black, no matter what color of the cat so long as it can catch mice). The intellectual narrative is to "let some get rich first."[10] This race to get rich first is also a race to the bottom for migrant workers. The average monthly wage for migrant workers has remained stagnant at the rate of RMB 600–800 for about 20 years, and that is how the so-called "made in China" commodities have remained competitive.

---

9   The brainchild of Italian statistician Corrado Gini, the Gini coefficient, which is a measure of statistical dispersion, is commonly used as a measure of inequality of income or wealth. A low Gini coefficient indicates more equal distribution, with 0 corresponding to complete equality, while higher Gini coefficients indicate more unequal distribution, with 1 corresponding to complete inequality.

10   This is attributed to Deng Xiaoping as well. However, in the Western media and even in some academic works, Deng Xiaoping is reported to have said "to get rich is glorious," but I have never been able to locate where and when Deng Xiaoping said that.

By 2010, China already had the second largest number of individual billionaires after the United States. Of those on the list, many are property developers. There are also those Chinese who work for foreign companies and have become affluent, if not enormously rich. There are, of course, those who work in the large state-owned enterprises that have the monopoly on resources and the market, such as the big communication companies, the large iron and steel companies and oil companies, the railway giants and the banking sector. Most of all, there are those who became rich by seizing state assets when large-scale privatization started in the early 1990s. There are also some self-made entrepreneurs, such as the coal mine owners in Shanxi, or the button-making factories in Wenzhou, or new media tycoons like Ma Yun, or indeed even comedians like Zhao Benshan, who is reported to fly in a private jet.

There is therefore a rapid process of a growing gap between the rich and the poor in China. The poor include not just the rural Chinese. One decade into the 21st century, the urban Chinese, including the educated urban elite, do not see much of an upward prospect. Housing is too expensive for the young. Many a university graduate cannot find employment. For those who do work, earning something like an average of RMB 3,000 a month is hardly enough to survive on, because rent is high and inflation is soaring. Some urban Chinese people resort to selling bits and pieces in the street, to supplement their meager income. On the Tsinghua University campus in Beijing, for instance, I saw small vendors on street corners, especially after official work hours. Some were just trying to sell a few pieces of vegetables and fruit. Another thing I noticed inside the Tsinghua University campus is that there were a lot of sheds here and there, squeezed under a tree or around a corner. I was shocked by such sights because they looked like ghettos or olden-day rural dwellings. Compared with any university campus outside China, say, in Hong Kong, which are neat and tidy, some areas of the Tsinghua University campus, which is one of the best-endowed universities in China, looked like a rural China area that I remember. I was told these were sheds put up by the university staff and were used to rent to migrant workers or people from outside the university as extra income.

On the other hand, keeping pets has become a fashion and a way for the rich to show off. In 2010, my wife bought a kitten for our two young children who were learning Chinese in Shenzhen and it cost us RMB 1,000, a little more than many Chinese people's annual income. This shows how expensive it is to keep pets in China. One woman from Xi'an was widely reported to have paid RMB 4 million for a single dog that was escorted to its new home in a motorcade consisting of 30 Mercedes (Wines 2010).

Environmental Destruction

At the 2009 Copenhagen Climate Change Conference, China was widely reported by Western media to have been nationalistic and uncooperative, but that is not how the Chinese felt about it. For them, the developed countries just wanted to shift their own responsibilities. It is true that China has become one of the world's largest polluters, if not the largest one, but the Chinese could say that on a per capita basis, China is not one of the worst polluters. They could argue that after Western countries polluted the world by developing first and grabbing the world's resources, they now want to stop developing countries to progress so that they can have clean air. By far, the most neglected point in talking about this subject is the fact that by being the world's assembly line, China is polluting itself while providing convenience for the developed world. In other words, China is importing pollution indirectly by accepting the polluting industries and directly by importing rubbish from developed countries. At one point, a government official in the UK tried to justify its exporting of rubbish to China by saying that otherwise, the cargo ships would have to return to China empty. One Chinese blogger commented that that was right, the British did the same thing in the 19th century when the cargo ships carrying Chinese tea and porcelain to the island would return to China with opium (Watts 2010). As a historical fact, that accusation is not true, since opium was not produced in the UK but in India. But the point is clearly made.

Photo 2. China's largest freshwater lake, Poyang Lake, is a desolate sight. (humphery/Shutterstock.com)

According to the China Geological Survey, 90 percent of underground water has suffered different degrees of contamination, with more than 60 percent suffering severe contamination. Also, according to statistics released by the Xinhua News Agency, out of 118 Chinese cities, only three percent have underground water that is considered moderately clean (Zhang and Harrison 2013)

Under normal circumstances, Poyang Lake covers 3,500 square kilometers, but by 2011, only 200 square kilometers had water. The cracked earth should be covered with water during this season under normal circumstances. Whatever the cause, the impact is directly felt in Gao Village, as the village borders on the edge of the lake. There used to be a virtually unlimited source of marine life from the lake, providing food for both humans and animals, but now there is virtually nothing, though the process of destruction started in the 1970s.

Issues of Land and Land Ownership

That land is fundamental to farming and rural life never changes, but issues with land have undergone great changes in China. To start with, rural income is no longer tied to land. In fact, rural Chinese could not and cannot sustain a livelihood by just working on the land. The fact of and reason for that has also been discussed in *Gao Village*. According to He Xuefeng (2013), who heads a rural research center in Wuhan, since 1990 income from farming and income by migrant workers in urban areas have been about the same. There are roughly an estimated 1.8 billion *mu*[11] of arable land and about one million rural households. That means an average household's land holding is only about six to seven *mu*. This is a national average. In Gao Village it is half of that. Therefore, no matter how much labor is invested into their land and no matter how hard they raise their production output, the current state of technology and the current price of agricultural produce means that there is a limited income for Gao villagers.

At the closing of the annual National People's Congress (NPC) meeting held in Beijing in March 2011, the NPC's figure head chairman, Wu Gangguo, said something that aroused wide interest. Wu said that the Chinese government would not support privatization. The debate, both in public and in private among the CCP hierarchy, has been going on for at least a decade. Among academics and intelligentsia there are also two camps on the issue. One camp largely consists of economists and those who hold right-wing political values. The polemics in this camp argue for definitive and authentic private ownership of land. Currently, land in China is not privately owned, and even land on which a house is built is supposed to be on lease for 50 or 70 years. Theoretically, all land belongs to the state and any individual or enterprise can only have land use rights, the terms of which vary from place to place and time to time.

---

11   One *mu* is equivalent to 614 square meters.

In rural China, land is theoretically owned by the collective. What that means, in practice, is that whatever land that was historically owned by people of one village is owned collectively by all the people in that village. Once you move out of the village, say by marriage to a man in another place, the woman automatically loses the right to any land in that village. For the same reason, a woman who marries into the village will automatically have a per capita share of the village land. The current arrangement is that land that is collectively owned by the people in any particular village is distributed equally on a per capita basis to the households. The household has the right to use the land that is allocated to them and grow whatever they wish, but they cannot sell or rent their allocated land to anyone in or outside the village; however, they can lease the land use right to someone else on an annual basis. In places like Gao Village it is difficult for villagers to lease their land on a long-term basis because land is reallocated every five years to cater for the demographic change among the families, like new births, deaths, permanent migration like marriage, or change of household registration. However, the process of leasing out land is currently changing rapidly in China, an issue that will be dealt with later.

One strong argument, against which there are also strong arguments, is that in order to move fast to urbanization and modernization, not only land use rights, but also the very ownership of land in China, should be privatized. There are three main arguments, mostly from the right wing, for wholesale privatization. The first argument is that efficiency is not possible with household farming and only privatization can enable the sale and purchase of land legally. The final outcome of a market economy would mean that the aim of efficiency will lead to large-scale farming. The second argument is that farmers would not carry out any long-term investment on any land until and unless the land is legally theirs. The third argument is that this would stop once and for all the "land seizure" problem that is frequently reported in the news, referring to the fact that a developer, together with state agents, can take land away from a household's private ownership of use rights.

Those from the left, however, do not agree, not because they are fundamentalist communists but because they believe that economical rationalists ignore the Chinese reality. First of all, long-term investment such as irrigation projects require coordination from the government, and no private person or company can do that since large irrigation projects usually involve areas across villages and even counties. Furthermore, in much of the terraced land in south China, large-scale farming is difficult even if one person owns all the land. In areas like the north and northeast of China, where land is level, large-scale farming has already taken place and there is already mechanization under the current collective land ownership system. In those areas, farmers form groups and communities themselves to decide what crops to grow together and in what to invest, like farming machines. Secondly, the land seizure issue does not apply to the vast area of rural China where land does not have commercial value, since it is far away from any urban center. According to He Xuefeng (2014) only about five percent of China's land is close enough to an urban center to have speculative or commercial value. Therefore, the idea of privatization in order to protect individual rights does not apply. In any case, privatization would probably lead to more abuse at the expense of farmers because the collectives actually have more bargaining power than one individual against wealthy developers or local authorities. Finally, the most compelling argument from the left is that land is actually the last and only type of social security for vast numbers of rural people. This argument can be underlined by the fact that there are few shantytowns left in China's urban centers. One may notice beggars along the roads and occasionally someone picking things from the rubbish bin, but one does not see massive ghettos or children feeding on rubbish dumps in China. Occasionally, and in some places maybe, but ghettos are certainly not a defining feature in China as they are in some other developing countries. This is the case because every rural person has a piece of land in China. If and when they cannot find a job in an urban center, a rural migrant can always return home to work on the land. That is at least enough to survive.

Urbanization and New Rural Construction

Different experiments have taken place all over China to deal with the process of urbanization. In Shandong Province, for instance, people have started what they call the *shanglou* ("go upstairs") experiment. What they do is round up all the villagers scattered over the fields and put them together in one area. New houses are built for them, equipped with modern facilities like toilets and running water. The houses are multi-storied apartments, unlike the traditional houses in the north where there is always a one-story house with a big courtyard. These houses will be built along a street, with schools and shops and other amenities, creating a small town in one stroke. There have been criticisms of this experiment, not surprisingly, in the media. One of the points made in criticism is that the local authorities might have an ulterior motivation in launching this experiment, i.e., to make more land available for commercial use. Beijing imposes conditions on local authorities if the latter attempts to turn arable land into commercial use. One condition is that for any amount of arable land made for commercial use, a replacement amount of arable land must be found, such as making a plot of wasteland arable. Therefore, to remove farmers from their homes and place them in artificial centers is an excuse in the name of urbanization to make land available for commercialization, because concentrated tall buildings to house the same amount of people save land.

This experiment is actually in line with what is called the New Socialist Rural Construction movement, which, ironically, seems to have been inspired by a similar movement initiated by Yan Yangchu and Liang Shumin before the Communist Revolution in 1949. By the time the CCP had installed its new government, the rural construction efforts by those people were considered a failure. Now, since the collective system in the Mao era is considered a failure, the idea of rural construction has arisen again.

Song Dian Xiaxiang and the Number One Document

As the detailed descriptions of Gao Village later in the book will show, the Chinese central government has been paying more attention to rural problems in recent years. One landmark decision in this direction was the central government's decision to implement nine-year compulsory education for rural people by allocating RMB 200 billion a year for this (Li Changping 2011). Another important decision was taken soon after what is called the global financial crisis of 2009. Beijing decided to launch a large stimulus package to prop up the economy. Part of that package was to boost consumer spending in rural China. This is what has been referred to in China as *song dian xiaxiang* ("sending electrical items down to the countryside"), which involved subsidies paid by the central government for companies to sell television sets, washing machines or fridges at reduced prices so that rural people could afford to purchase them. This again had some mixed results. The subsidies certainly helped many electrical manufacturers and retail shops, but it was also alleged that the retail shops only gave the rural people outdated and faulty products to clear their stores. It was also revealed that many rural people actually did not make use of their newly acquired gadgets because they soon discovered that it was too expensive to run them as the cost of electricity proved to be too much for them.

For a number of years, a central government document known as the Number One Document, issued each year from Beijing, has been about rural China. Whether these documents entail good policies for the rural sector on paper, and whether they can be implemented, is another matter. For instance, the central government has introduced labor laws to protect migrant workers, like limited weekly working hours, overtime rates, and the necessity of having written contracts. Local authorities tend to sideline these measures, however, and whenever there is labor unrest, like protests or strikes, the local government authorities tend to be on the side of the employers as the local authorities do not want to scare away business. They want to attract more capital, have more projects and encourage more development so that they can have more

GDP growth to report, as that is the most important performance index for their career. Furthermore, continued development and more projects have driven the value of land up, and in the process the local governments have collected more revenue. Gleaming skyscrapers make the place look modern, more taxes make the pockets of these officials fatter, and more GDP means upward promotion. As well, with all the bribes and thank you money they keep collecting along the way, why would they care about the increase of a few dollars in wages for the lower class migrant workers?

What is interesting is that the Number One Document in 2011 was about irrigation in rural China. According to the Xinhua website's official interpretation of this document,[12] Beijing plans to spend RMB 4 trillion on rural irrigation in the next ten years. The reason why this is interesting is that it took 30 years for the Chinese authorities to realize that they could not ignore this matter any longer. It took that long due to the fact that the sound irrigation infrastructure that was built in the Mao era worked well for so many years. The dismantling of the collective system meant that even elementary maintenance has been neglected. A lot of the infrastructure fell into disuse and the droughts in the north and southwest have shown the effect of this neglect.

According to one study, 1988 statistics for Anhui show that, of the province's 98 middle-sized reservoirs, 70 were built between 1966 and 1979, and of the 2.79 million *mu* effective irrigated areas 1.96 million *mu* were built in this period. There was a severe drought in 1978 but grain production was not effected as a result of the irrigation infrastructure built in the Mao era (Li Changping 2011; Xu Hailiang 2012)

Li Changping further argues that although four trillion RMB may sound like a lot of money, compared to what was invested in the Mao era, it is not much. According to Li, on average there were two to three

---

12 The document is titled "Zhonggong zhongyang guowuyuan guanyu jiakuai shuili gaige fazhan de jueding" (〈中共中央國務院關於加快水利改革發展的決定〉[Decision on the reform and development of irrigation and waterworks by the central committee of the CCP and the State Council]).

hundred million laborers working on irrigation projects each year in the winter. If each laborer worked 30 days each winter at the cost of RMB 100 a day, at today's value the investment on irrigation each year was about RMB 600–900 billion a year.

Conclusion

In this chapter, I have sketched out some prominent politico-economic problems and issues in current China as a context for the later discussion of Gao Village. The general tone may sound gloomy but it is not meant to be. Ironically, one of the reasons that I think China is not going to collapse easily is the diversity of China. This diversity ironically provides coherence in that the gaps can be and actually are spaces for people of different sectors of society to move and to change.

There are so many different sectors and strata in Chinese society, due to ethnicity, region, gender, class, background, personal interest, profession, education, politics, economic history, or climate. As a result, there are countless different types of people in Chinese society. This is in total contrast to developed Western societies, where there are clear, but few, very well-structured interest groups and sectors. Developed societies in Western countries, or in Singapore for that matter, are highly structured and highly regulated.

In China everything looks so chaotic, and as a result there is more freedom for all kinds of activities, like setting up a food stall at the street corner. You may find someone on a flyover bridge selling pawpaw fruit, or fake Mao badges. By Western standards they may not make much money, but they might be able to make enough to survive and so, in many ways, Chinese society is actually a much more diversified society, for the very reason of which there are as many problems as solutions. And for the same very reason, there are so many problems if you want to look for them, and at the same time the Chinese have found so many solutions if you care to identify them.

CHAPTER 3

A Brief Survey of Gao Village since the Late 1990s[1]

Introduction

In this chapter I would like to convey to the reader some sense and feeling of how Gao Village has been since 1997, when *Gao Village* (Gao 1999) left off. Furthermore, this chapter aims at giving the reader a general sketch of various aspects of life and reality in present-day Gao Village. These aspects include population, family and family planning, income and living standards, healthcare, and land.

I will start with some personal experiences. In August 2011, I took my two Australian-born and raised daughters to Gao Village: two Aussies, eight-year-old Saskia and ten-year-old Olivia. As part of the journey to Gao Village, we took a train from Beijing to Nanchang, the capital city of Jiangxi Province. During the 24-hour train ride, the girls were very excited, asking about the plants and animals in Gao Village. After a few days in Nanchang, a friend drove us to Jiujiang, where my brother Gao Changxian picked us up for the last leg of our journey to Gao Village. As soon as we got out of the car upon our arrival at Gao Village, after about a three-hour car ride, Olivia wanted to see frogs and so went straight to the rice field. I followed her with Saskia on a muddy

---

1   Some of the information in this chapter is also in Gao 2017a and Gao 2017b.

Photo 3. The kind of Gao Village that my daughters had not expected to see.
Taken by the author in 2015.

path dividing the paddy field. But there were no frogs to be found. We searched around in a little stream where when I was a child we children used to catch fish, eels, frogs, and shrimp. But now my excited girls could not find frogs of any significance except occasionally a couple of tiny ones that disappeared quickly.

Then Olivia and Saskia wanted me to make bows and arrows to shoot at animals in the forest. With the help of my brother-in-law, we cut some bamboo and made some very nice bows, like the ones that I loved to have when I was a child. However, we could not find anything for them to shoot at, and they could not find any animals except dogs when they walked around the village, though Olivia at some point discovered a tiny dead snake on the road. Saskia protested: this is not a village! This is like Jinan, she declared. Jinan is the capital city of Shandong Province, one of the biggest and richest provinces in China where, prior to our stay in Beijing, we stayed for three months when I was a visiting scholar at Shandong University. The girls expected Gao Village to be something like they had probably seen on TV: mud houses with straw roofs in the middle of thick forests. They did not and still do not know that Chinese villages have never been like that. Nor did they realize that rural China has changed so much that houses like my brother's house, where we were staying, and the houses surrounding it are actually better than urban dwellings, at least as seen from the outside. These rural houses are modern and beautifully decorated. In my brother's house air-conditioning was installed for the benefit of our arrival, the kind of modern convenience that we did not have in our rented apartment in Jinan.

There were things that were "un-Australian" for them of course. For instance, the mosquitoes were far less ferocious but so massive. Almost every night when we were in Gao Village, my brother Gao Changxian would gather the villagers to play mahjong in the front hall, leaving the front door open. They would use insect control spray to fight the mosquitoes. The next morning we would get up to find that the floor was totally black, covered by a thick layer of dead mosquitoes that carpeted the floor.

Changes in Gao Village: For the Better?

The girls were somehow disappointed by the lack of exotic "backward-ness." There would be no hunting trips and no scary walks in the depths of the forest. And it was so hot. So they preferred to stay in the air-conditioned room all the time. But their other casual observations could also be so surprisingly insightful. One day, Saskia asked me why the Gao villagers were so old. I was taken aback by the question. It was of course true that the villagers we met in August 2011 were almost all old, except for the schoolchildren. The reason is, of course, that the young Gao villagers were far away, working as migrant workers or looking for work, all over China.

So this is a village that, since the 1949 revolution, has witnessed tremendous changes both physically in the village and mentally for the villagers, the kind of changes that have brought the village from the end of the 18th century to the 21st century in just 60 years. According to Gao Village clan records, the first Gao villagers migrated to the present location about 200 years ago. From then on the Gao villagers lived more or less the same kind of life, in the same style of dwelling, eating the same kind of food, wearing more or less the same kind of clothing, receiving the same kind of education, getting the same kind of healthcare (if any), in the same kind of social structure and family formation, and using the same mode of production for one and a half centuries until the 1950s. The 1949 revolution led by the Chinese Communist Party changed the social structure, education, healthcare, and mode of production, much for the better for the majority but with tragic cost for some.

The changes continued in the post-Mao era, the most dramatic of which was not the dismantling of the collective system, as normally assumed by many in and outside of China, but that of migrant workers moving from Gao Village to urban areas. Physically, the newly built large, decorative houses in Gao Village are overwhelmingly impressive. Some of the houses have not only flush toilets and tap water but also marble top kitchens. There is electricity in every household, whereas until the mid-1980s Gao villagers had to use oil lamps. The clothes that Gao villagers wear are not much different from what the average urban Chinese wears, and the clothes of the average urban resident in China are not much different from that of the average resident in a Western country.

That is the exterior of Gao Village, the physical side of the village. How about internally, the mental side of the village, so to speak? How do the villagers think and feel about their life and the world? A comparison and the contrast I experienced between the urban and rural are of interest and relevance to this question. Before my August visit to Gao Village in 2011, I had been staying at the Research Institute of Social Sciences and Humanities headed by Wang Hui, Wang Zhongcheng, and Zui Zhiyuan at Tsinghua University in Beijing, as a Weilun Professor for six months. I participated in seminars with visiting speakers from all over the world who came there frequently because it was Tsinghua

University and because of Wang Hui's reputation. I held a reading workshop for a dozen postgraduates from Tsinghua University, Peking (Beijing) University, and the Chinese Academy of Social Sciences. To get into these institutions, academics are supposed to be la crème de la crème in China. So I had a plenty of opportunities to find out on the ground what the Chinese intellectual elite thought about the state of affairs in China and the world.

Basically, though there was no feeling of absolute despair, the sentiment was of resentment and complaint, against and about corruption, the unaffordability of housing, the increasing gap between the rich and the poor, the decline of the number of students from rural China in prestigious universities, the increasing signs of structural problems of the economy, and the lack of initiatives for political change. In a word, there was a widespread frustration over the lack of a narrative that can direct what the next step for China is.

However, when I arrived in Gao Village after my rather long stay at Tsinghua University, I was surprised to find that the Gao villagers I talked to were much more optimistic. This is consistent with a large-scale and comprehensive citizen satisfaction survey carried out from 2003 to 2011 under the leadership of Anthony Saich (Xu Qinghong, 2011), which shows that the rural and the more marginalized sectors of Chinese society are more satisfied. The Gao villagers smiled broadly, and carried out their work and life with confidence and vigor. This is not a patronizing observation by an outsider who visits an exotic place and finds nothing but happy people of blessed ignorance. I know these villagers very well because I lived and breathed with them for about 20 years. I know intimately and instantly what they think when I talk to them. I was surprised because there was a genuine happy mood in the village. I was also surprised because it was such a reverse contrast between the urban and rural, between the elite and people at the lower strata of Chinese society. One would expect that the urban and the elite would be happier than the poor rural beasts of burden in the current state of affairs. In fact, it is the first time since I left Gao Village permanently in the late 1970s that I felt this reverse contrast.

In my numerous previous visits to Gao Village I always encountered complaint, resentment and sometimes despair among the villagers (Gao 1999). But this time it seemed different. This is the reverse of what I had expected, certainly the reverse of the late 1980s and early 1990s. Previously it was Gao villagers who would come to me and complain about this and that. There is, of course, visible evidence for the cause of this contrast. For the first time in more than 2,000 years of history, the rural people are not taxed anymore. There is no longer a tax per head or tax on land. Instead, there are various kinds of subsidies for production inputs such as costs of seeds and pesticide. The Chinese authorities have been trying to invest in country roads, healthcare and social security. For instance, for the first time in 20 years, the two disabled sons of Gao Guoneng have been getting about RMB 2,000 as disability benefit, starting since 2011. After more than 20 years of stagnation, migrant workers' salaries have been on the increase in the last few years and especially since 2009. As I will describe in Chapter 9, there is real estate boom happening in Gao Village.

Population and Family Planning

As Sautman points out:

> China's natal program is inaccurately termed a one child–policy … it actually is anywhere from a 2.1- to 2.6-child policy. A PRC official has been quoted as stating that 90% of rural families have two children and others have more. (Sautman 2001: 123)

Since 1996, there have been 69 males and 58 females born in Gao Village; the village has clearly expanded since 1999 when *Gao Village* was published. It had 105 households and 412 people registered as Gao villagers as of 2015. Of those, more than a couple of them actually have obtained urban household registration, even though they might not have deregistered as Gao villagers. One of Gao Chaozuo's sons, for instance, works as a house painter in the city of Leping, a small city by Chinese standards in Jiangxi, and married a girl from Hunan. Now they have settled down in Leping, though he is still considered a Gao villager. On the other hand, what is considered urban in Chinese official statistics is not what it seems. According to official statistics, by 2010 the percentage of urban residents in China had reached 49.68 percent, while the percentage of rural residents had decreased to 50.32 percent. The percentage breakup is based on those have lived and worked in an urban area for six months or more. According to this approach, nearly 30 percent of the 412 Gao villagers would have to be considered urban residents. However, those Gao villagers do not consider themselves urban residents. Nor are they de facto urban residents: they have their per-capita share of land in Gao Village, and they have children mostly back in Gao Village and no access to most of the urban facilities or social and economic welfare measures where they live and work. They are barred from most of the job opportunities in the cities where they work. Their children cannot go to the schools where they work. Nationally, the so-called urban residents whose *hukou* are somewhere other than where they work and live amount to 261.39 million, and of these 240 million are migrant workers from rural China (Wang Su 2011).

Family planning has been practiced in Gao Village, though in a much more relaxed fashion since the end of the 1990s, for four reasons. One reason is that more and more people can afford the fine. In fact it is not called a "fine" or "penalty" anymore; it is called *shehui fuyang fei* ("social maintenance fee"). Up until 2015, the rule stipulated that a couple could have a second child if the first one was a girl. If the first one was a boy, then a fine of RMB 10,000 would be imposed if a second child was born. Many villagers were ready to pay to have another child and the local authorities were happy to collect the revenue without being seen as brutal. The second reason is that some young couples might have babies born somewhere far away from the place where the family was registered. Therefore, monitoring has become difficult and some local authorities have just given up. The increasing ability of villagers to pay this fee also meant that the desire for male children can be met by having a screened abortion, that is, selective abortion on the basis of gender. Screened abortion is illegal in China but a "backdoor" approach of payment can be used to make the doctors violate the law. In this context, many young people have attitudes different from their elders. When I talked to the villagers I found that many young people had come to the idea that girls and boys were the same. Lastly, some of them think they are too busy to have more children and that to have children is too expensive. Underlining this kind of attitude change are several factors including a modern education, jobs far away in urban areas, and the changed expectations of children such as getting a higher education. There is also an important socio-economic factor: infant mortality rate is very low now. As a result, the Chinese do not have to consider having more children as a security measure in case one or more of them die.

During my recent visits, family planning has not been a topic that the villagers were willing to talk to me about, as it used to be. During the 1990s, family planning was a big deal for everyone: for the local authorities because population control was their key performance index, and for the villagers because their very existence was under threat. The local authorities were not happy either because they were made to be brutal to their fellow villagers. I used to hear complaints from both parties—the villagers who bore the brutality and the local officials who had to impose the brutality. Then it was considered by both the intellectual and political elite in China that the control of the Chinese population was a national emergency, a war strategy, as if China was being invaded. Now the considerable arrest of population growth and the seeming shortage of labor have finally made the Chinese political and intellectual elite feel more relaxed about population control. In fact, there have been calls for reconsidering the priority and a reassessment of family planning policies. In 2015, a "two children per family" policy was finally promoted.

For a long period of time, the post-Mao official propaganda repeatedly stated that Mao had encouraged the rapid growth of the Chinese population and that the criticism of Professor Ma Yinchu, who advocated population control, resulted in the explosive growth of an extra 200 million people. Xin Zilin even went so far as to say that the negligence of Professor Ma's advice led to the birth of an extra 400 million people (Xin Zilin 2007). Such an outrageous claim could have been believed by many intelligent people simply because any accusation of communism or Mao is believable. Now new evidence is allowed to be published that shows that Mao actually supported population control, that there was a population control policy in the Mao era, that Professor Ma Yinchu was not an expert on demography, and that Ma was not criticized for population control per se but for advocating Malthusianism(Gao 2008a; Liang 2012; Qian 2008).[2]

An example that illustrates the current state of affairs of family planning is what happened to Gao Anyuan, a school teacher at the local school. He had a son who was 18 years old (when I visited) and had enrolled in a college in 2011. However, less than two years earlier his wife, a woman from the nearest town center, Youdunjie, gave birth to a girl. Gao Anyuan was obviously a happy father, as he is fond of taking his little daughter on a motorbike wherever he goes. This is an indication of two points. One is that Gao villagers actually do like having girls, at least if they have a son at the same time. Secondly, after 16 years a second child was added to Gao Anyuan's family, an indication that family planning is not as rigid as it used to be.

Income and Living Standards

There is no absolute poverty in Gao Village anymore. Even the poorest have shelter, very good quality shelter compared with what some of them used to have. Every household has some land to grow grain and vegetables for self-consumption and therefore nobody goes hungry. They are much better clothed than ever before in Gao Village history. In terms of material life, Gao Village is at its best ever. Education has been improved since I wrote *Gao Village*, largely because the nine-year

---

2   For a very detailed chronology of the family planning policy, see Chen (2015).

compulsory education became truly implemented. It is now indeed free education for rural people for nine years, though the villagers still pay some fees.

The two poorest families in Gao Village are Gao Renfang (nickname Lati, to whom a chapter is devoted later) and Gao Changfan. Gao Renfang is poor for two main reasons. One is that he suffers from a long-term respiratory illness. He cannot work to his full capacity and he also has to pay considerable medical costs. Another reason is that neither of his two sons have made enough money. One son died in 2000 at the age of 20 because of epilepsy. The other son is just able to earn enough to support himself as a migrant worker.

Gao Changfan became poor for the opposite reason. He was determined to get his son educated. His son was kept at year 12 for five years, repeating his course of study each year in the hope of obtaining a better national tertiary entrance examination result so that he could be enrolled in a college or university. His son did succeed eventually to enter a college. But after eight years of senior high and four years at a college, this son of Gao Changfan has not been able to find a stable and reasonably paid job. Either a job is paid too low or not to his liking. Gao Changfan's son moved from one job to another and therefore is not able to earn a good income for the family. This is on top of the fact that the family incurred a considerable debt for the son's education, with the hope that once the most promising member of the family graduated there would be money enough to pay the debt. But the most educated son in the family has not been able to do that.

It is hard to earn a living by just farming the land. Take the case of Gao Lati as an example. The over 60-year-old Lati is too old to be a migrant worker. He and his wife work on 2.4 *mu* of land, one *mu* of which was leased from another villager. For that one *mu* of land to grow rice, Lati has to pay RMB 200 for the rent, RMB 100 for chemical fertilizers and insecticides, and RMB 100 for machines to harvest the rice crop. The crop usually yields a little more than 500 kilograms of rice. The selling price at the market in 2010 was RMB 108 per 50 kilograms; therefore, the total return in cash for working on one *mu* of land is a little over RMB 1,000. Taking away the RMB 500 input including rent, Lati gets only RMB 500 for all his and his wife's work on the rice crop that year. Since Lati did not have to pay rent for the other 1.4 *mu* of land, Lati's income from one rice crop is about RMB 1,500. Typically, Gao villagers plant and harvest two rice crops a year, one in summer and one in autumn. So the total income of Gao Lati for a family of four is RMB 3,000, or RMB 750 per person.

Nowadays, unlike in the Mao era, the villagers do not have to sell what they have produced to anyone. They could keep their produce, or sell it at a market any time they choose. So, as I witnessed when I was there, there are trucks plowing through villages in the area all the time, looking to purchase agricultural produce. One day, I saw Gao Changkuan, his wife and their school-aged daughter passing by, with Changkuan pushing a wheelbarrow. They had just finished harvesting peanuts. While they were walking along the main road running through the village, within no more than three minutes three passing trucks stopped, attempting to buy the peanuts that had just been harvested and were still in the wheelbarrow. The first truck driver offered RMB 1.40 per 500 grams of peanuts. Changkuan declined the offer and eventually sold their peanuts to the people in the third truck, who offered RMB 1.5 per 500 grams. Changkuan harvested 73 kilograms of peanuts on half a *mu* of land. According to him, the amount of money he got from selling them could barely cover the cost.

The Chinese government has actually been trying to implement measures to maintain some level of agricultural income for farmers. When I was in Gao Village in August 2011, the rice had just been harvested and dried under the scorching sun on cemented ground in every household's front yard. Constantly there were trucks passing by Gao Village, carrying bags and bags of rice. A truck stopped at Gao Village and I witnessed some Gao villagers selling rice at RMB 110 per 50 kilograms. I asked the people who were buying how the price was determined. I was told that the Chinese government had assigned a "protection price" (*baohu jia*) at RMB 102 per 50 kilograms for 2011. So the market price had to be higher than that, or else the farmer would not sell.

What is also interesting is that the people who were buying the rice are actually from the local grain stations (*liang zhan*), which used to be collective. Now all these grain stations have been privatized. What happens is that they buy the grain locally and store them in their stations and then sell the grain to whoever and whenever they can get a profitable price. The buyers and Gao village sellers seemed to know each other—there was no receipt needed and no cash involved on the spot. All they did was weigh the rice, write down the figures in a notebook, and then they disappeared in the truck. The Gao villagers would get the cash sometime later.

At least in the case of Gao Lati, the cash income from farming is far below the Chinese government's official line of poverty in China. According to an official white paper published by the Chinese government in 2011, the definition of poverty includes those who earn less than RMB 1,274 a year (Krishnan 2011). But Lati's family's earnings from farming are only about RMB 750 per capita a year. This calculation does not take into account the vegetables that Lati grows on his dry land plots for self-consumption. Nor does it take into account the earnings by Gao Village migrant workers. Lati is one of the poorest in Gao Village for the very simple and basic reason that his family does not have much income from migrant working.

However, Lati does manage to find ways of earning some income now and then from short-term work in and around Gao Village. Short-term work includes planting rice in the busy season, carrying bricks or making cement at construction sites, and so on. For instance, when I was in Gao Village in August 2011, there was hardly any farming work since the first rice crop had already been harvested and the second rice crop had already been planted. Periodically the villagers would have to spray insecticide on the paddy fields. That was about it. But Lati had been working for Gao Wenshu at the latter's housing construction site. Usually, for this kind of short-term work, the employer would pay RMB 80–100 a day, plus a free lunch and a package or two of cigarettes, the last freebie especially appreciated by Lati, though he looks like he is dying from lung disease.

In the Mao era and even until the late 1990s there was hardly any short-term work like this. In those days the villagers would help each other in this kind of work for free, paid at most with some food and a few cigarettes. Now it is all commercial and at market price. This also explains partly at least why there seems to be a shortage of laborers in southeast coastal cities. In other words, the economic development has been shifting from and trickling down from the southeast coastal areas to inland so much that there are job opportunities not far from their home villages or even within the villages. The real estate boom in Gao Village, discussed in Chapter 9, is an obvious and the foremost illustration of this change.

As an indication of the kind of living standard and income in Gao Village, my research finds that by the first decade of the 21st century, 20–30 percent of households had air-conditioning, 60–70 percent of households had fridges, and almost every family had one electric bike or a motorbike. Some of them had mobile phones, but I found only one Gao villager who had access to the internet. That was Gao Anyuan, who, though a full time school teacher at the local school, also drove a truck to earn some extra money. This is not surprising because mostly only young villagers use the internet. There is no use installing internet access since young Gao villagers do not work and live in Gao Village. Gao Anyuan's wife used to run a corner shop in Gao Village, but the shop was closed down a couple of years ago due to a lack of business, since the village was quiet most of the year because of migration and there was so much competition. Now there is only one corner shop in Gao Village, run by the son of a former rich peasant. He and his wife, a girl from the nearby Cao Village, also run a sewing business in the shop. When there are no customers, the two just work on making clothes.

Family and Marriage

For Gao villagers, the concept of family is the same and yet different from what they used to know and value traditionally. It is the same in that they still think their roots are in Gao Village, that they still have to look after their parents, and that they still think their kids are Gao villagers. It is very different in that they might marry someone from another province, and that they want their children to grow up in cities. All the migrant workers that I have talked to indicate to me that when they are old they would like to go back to live and die in Gao Village. At the same time, they would like their children to succeed in being able to work and live in urban centers. This is consistent with the results of a large-scale survey done by the Chinese Academy of Social Sciences, which showed that only 3.9 percent of the surveyed rural people wish the next generation of their families to live in rural China (Ding et al 2016). This is in some way contradictory: On the one hand, the villagers are found to be content and optimistic about their life, and on the other hand they would like their children to be different.

One of the explanations for this seeming contradiction is that the concept and structure of the family in Gao Village is different from tradition in that the family is usually split into two. Either the husband and wife is in one urban era working while their children and parents are back in Gao Village, or the husband is working away from home as a migrant worker and his wife and children are back home in Gao Village with his parents. This situation is so uncertain and unsettling that the consequences are hard to assess. Although the villagers see improvement of life now and they are happy about that, they are uncertain as to what the future will be. In the final analysis for them, success in life ultimately means becoming urban.

Therefore, one crucial issue concerning rural China is the final destiny of migrant workers. For many years, the usual practice and outcome has been that a young man or woman, usually a teenager, would leave the village to be a migrant worker. They might work for a few years or even 20 years and would send money home to help the family for their siblings' education, for medical costs and above all to save up to build a house as a first condition for marriage, if it is a male. Then they may get married but leave the village again to work far away to earn money for their own kids. Finally, when their kids are teenagers and they are too old for the factory or workshop, they would return to their villages and their children in turn will become migrant workers. This has been the case up until 1996, when I finished *Gao Village*.

In this update of Gao Village, I want to find out whether this pattern has changed and I want to find out to what extent and in what way Gao villagers can be part of China's urbanization. As mentioned above, according to some sources, currently more than 46 percent of the Chinese population are already urban, judging by the international standard that one is considered urban if one continuously works and lives in an urban area for six months. But I don't think this percentage can be taken at face value. Many of the hundreds of millions of migrant workers from rural China may work and live in an urban area for 20 years while their families are still rural. A migrant worker would not be able to access any of the social and economic welfare measures the urban population has, though it is increasingly the case that many of the urban residents have lost their welfare entitlements.

My sister Lingli married a man with an urban household registration and became an urban person. But that was in the 1950s. In fact, there were only five women in Gao Village who became urban by marriage in the 1950s and 1960s. What is surprising is that since then, even fewer women have become urban by marriage. The divide between urban and rural has become greater because an urban man does not come to rural China to pick a woman to marry, not anymore. Since 1997, there have only been a couple of women in Gao Village who have succeeded in becoming urban by marriage.

It is very difficult for a migrant worker to become an urban person in both name and reality. There are only a couple of men who succeeded in doing that, one of whom is named Gao Chaoqiu. When Chaoqiu started as a migrant worker in the late 1980s he was barely 17 years old. After many years of dedication and hard work, Chaoqiu was handpicked by the factory owner to be a shop floor supervisor. To reward him for his hard work, his boss also got him a Xiamen *hukou* registration. He also registered for social security, half of which was paid by his employer.

Now his children can go to school like a local Xiamen person and his family can have access to government subsidized medical services.

It used to be the case from the 1950s to the 1990s that if a rural person got enrolled in a college, an urban *hukou* status was guaranteed because the state had the responsibility of assigning work for all the graduates. Now that system is no longer practiced. All graduates have to find work themselves, thus they have gained freedom but lost certainty. A rural person who is enrolled in a college or university will take his or her *hukou* to where the school is located. However, upon graduation the *hukou* status goes with them wherever they work. If they cannot find work, they will have no *hukou* anywhere. An example of that is Gao Wei, the son of my brother Changxian. After graduating from Central China Agriculture University in Wuhan, Gao Wei found work in a company in Guangzhou. His *hukou* was temporarily held in Guangzhou though he then worked in Hainan, sent there by his company. If he marries and has a child in Hainan, he will have no access to any of the social welfare there because his *hukou* is in Guangzhou.

One other notable and potentially significant phenomenon is marriage between migrant workers. For a long time Gao Village migrant workers, male or female, though working far away, say in Beijing or Shenzhen, would, through a go-between, find a marriage partner in villages and areas near Gao Village. Now that has changed. By the mid-2010s, there were a dozen Gao villagers who had married partners from Hunan, Henan, Hainan, Fujian, and Guizhou, provinces where most migrant workers come from. It is interesting to note that it is always the case that in a marriage involving a Gao villager and someone outside Jiangxi Province, the husband is a man from Gao Village and the wife is from some other province, mostly from Hunan. I did make some enquiries about this but failed to get a satisfactory explanation. It seems that no Gao Village girls did not want to venture a marriage with someone that was good enough from other province. For example, Gao Chaoxin's second daughter married someone from Hunan, but she divorced the Hunan man after she found out that the man's family lived in a very remote poor mountainous area. It is mostly the case that the wife goes with the husband to his home village to settle, not the other way around.

There are other cases of family changes because of marriage that go beyond the simple urban and rural divide. One of my students at the Gao Village School, when I was a "barefoot teacher" during the early 1970s, married a man from a village near Gao Village. They managed to move to and live in Shenzhen, where her son studied English and became an interpreter for a company that did business with the USA. So he now travels to the USA, her grandfather proudly told me. The daughter of Gao Chaodong, who is one of the sons of Gao Changyin, the party secretary of the brigade that Gao Village belonged to and who was toppled during the Cultural Revolution (the details of which are described in *Gao Village*), now works in Singapore. But then Gao Chaodong has not been and has never been seen as a proper Gao villager ever since he attended boarding school in the county seat Poyang when he was a teenager.

Gao Shenneng, another student of mine, first was a bamboo furniture apprentice for three years and then went to join the PLA. After he finished his service in the army, he was assigned to work in a collective shop in Jingdezhen. When the economic reform went into full swing, his collective shop was privatized. Shenneng volunteered to rent the shop and ran it with a couple of colleagues for a few years. Then he became a taxi driver, after which he bought two taxi vehicles and rented them out. He also bought two apartments in Jingdezhen, so the family has Jingdezhen urban resident status, although one of his sons still built a house in Gao Village, where their grandparents now reside.

Healthcare

Although China has made remarkable economic progress over the past few decades, its citizens' health has not improved as much. Since 1980, the country has achieved an average economic growth rate of ten percent and lifted 400–500 million people out of poverty. Yet Chinese official data suggest that between 1981 and 2009, average life expectancy in China rose by only about five years, from roughly 68 years to 73 years. In contrast, life expectancy had increased by almost 33 years between 1949 and 1980. One might propose that once life expectancy gets to certain threshold, any increase will have to be slow and less dramatic. While this may be true, it is not a good reason to congratulate the post-Mao authorities. In countries that had similar life expectancy levels in 1981 but slower economic growth thereafter—Colombia, Malaysia, Mexico, and South Korea, for example—by 2009 life expectancy had increased by 7–14 years. According to the World Bank, even in Australia, Hong Kong, Japan, and Singapore, countries that had much higher life expectancy figures than China in 1981, life expectancy rose by 7–10 years during the same period. As Huang (2015) argues, the post-Mao leadership has single-heartedly pursued a policy of economic growth for a long time, ignoring issues of public health.[3]

That being said, Gao villagers on the whole are much healthier than before. With the improvement of living standards such as the absence of starvation and a better diet, better living conditions such as modern housing with sufficient light and hygiene, sufficient protection from rough weather, fridges, air-cons and so on, signs of formerly common diseases such as smallpox, cholera, leprosy, and furuncle are absent, while other common problems such as fevers and diarrhea are easy to handle and can be controlled. The last time that I visited Gao Village, I was surprised to find that there were six men and two women who were over 80 years old and still healthy. By the time I finished writing *Gao Village* in 1997, there was not a single person there who had lived beyond 80 years old. My mother managed to reach the age of 79 and died in 1998. This clearly is a sign of improvement of health. What was not surprising was that none of the eight Gao villagers who were over 80 and healthy smoked. Smoking is probably now the biggest killer

---

3   For the mistakes that the Chinese authorities made and their subsequent efforts to correct their mistakes in health policies, see Blumenthal and Hsiao, 2015.

in Gao Village and in rural China. It is still customary to offer a male villager a cigarette whenever a man comes to visit you; otherwise you will be considered either as stingy or rude. Every man smokes, it seems. Gao villagers are increasingly found to die of cancer, lung cancer, liver cancer, throat cancer, and heart disease; in fact, the word "cancer" was one of the most often heard from villagers when I talked to them.

In spite of huge improvements in health, medical costs remain a great fear for Gao villagers. Mostly the villagers do not go to the doctor if they have a complaint. They mostly rely on their body's natural resistance or just let the illness take its natural course. Decades after the abandonment of the effective and affordable "barefoot doctors" system, along with the dismantling of the collective system, the Chinese authorities have begun to realize the stupidity of throwing out the baby with the bath water. In August 2011, I found that they even refused to pay the RMB 10 that is required to join the system. I was very perplexed about this, since RMB 10 is really nothing much for the villagers now. They could spend RMB 10 easily on anything. For instance, while I was there in the village a truck stopped by one day. It turned out that it was a fruit seller truck, selling pears and apples. At least half a dozen Gao villagers spent RMB 10 or more to buy fruit that day. That was a little surprising to me because I know that Gao villagers did not used to eat fruit. They used to and still do eat a lot of vegetables, but not fruit. If they had anything to do with fruit it would be that grown on the trees around their houses. Or if they bought some it would be for special occasions. In any case, the fact they did not hesitate to spend RMB 10 or more on buying fruit from a passing truck meant that RMB 10 to join the medical insurance system should not be a big deal for them now. But they were reluctant.

The way the system works is that for some daily complaints, the medical insurance system does not reimburse the cost. One can get reimbursed by the system only if one has to be hospitalized and only if the patient goes to a designated hospital in the town of Youdunjie, about 15 kilometers away from Gao Village. Even then one can only get reimbursed for 70 percent of the cost. In any case, for Gao villagers, by the time one has to be hospitalized, one might as well die at home.

For Gao Villagers, the current medical insurance system is not just useless but also a concerted way by the various interest groups to rip the villagers off, at the same time pocketing the government medical insurance investment.

However, as I describe in Chapter 11, the situation has gradually improved. This medical care insurance system started only in 2011 in Gao Village, and the villagers did not trust it, understandably, since state agents, i.e., party officials and government bureaucrats at various levels of the hierarchy, have been consistently trying to get themselves rich first in the post-Mao era and since policies have been changing all time. By 2015, when I last visited Gao Village, the villagers had seen the benefit of the policy and most of them were happy to pay the premium.

The Issue of Land

For any rural community, land is of the utmost importance. They live on it and they are emotionally attached to their land. For Gao villagers this also should be the case, but this cannot be taken for granted anymore. The Chinese media has been full of reports and news of stories and horrors resulting from what are called "land seizures," that is, commercial companies, or local authorities, or the two conspiring together, with the support of the police and the laws, take land away from farmers and owners of residential houses. The land is then turned into a commercial development with huge profits, while the original "owners" of the land are compensated with very little for being forcibly removed. I have placed quotation marks on the word "owners" because in terms of legal status as stipulated in the Chinese Constitution, nobody owns any land in China. All land belongs to the state or the collective community. So theoretically, a body, be it a company, an institution or an individual person, only has land use rights. Therefore, there have been constant and sometimes fierce debates on whether China should privatize all land. The most seemingly convincing argument for such wholesale privatization is that it will solve the "land seizure" problem once and for all. The underlying assumption for such an argument is that the reason local authorities and commercial companies can forcibly remove occupiers of any piece of land is the lack of legal ownership.

But there are also two pervasive arguments against wholesale privatization of land. One is that "land seizure" problems arise in only a small percentage of the land in China, that is, the land that is near a commercial center, such as towns and cities or where concentrated industry is located, like some areas around the Pearl River Delta and the Yangtze River Delta where commercial developments are profitable. For the majority of land in China, there is no commercial or developmental interest, just as there is no such interest in Gao Village. Therefore, there is no "land seizure" issue justifying privatization. The second argument is that the current land system acts as a social safety net for the majority of Chinese people, that is, the rural Chinese. This argument reminds us of the fact that the absence of large urban ghettos in China, not uncommonly seen in developing countries with large populations, is a beneficial result of the current land ownership system. Every household is guaranteed to have a piece of land, no matter how poor the family is. A villager might venture to urban areas for work; but if there is no work he or she can always go back to that piece of land in the village and grow food. It is this land system that enables China to have cheap labor at almost no financial cost for the Chinese government. It is also this system that has given rise to a hybrid form of existence for rural Chinese: migrant workers are urban but also rural; rural Chinese are agricultural and yet also earn income from industry. With this contextual big picture in mind, it should not be surprising for the reader to hear that Gao villagers are not interested in "land seizure" problems, not yet.

Though there is less than one *mu* of land per capita in Gao Village, which consists of 0.6 *mu* of rich paddy fields and 0.2 *mu* of dry land per capita, quite a large percentage of land in Gao Village lies untilled and unattended. This is either land that is a little further from the village center, land that is not so fertile, or land that is prone to floods, similar to what I observed in the vast Chinese countryside while I took the train from north to south many times in the past couple of years. It is very pleasing for me to see that there are now marshes and wastelands covered with tall grasses, bushes and different vegetation. This is what it should be, I would tell myself, after having lived many years in England where there is this overwhelming sense of greenness and lush vegetation is visible everywhere. This newly emerged greenness is a result of an increasing phenomenon all over China's countryside called *paohuang*, which refers to arable land that is abandoned and becomes wasteland. This is in total contrast to the state of affairs during the years when I was living in the village, when every inch of land was cultivated for growing something. There was a term in those days called *kaihuang* ("open up wasteland"). Those days in Gao Village, even tiny narrow footpaths between paddy fields and plots for planting were stripped bare by human activities, as people were trying to make use of everything, such as grass burned for fertilizer and bushes cut for firewood. Now there is coal, electricity or even gas for cooking. Trees are growing back, roads are covered with bushes, with grass growing taller than human beings, and the birds are all coming back.

In Gao Village land is distributed to each household on a per capita basis. Currently the per capita land is 0.6 *mu* of paddy field and 0.2 *mu* of dry land. In order to account for the demographic change as a result of birth, death and marriage, land is redistributed every five years. So now Changxian has land only for himself, because his son has left the village after finishing university, his two daughters are married to men outside Gao Village, and his wife has urban registration because she was born to a state paid teacher. But land used for growing crops is not much valued these days, especially land that is not fertile, such as marshland and hillside land. As mentioned above, much of this kind of land has been left unused for years and therefore has not been included in distribution.

I was actually very surprised to learn that one piece of land measuring 40 *mu* has been contracted to a non-Gao villager who lives 50 kilometers away. That piece of land was left uncultivated after the 1998 flood because not only it is a little further away from the village center, but also it is in a low position near the river running through the east of Gao Village and is therefore prone to even the slightest possible flood. One way of preventing flooding is to build a dam around this piece of land. However, it is very difficult to mobilize enough labor to do a project like this in post-Mao China. So the village collectively decided to lease that piece of land rent-free for ten years to whoever was willing to build a dam around it. A truck owner and driver named Gao Chaoliang took up the lease. But he himself did not do the job. Instead he sublet the lease to a relative who lives in Yaquehu. Gao Chaoliang gets something out of the deal, the nature of which is kept secret, while his relative works on the land more or less free. The contract was signed in 2009. It is still hard for me to believe that Gao Village is willing to lease a piece of land to someone for free.

One reason for this lack of value of agricultural land is that the return is so low, as described in the case of Lati. Some villagers are content to just produce enough for self-consumption, which has become easier in the post-Mao era for two main reasons. One reason is that though the population has increased, the people needing food in Gao Village have become fewer because many migrant workers are away from home. The second reason is that production output is higher, not because the dismantling of the collective system has given farmers more incentive to work harder, as assumed and propagated by the post-Mao authorities and intellectual elite, but because of the availability of new technology such as hybrid rice crops and the intensive use of chemicals (Gao 2008a). Some households may not have any laborers to work on the land in any particular year, in which case they let their neighbors or relatives or friends work on the land, and in return the person who works on the land will give the land owner 50 kilograms of rice.

Virtually none of the young Gao villagers works on the land anymore, because they are either working or looking for work far from home. Mostly the land is worked by the elderly and by women. Some—but very few—young women stay in the village to look after kids. Gao villagers still mainly grow rice, but also grow soya beans, peanuts, sesame, wheat and canola seeds. Every household grows some vegetables for self-consumption. There is limited use of small machines, like rice harvesters (rice is still the main crop) and machines for tilling the rice fields. Gao villagers do not use draught animals to till the land anymore. In fact, the main draft animal, the water buffalo, has been banned by the local authorities: the villagers have been told that water buffalos are the main source of transmitting schistosomiasis, or snail fever (for a description and impact of this disease, see *Gao Village*), because when the animals feed themselves along the lakes and creeks, schistosomes will get into their bodies and in turn, their droppings in the rice fields can spread schistosomes into the environment. When I visited Gao Village in 2011, there were still half a dozen yellow buffalos, but there were none of the tame and hardworking grey water buffalos in Gao Village. I was surprised and disappointed by this fact, because not only I did I have fond memories of these animals, but also I promised my two daughters that they could have a buffalo ride in Gao Village. One cannot ride on a yellow buffalo because it would never allow someone on its back. By my visit there in 2015, there was not one water buffalo to be seen, whereas in the past up to the 1990s water buffaloes were the most precious animals for villagers in the area.

Photo 4. The last yellow buffalo in Gao Village.
Taken by Wu Yegen in 2013. In 2015, there were none in Gao Village.

The once-prized water buffalos have all but disappeared. Farming work, at the same time, is much less demanding since it is very much dependent on chemicals, for fertilizing the crops as well as for insect control and in fact even for weeding. The villagers pay a tractor owner RMB 80–90 for tilling one *mu* of land and RMB 60 for harvesting one *mu* of rice. The plowing machines are small and handy ones that are made in China especially for small plots of land in terraced fields. Several Gao villagers own such equipment, and those who don't hire one when needed. However, no Gao villager owns a combine harvester, which has to be hired from outside Gao Village.

Education

One major progressive development in rural China since the beginning of the 21st century is the genuine nine years of free education for all. However, anecdotal evidence, as I found when I was at Tsinghua University, suggests that the percentage of students from rural China at China's best universities has been on the decline. This seems paradoxical if one assumes that free education would mean an increase of the percentage of students of rural backgrounds at the tertiary level, since the majority of Chinese are rural. The fundamental reason for what is seemingly a discrepancy is that the income gap between rural and urban people is still too big, even after the abolition of agricultural taxes and agricultural subsidies. When they finish their nine years of education, most children in rural China leave their hometowns to become migrant workers, whereas children of urban backgrounds can—and most do— continue their education with the aim of entering tertiary institutions. For the tiny percentage of rural children who manage to make it to tertiary institutions, they are at a disadvantage in terms of academic performance and in terms of finding jobs after graduation, as the case of the son of Gao Changfan shows.

Another development in education since the 1990s is the flourishing of private providers who have entered the market to make profits.

By 2011, there were already three private middle and high schools in Poyang Town, the county seat of Poyang County. The principal of one such school, Jiang Huigong, is actually from a village not far from Gao Village and used to be the deputy director of the Education Bureau of Poyang County. I was quite shocked when about ten years ago he was earning RMB 10,000 a month as a school principal in the first private school in the county (as a comparison, that is about the same amount a professor would earn at Peking University ten years later, in 2011). These private schools enroll only children of the rich and the powerful, and occasionally gifted students by giving scholarships. The average fee is RMB 10,000 a year, which includes boarding. In order to build up a reputation, the private schools have now started to compete to get some of the best students. One of the most treasured indicators of success and reputation for students is to enter the two most prestigious universities in Beijing, Peking University and Tsinghua University. One private school, Raozhou School, actually goes around all the rural schools in Poyang County and handpicks the most promising by giving scholarships, which can be as much as RMB 20,000, more than the fees and the cost of entering Raozhou. Once a graduate is accepted by Peking or Tsinghua University, the student will wear big red flowers and lead a parade with music as it goes through the main street of Poyang Town.

One other consequence of the marketization of education is the brain drain from public schools. Because private schools have better resources and the teachers get rewarded better in terms of salary and living conditions, they can attract the best teachers from the public sector. It is widely reported in the news that a large number of rural schools have had to close down as a result of the shrinking number of students and the lack of qualified teachers (Wang 2013). As a result, some rural children have to travel further or board at the school even in order to attend primary school, a disincentive for school education even though it is free.

The Environment

Environmental developments since 1997 have brought both good news and bad news to Gao Village. Let me start with the good news first. Since more than a quarter of Gao villagers do not live in Gao Village on a permanent basis (migrant workers), the ecological pressure has been reduced considerably. There is less demand on water resources and less demand on the land, a situation that could be good for the environment. Furthermore, since the late 1990s, Gao villagers started using coal to cook and then moved to gas and electricity. Only when the villagers hold big banquets like weddings, funerals, occasional celebrations or Chinese New Year dinners do they use wood to cook in a big wok. So there is no longer any pressure to hunt for firewood. When I was a child, one of my main and constant jobs was to cut bushes and even grass as firewood for cooking. The trees were gone, the bushes were gone and then we turned to grasses, grasses along the footpath or anywhere. Eventually we had to buy firewood from nearby mountainous villages, whose firewood resources would be exhausted as well by the increasing demand. The supply source would move from nearby places to farther mountains and hills. Eventually, in the 1970s when I was still in the village, one of the most arduous tasks was to push a wheelbarrow for 30 kilometers to get something like 100 kilograms of firewood and bring it home in one day. It was one of the most dreadful tasks I can remember and even now I recall it with fear. I had to get up at four in the morning and push the wheelbarrow to where we could buy the wood. By the time we arrived at the destination it would be about lunchtime. We would cook lunch at a villager's house, with our own rice and some pickled vegetables with a few pieces of meat or fish thrown in. Everyone would eat as much as one kilogram of rice for one meal. We would then tie the firewood (mostly bushes with leaves, not like the kind of nice and neat firewood we are used to having in the West, because there were no trees like that to cut) onto the wheelbarrow and start to push it back home, step by step, along the dusty roads. When I arrived home it would usually about six or seven o'clock in the evening. I would have sunken eyes, sore legs and blistered feet. I would feel weak and as if I were recovering from a disastrous illness.

Now in Gao Village one can see trees everywhere, though they are still young. Bushes are everywhere and grasses and reeds grow taller than humans along the footpaths. The marshes and wetland are full of grass. Occasionally I can see yellow buffaloes grazing on the grassland here and there. It really gives you a sense of wealth and wellbeing, just like the feeling I had when I first went to England, when I was overwhelmed by the greenness and lushness of the English countryside. Because there are trees, the birds have all come back, including sparrows, crows, magpies, little yellow birds and all kinds. However, that is the good news; but there is also the bad news.

The bad news is that the chemicals have wiped out many animals that I used to encounter and love, like frogs, all kinds of fish, shrimp, prawns, eels, turtles, shellfish of all kinds and so on. We could find them in the ponds, streams, ditches, rivers and lakes. But you cannot find that anymore. When I walked among the paddy fields full of rice shoots, I could see the used packages or bottles of fertilizer and pesticide scattered here and there. The villagers really do not have much of a sense of environmental protection. They throw rubbish everywhere they can, in front of their own houses, along footpaths or roads, including foam, plastics, and waste paper. It would have been worse if China had not had a vibrant recycling industry. The worst is the destruction of the biological system that is related to water and soil, as a result of chemical applications. During my stay in the village, I witnessed a couple of times when men and women were out carrying sprayers. It turned out that they had to do the pesticide spraying together, otherwise the insects would fly from one to another field. I was told they need to spray their crops once a week. They have to spray on any and all crops. When I was in the village up until the early 1970s, chemical spray would be applied only to cotton and rice crops. Now, even eggplants and sesame plants require pesticide.

My feeling about the environment in Gao Village was of despair and disgust. However, in early 2015 when I visited Gao Village the last time before I finished the writing of this book, I gained some hope.

Urged by the local authorities who themselves were urged by the higher authorities, Gao villagers have finally started to pay attention to their environment, at least in terms of dealing with rubbish. Details on this are in Chapter 11.

Conclusion

In this rather longish chapter of a general survey of Gao Village since 1997, I have dealt with what I consider to be the major themes in contemporary rural China: population and family planning, healthcare, education, family and marriage, the land issue, income and living standards, and environment. There have been some welcome and progressive developments such as the abolition of agricultural taxes, the first time in 2,500 years, and free school for up to nine years. There has been an attempt to build up an affordable healthcare system and there are some other more or less ambiguous developments, such as the emergence of private schools. Environmentally speaking, the developments since 1997 have been a mixture of both good and bad. It is good to have the grass and wetlands come back, to have the trees and the birds back. But marine life has become almost extinct, though the signs of this development were already evident before 1997. However, by 2015, there had been an improvement in awareness and in attempting to deal with the issue of rubbish.

Living standards in general have been improving since 1997, and there has been a flourishing development of housing construction. However, this kind of improvement in material wealth is not derived from farming, which is supposed to the main lifeline of rural China. This improvement of living standards is sustained by the sweat of the young Gao villagers who migrate thousands of miles away from home to work. This situation has been described in *Gao Village* with a note of uncertainty, but 18 years later this pattern has not changed. The village economy is still sustained by migrant workers who are thousands of miles away. The young Gao villagers still don't know where their future lies, just like China in general.

CHAPTER 4

The Resourcefulness and Entrepreneurship of the Rural Chinese

Introduction

As I have articulated in the introduction of this book, China's economic success—and with it the takeoff in development—have been built on the shoulders of the Chinese rural people. The Chinese government did not look after the rural Chinese in terms of welfare until the 21st century; in fact, it is the other way round. The rural Chinese have not only looked after the Chinese government, but have also made China the economic success that it is, in spite of an enormous amount and degree of injustice, unfairness and inequality against them. They have done this because of their resourcefulness and because of their inner strength to improve their lives.

The inner strength, resourcefulness and entrepreneurship of the rural Chinese that I have been discussing here are in sharp contrast to the influential discussion of what is called "the Chinese spirit" by Gu Hongming (1915), Lin Yutang (1935), Liang Shuming (1949), Arthur Smith (1894), Bo Yang (1986), and of course Lu Xun (1921). Even though there are discussions of Chinese entrepreneurs in old Shanghai, modern Hong Kong and Taiwan, and discussions on the topic of rural contemporary migrant workers (Solinger 1999; Chan 2001 and 2015; Pun 2005), the rural Chinese referred to as *nongmin* (peasants or farmers) are generally thought of as passive and ignorant. But this is not what I have found in contemporary Gao villagers. Gao villagers today are resourceful, innovative, active, and display great entrepreneurship in extremely harsh and difficult circumstances, as the subsequent chapters on individual Gao villagers will demonstrate.

However, in this chapter I will outline the extraordinary resourcefulness and entrepreneurship of one rural Chinese person named Yang Dongping, who I think has the quality and experience to capture most of the meaningful associations of the title of this chapter. This person is not a Gao villager, but the reason I have included Yang in this book on Gao Village is twofold. In this book, an important insight I would to bring out and an important understanding I would like to promote, is the struggle and contribution of the rural Chinese. The chapters on Gao Wenshu and Gao Changxian (Chapters 5 and 6) should correspond very well with this chapter on Yang Dongping. The second reason for providing a portrait of Yang Dongping is that Yang's case is not only more impressive than any individual in Gao Village, to the extent of being astonishing, but is also well-known and was broadcast on television nationwide. To include someone of national significance, someone outside of Gao Village, is to connect Gao Village to the national.

The Chinese Spirit?

Before I present the portrait, let me briefly outline the controversial nature of the topic of the Chinese spirit. I know a term like this can be dangerously misleading and easily slides into hopeless and meaningless essentialism. First of all, there is no such thing as something that is called "Chinese" in the whole of China. China consists of many nationalities and not any of them, not even the biggest ethnic group, the Han, can be said to be representative of all of China or Chinese. In fact, there is no such a thing as the real or pure Han Chinese (Gao 2008b). Secondly, no nation, ethnic group or culture of any place remains still and unchanged for any lengthy period of time. There is always the dynamic inside a place or a group, there is always the influence from outside the place and group, and there is always interaction. Thirdly, it is always dubious to talk about any group of people in terms of culture or spirit, without relating to economics and the material life of these people. There is always the dialectic between the concrete material life and economic structures (the base structures of a society) and cultural and spiritual life (superstructure) in that the base structure somehow configures the characteristics of spiritual and cultural values, and spiritual and cultural values in turn influence, and have an impact on, the continuous development of material life.

However, some description, discussion and analysis of the inner qualities of the rural Chinese can be justifiably said to help improve an understanding of Gao Village in particular, and Chinese in general, on the following rationale. Firstly, the discussion of the inner qualities of the rural Chinese in this chapter is closely related to the economics and material life today. Secondly, this is about rural China, at this particular time and place, which is changing fast and therefore none of what is said is supposed to be ahistorical, historicist or transcendental. Thirdly, this ascription of the inner qualities of the rural Chinese is non-ethnic. In fact, I don't even know to which ethnic group Yang Dongping belongs. Finally, it is precisely to counter the essentialist, ahistorical portrayal of the passive, backward and unenlightened rural Chinese that the current inner qualities are being written about in this chapter.

Gu Hongming, Lin Yutang, and Liang Shuming talk about the Chinese spirit on a cultural and philosophical level, and their treaties on the Chinese spirit therefore appear to be ahistorical and transcendental. Most of what they mean by "Chinese" is about the elite and high culture in the most abstract sense of the word. Arthur Smith talks about Chinese culture and ways of life from an outsider's perspective, and very often shows racial stereotypes, which is no more condemning than Bo Yang, who titled his once bestselling book simply *The Ugly Chinese*. Lu Xun's 1921 portrait of the Chinese spirit, or rather the fatal shortcomings and problems of the Chinese spirit, famously depicted in his novella *The*

True Story of Ah Q, one of the first pieces of literature in vernacular Chinese, is supposedly represented by a marginalized man, bordering a rural and township area in south China at the turn of the 20th century. Although Lu Xun has a deep sympathy with his character in the novel, the character Ah Q is seen as despicably weak, dishonest, cowardly, and lacking awareness of his own identity and his environment. Ah Q might have made a few attempts to change his life, but he certainly does not have anything near an aspiring entrepreneurship. For many Chinese elite, ever since the May Fourth Movement in 1919, Ah Q is typical of a problematic Chinese person who is to blame for the backwardness of China and her lagging behind the West in both spiritual and material life. Recently, scholars like Wang Hui, who writes in hindsight of the Republican Revolution in 1911, the Communist Revolution in 1949, and the success in modernizing China since then, have been trying to restore the positive, active and dynamic quality of Ah Q (Wang Hui 2011). But his voice is still that of a minority.

What a contrast if we look at Yang Dongping. He is so totally different from Ah Q. This chapter will bring out this contrast, but this requires an explanation. Lu Xun, at that time of frustration and despair, might have been unnecessarily too dark about China and too pessimistic about the Chinese. Ah Q was set at that time when China was besieged by Western colonial powers, as well as Japan. Maybe the two revolutions, especially the 1949 revolution that Lu Xun could not have foreseen, have made a great difference on the inner qualities of the rural Chinese, or maybe Ah Q is not depicting a real rural Chinese person though he is said to be rural. However, this chapter is not going to dwell on a defense or a critique of Lu Xun or his contemporaries. Suffice it to say that Yang Dongping was born and raised in a rural village into a very poor family. Because of this background, the story of Yang Dongping can and should bring insight to the life and changes of Gao Village, even though Yang Dongping is not a Gao villager.

Yang Dongping: A Peasant Entrepreneur

Yang is from Sichuan and was born in 1980. This sketch of Yang Dongping is based on a television documentary by CCTV Chinese International aired on June 5, 2011. The title of that documentary, in English translation, was "The Broom Sweeps Out a New World."[1] A large part of the documentary consists of interviews with Yang himself, as well as his family.

When Yang was a teenager his family was too poor for him to finish senior high school. Instead, Yang had to become a migrant worker to earn money. After working in a factory for a while, Yang decided to be his own boss, and his first attempt at entrepreneurship was to buy shampoo wholesale and then sell it to students by going around knocking on the doors of university student dormitories, selling it at a price 20 percent lower than at the local shop. He made a few hundred RMB in half a year. This income was too small for Yang, so he abandoned that line of work and changed to working on a building site as a laborer, which was at least out in the open and more interesting than working in a factory.

One day there was an incident that led to the change of his fortune. In a street near where he worked, he saw an old man fall to the ground. He went over and helped the man to get up but the old man lost consciousness and required medical help urgently, so he hailed a rickshaw and got the old man to the nearby hospital. The hospital required RMB 2,000 as deposit for any treatment, but the old man was unconscious and therefore unable to be responsible or responsive. Without much thinking, Yang decided to take out all of his savings from working on the building site for two years to pay for the deposit for medical care. By chance, the old man happened to be a construction businessman. After regaining consciousness and learning of Yang's

---

1   This is a retelling of the story that I watched on the Chinese CCTV channel *Zhongwen guoji* (中文國際). The Chinese title of the documentary is《掃帚掃出了新世界》(*Saozhou saochule xin shijie*).

circumstances, the old man decided to contract a construction business that was worth RMB 6 million to Yang as a gesture to thank this young man who more or less saved his life. That project alone earned Yang more than RMB 60,000. Yang could not believe his luck: how could one earn so much so quickly and so easily? He had hardly done anything. Before he could think of anything else, he bought a brand new car and drove it home to show his parents and his villagers, the owner of a new car and a successful businessman. In the late 1990s, for a poor villager to own a new car was really something special.

What happened next echoes well the Chinese Taoist idiom, *Saiweng shima yanzhi feifu* ("you cannot be sure whether it is bad luck or good luck when someone [here a man named Sai Weng] loses a horse"). By driving his car to show off, the excited Yang had a car accident. He was lucky not to be seriously hurt, but the car was damaged beyond repair. The accident shocked him and made him realize how fragile life was, and how money earned without hard work was not valued as much and was easily squandered. Yang decided to do what reflects a person of initiative and effort. He decided to go to the city that was nearest his village, Luzhou, to set up a cleaning business. He knew that the city had 400,000 households but not one single cleaning company, so Yang registered a company and named it Xiao mifeng ("small bee"), meaning a small business that is working hard to bring sweet rewards to you. But it was a typical *san wu* company ("three withouts": i.e., without an office, without any workers, and without any clients). Yang walked aimlessly backwards and forwards in the street for hours thinking what to do when he noticed that there were many young men and women idling in the street doing nothing. Yang approached them, one by one, and asked them if they wanted to join him in his cleaning company. He of course told them the pay might be low at the start, but it would be better than nothing since they had nothing to do.

The next problem was how to find clients. He decided to lead a couple of the agreeable workers, holding a bucket and a mop in hand, and knock on doors asking for work. They went from one household to another offering cleaning work. Most of the residents thought they were simply crazy. Some just looked at them with contempt. To start with, the idea of employing someone to clean your house had not even occurred to residents of the city of Luzhou during the 1990s. They would do this kind of work themselves, as they had done for generations. Only the very rich and privileged could afford to have a housemaid in the household, and that was the case only in traditional China. Since the 1949 revolution, the idea of employing someone to clean your own house has been alien. For the vast and absolute majority of Chinese, the idea was unthinkable. Moreover, who would pay for a couple of untidy-looking youngsters holding a bucket to clean your house?

Yang then decided on a different promotion and publicity strategy. He used what was left from his building contract money to buy some paper to produce leaflets. Yang could not afford printing or photocopying and so decided to hand-write the leaflets. He wrote the leaflets at night and distributed them door to door in the daytime. The part of the city where he could afford to stay did not even have electricity at that time, so Yang would light a candle and write them. For the next three months he hand-wrote 30,000 leaflets introducing his cleaning company and asking potential clients to telephone if they were interested. For the first three months all he received were two calls; one from his parents from a public phone booth to ask how he was doing, and one from his landlord to say that his rent was RMB 80 overdue. By then, Yang had only had 30 cents left.

In desperation, Yang decided to offer free cleaning first to prove himself. Yang went from door to door, offering free cleaning service. Most of the residents just shut their doors on his face, for who could trust a young man offering free cleaning. But one quality that Yang admitted several times during the television interviews that he gave is that he is persistent. Once he knows what is right, he never gives up. Yang put this into a nice couplet: *Nuli bu yiding chenggong, dan fangqi kending shibai* ("you might not succeed when you try, but you will certainly fail if you don't try"). Yang believed that there was a market there for the many increasingly affluent and busy households. He kept on trying until one day a woman asked, "Are you really offering free service?" to which he replied, "Yes, let me show you." The woman let Yang in the house, and for the next three hours while Yang was cleaning the house, the woman watched, firstly to see how Yang was doing his job, and secondly to make sure he did not do anything dubious like damage the furniture or steal anything. After three hours the house was sparkling clean and the woman was very happy. Yang went on to clean 500 households for free, of which eventually 200 households offered him cleaning contracts!

This was his first real substantial success, but Yang did not stop there. He started to think of better ways to promote his cleaning business. He first went to the local newspaper, the *Luzhou Evening News*, and negotiated a deal for free advertising whereby whoever bought a paper for the first time could have a free cleaning service. It was good for the paper but also good for Yang since he could not afford to pay for an advertisement. He would also offer a similar deal to a car dealer or a supermarket, in that if someone bought a certain product, they could have one free cleaning. In this way, Yang's cleaning business expanded.

Yang's persistent resourcefulness proved to be a crucial element for his success, as can be seen in another example. Once he was taking a flight from Chengdu to Xiamen, because now with his business expanding, he flew a lot. When everyone else got off the plane, Yang stayed until the plane was empty. When the flight attendants asked Yang what the matter was, Yang said he would offer to clean the airplane for them. Yang then pointed his fingers at this and that spot to show how dirty and unclean the plane was. Some of the attendants just laughed at this strange encounter, while others told Yang to simply get off the plane quickly. Yang insisted and asked to see someone in charge. Eventually, Yang had to get off the plane in order to talk to a person with responsibility for cleaning services, and to whom Yang offered a deal: his company would clean one plane for free, and all he needed was three hours for them to see the difference. The arrangement was made and the cleaning clearly made a huge difference, as it resulted in the airline company offering Yang a RMB 1 million annual contract to clean the company's planes.

Another business deal was also the result of such persistent resourcefulness. Because of the success of his business, Yang was selected to be given an award and was invited to attend a ceremony at the Great People's Hall in Tiananmen Square in Beijing, with other successful entrepreneurs from all over China. After the ceremony, Yang decided to stay behind, again, because he saw the dirt and untidiness of the thick carpet at this great symbolic place at the nerve center of China, the Great Hall of the People. The Chinese authorities actually employ many cleaners in those state bureaucratic institutions, but the floors and many other places are permanently dirty because the cleaners just use wet mops, which just move the dirt around. They don't use new technology, nor do they try new cleaning products.

Yang pointed to the dirt and traces of dirt on these beautiful carpets, and said to the personnel in the Hall that he could clean them. The attendants could not believe what they had just heard; had this man just offered to clean the Great Hall of the People in Beijing, where the state leaders gather for grand occasions? Who did he think he was? Naturally, Yang refused to leave without being allowed to talk to the person in charge. The supervisor, greatly irritated, reluctantly received Yang, just to get rid of him quickly. Yang introduced himself and his company and told this person, who was looking at him in contempt, that he ran a successful cleaning company and that was why he was invited to be at the Great Hall. The person in charge dismissed Yang before he could finish his introduction. Things just do not work like that in Beijing. The Great Hall of the People employs reliable cleaners and they work there every day to clean the place and they are paid regular wages. Their jobs are secure and permanent. The Great Hall of the People has nothing to do with people like him who run a private company, a company from Sichuan. You must be joking!

One might find it hard to believe what Yang did next. He decided not to go back to Sichuan but to stay in Beijing to negotiate a deal. He rented a room near Qianmen, the front gate of the old Beijing City, near Tiananmen Square, and he stayed there for six months! Yes, he stayed in Beijing for half a year just to convince the manager of the Great Hall of the People to let him offer one free cleaning service. He would wait at the gate of the Great Hall, day after day, and continued to talk to anyone that he could. Eventually, either because the staff at the Great Hall of the People were tired of this nuisance and wanted to get rid of him, or because there was someone in the Hall who was imaginative enough, or because China had moved far enough ahead within six months (that is possible because China really moves fast) to think of the possibility to contract a private company to clean this Great Hall, Yang was allowed to have a try. In three hours, on one carpet, Yang and his company's workers tried different cleaning products, working furiously under the watchful eyes of the personnel and management. Eventually the carpet looked stunningly different from before. Yang was able to secure a deal to clean 16 of the rooms in the Great Hall of the People for RMB 300 million for one year, and the contract has continued since that time.

Yang now has more than 50 cleaning companies all over China, including Shanghai, Beijing, and Hong Kong. Yang even has cleaning companies in Malaysia and claims that he has 300,000 clients in Malaysia alone. In order to build a successful business, Yang developed three strategies: one is what Yang calls innovation, the second he calls standardized procedures, and the third is to pay attention to details.

An example of how Yang pays attention to details is significant, because the Chinese are always thought to be sloppy, with a lack of standards, unlike the Japanese and Germans. Once Yang noticed a female worker's hair was very wet after completing cleaning at a household. Yang stopped the worker and asked her whether she had taken a shower in the client's home. The worker admitted that she had. Yang personally took the worker to the household and apologized for the worker having taken the liberty of having a shower at their home. Yang was determined to stop this kind of thing from happening again, of course, so he developed around 20 small, simple booklets setting out the procedures for cleaning and a code of conduct for staff. These included, for instance, using different colors of cleaning cloths, so that the cloths cleaning the toilet would not be mixed with the cloths that clean the kitchen, which in turn should be different from those that clean the lounge room. Other rules included knocking on the client's door gently before entering and changing one's shoes upon entering the house. All these rules and regulations were standardized so that it was clear for the workers to follow.

One example, which shows Yang's idea of innovation and continuously improving service, can be seen as follows. Once, some of his workers came back to report that their cleaning on some exterior walls had resulted in the walls being marked and that there was nothing that they could do about it. Yang knew immediately that the cleaning product that was being used was not suitable for that wall. Yang recalled the workers, apologized to the client and promised to rectify the situation. Yang then went to a library and bookshops to find out about building materials and chemical elements that deal with different materials. As he had already set up a chemical laboratory for experiments, Yang used it to trial different products, and then he went to the wall himself to try to clean it, often at night so that he would not be seen. Eventually he hit on one combination of a cleaning product that worked. He and his laboratory have now developed more than 30 cleaning products.

Yang's daring in business goes with his care for his clients and society. This can be seen by the fact that he did not want to monopolize the cleaning business in Luzhou. Now there are more than 400 cleaning businesses in Luzhou, mostly as a result of Yang's inspiration and moreover because of Yang's help. It happened like this. Yang wrote to the mayor of Luzhou and offered a deal. If the city authorities could offer space and in-kind support, like publicity and organization, his company would offer free training for the workers who had been laid off and for the unemployed youth. The mayor, of course, replied straightway and a deal was made. Yang's company trained more than 100,000 workers in Luzhou as a result of this joint effort. Some of these people were employed by Yang and his franchised company outlets. Now Yang's Small Bee Company employs more than 10,000 people, and has expanded to include the business of looking after the elderly and an agency for nannies.

What are Yang's further ambitions? Yang has said that he wants to clean the United Nations. He was not joking, because he has already written four letters to the secretary-general of the United Nations. But he has yet to receive a reply.

Conclusion

This is an extraordinary story that demonstrates the ordinariness of rural Chinese people: resourcefulness, persistence, an optimistic outlook, and the tremendous inner strength to endure hardship. Yang's unlimited resourcefulness, willingness to try to get ahead, and above all, his ability to endure hardship under overwhelming unfavorable circumstances, are demonstrations of inner qualities of the rural Chinese. These were the inner qualities of the rural Chinese during the construction of the Western railways in the United States, during the Gold Rush there and also in Australia. These are the inner qualities of the rural people of this age, both in Gao Village and China. These are the qualities that enable the Gao villagers to struggle to succeed in today's China. But these qualities may disappear once Chinese society becomes more affluent. China has not reached that stage yet, not for the rural Chinese anyway, as the main contents of this book will demonstrate.

CHAPTER 5

Gao Wenshu:
From Troublemaker to Entrepreneur

The First Car Owner in Gao Village

The traditional word for "car" in Chinese is *jiao che* ("sedan chair ve-hicle"); the car is a symbol of wealth and status in China. That at least partly explains why those behind the wheel like to honk the horn, because they are annoyed if the pitiful pedestrians do not give way to them quickly enough. In 1981, when I returned from the United Kingdom to Gao Village, my fellow villagers, as I had feared, were terribly disappointed that, instead of being driven to the village in a car accompanied by Chinese government officials, I got off a bus with a suitcase. In those days, as someone who had been sent to the United Kingdom to study for three years, the only one in the whole county of 800,000 people at that time, and the first in Jiangxi Province since 1949, Gao villagers thought that I was sufficiently important enough to be carried in a *jiao che*. I knew the difference between reality and what the Gao villagers thought, but looking back, I could have made a fuss at the County Government Office to get them to lend me one of the only two cars in the whole county of Poyang so as to give the villagers some *mianzi* ("face"), or honor.

Owning a car is one of the greatest aspirations of the upwardly mobile Chinese these days. According to one estimate, by 2010 there were more than one million private cars (excluding trucks, taxis, and official cars) in Beijing.¹ Beijing is one of the wealthiest cities in China, with a population of about 20 million if you include migrant workers. Nonetheless, that is still only one car for every 20 people. One can therefore imagine the social value of owning a car if you are a rural migrant. Wenshu is one of those rural people who owned a car, and for some years he was the only one who owned a car in Gao Village.

Gao Wenshu has other achievements that make Gao villagers feel proud. The Chinese saying *wang yang xingtan*, which means to lament one's smallness before a vast ocean, is probably a more appropriate description of the feeling of some Gao villagers about Wenshu. For instance, one of Wenshu's many achievements, of which many Gao villagers of his age are probably jealous, is that he has two sons and a daughter. I asked him how he managed not only to have three children, but also to have them officially registered as persons at a time when the one child per family policy was most vigorously implemented in rural China. It should be noted that if a child is not registered at birth, he or she is considered an illegal person and is not allowed to enroll in school, for instance. His way of getting around it at that time was very easy, according to him: just throw a banquet with enough food and wine for the village committee officials.

Gao Wenshu: *Xie Laoguan* (the Evil Fellow)

A couple of decades back, Gao Wenshu would have worried about whether he was in any position to find a girl who would marry him. Wenshu is one of five sons and was considered one of the most hopeless children in the family. He was one of the thugs in the village, always fighting, stealing things, hurting people, and giving his parents many problems. As a result, his nickname was *xie laoguan* ("the evil fellow") and he was a troublemaker since childhood.

---

1   Since 2010, the car ownership rate has increased rapidly in China, especially in Beijing.

All the same, Wenshu was not a child without a total sense of what was right and wrong. In the late 1980s and early 1990s, when there were so many taxes and levies, as described in my first book on Gao Village, the villagers hated local officials, especially when they came to the village to collect grain from the village households as payment of these taxes and levies imposed on them. When Wenshu was 12 years old, there was a huge flood and the Gao villagers did not have enough to feed themselves. Nonetheless, the village committee officials still came to the village to collect grain from the households, with a truck and a portable weighing scale. In order to sabotage their grain collection mission, Wenshu took the sliding weight off the scale and hid it in a bush on the hill and so succeeded in thwarting the tax collection team, at least on that day.

Wenshu would always be fighting with someone. The standard reference used to describe him was that he would have at least three fights a day. He performed terribly at school and was often a truant. Very often he would rebel violently against a teacher who dared to try to discipline him. One of his teachers was from the neighboring Cao Village, a young woman of striking beauty. One day, Wenshu yelled at Teacher Cao: "It would be great to f*** you!" As a result, Teacher Cao took a stick and whipped him hard. It was so painful that he cursed the teacher loudly in front of everyone. Wenshu was subsequently kicked out of the school without even finishing year three.

Gao Wenshu is now one of the most respected personalities locally, but back then he managed to get married only as a result of his family's misfortune. One of his brothers, the elder and most promising one, was engaged to a girl from the neighboring Cao Village. However, just a few days before the wedding when everything was prepared for the big event, his brother died suddenly from a mysterious illness. The two families were not only struck by sadness, more so on the boy's side of course, but also panicked. Clothes had been made, wedding banquets of several hundred people had been paid for and arranged, guests had been invited and the dowry was prepared; a bike, a sewing machine, silk quilts, furniture, and even washing basins had been bought. Worse still, the girl would be a de facto widow, which was considered symbolically a person of bad luck, and therefore she had very bleak prospects for remarriage. Like all resourceful rural Chinese, the two families came to an agreement: the wedding should take place and everything should happen as planned, except that Wenshu should take the place of the groom. The girl had no choice but to agree. In any case, she did not know either of the two brothers and at least Wenshu was good looking. That is how Wenshu got married.

Gao Wenshu: A Bricklayer and a Migrant Worker

The delinquent Gao had nothing to do after being kicked out of school, so his parents arranged for him to be a bricklayer apprentice to his own nephew, and he did that for three years. As standard practice he earned virtually nothing, except food and board when he worked with his nephew at various construction sites.

In 1992, he completed his apprenticeship and went to the city of Shantou as a bricklayer. Shantou is located in the Pearl River Delta area, where there is more convenient access to Hong Kong in terms of both capital and skills as a result of historical exchanges between the two places. By the early 1990s, the Hong Kong factor had already had a huge impact on the Pearl River Delta area, spearheaded by the establishment of Shenzhen as a Special Economic Zone, where the get-rich-first people were given all the tax and infrastructure concessions. Wenshu's bricklaying skills were made good use of, at the right time. He worked in Shantou for a year, earning RMB 8 a day, which was good money at that time. In 1993, he took his wife with him and worked his way up until he was earning RMB 13 a day. When his wife got pregnant, he sent her home.

So far there was nothing that Wenshu had done that showed that he was anything special, though leaving home to work far away in Shantou was considered brave at that time for Gao villagers. By then there was still no electricity in Gao Village and most of the villagers had never traveled beyond the surrounding villages. For restless and rather disliked Wenshu, leaving Gao Village was exactly what he wanted.

From *Baogong Tou* to Entrepreneur

By the second half of 1993, Wenshu displayed his imagination and intelligence. Because of his daring and readiness to take risks, he was a natural ringleader. There were migrant workers from all over China, "floating" to the south and east coast cities to look for jobs. Wenshu invited a dozen of those "blind floaters" (thus referred to by the official Chinese press and the liberal intellectual elite at that time) to form a team. He then would negotiate with any construction site managers for contract work, such as digging a ditch, constructing underground sewerage systems, building a temporary toilet, and so on. Wenshu would be paid a total contract fee and he would then pay the gang members of his team individually. He was then referred to as *xiao baogong tou* ("head of a small contract team"). Wenshu could then use this control of the money to reward those who were loyal to him and to punish those who were not. Furthermore, he could make some handsome profits, without physically exerting himself too much. For construction management, this was a good deal since this meant that there was only one person to deal with, instead of dealing individually with a group of people who were considered troublesome, rural ignorant unskilled laborers. Of course the contract fees could be so arbitrary that it would not surprise anyone if the manager himself (always a man) could pocket some cash. By doing this, Wenshu was able to make more than RMB 2,000 within half a year in 1993.

In 1994, Wenshu's wife and son joined him in Shantou. The construction contract team became bigger and Wenshu was leading more than 30 people. Wenshu's wife started to participate in the management of the contract business. That year, Wenshu and his wife together managed to make more than RMB 6,000, an astronomical amount for a Gao villager at the time.

By the middle of the 1990s, China's economy had started to expand more rapidly, and more and more rural youth started to move to the southeast coast. Wenshu saw another opportunity: those young migrant workers were bored witless after 10–12 hours of monotonous work a day, often for six days a week. They needed some entertainment. It was at that time that the game of snooker began to become popular all over China. Wenshu persuaded a friend to invest with him, and each paid RMB 1,000 to rent a shop just in front of a large shoe factory. What they did was simple: they bought two snooker tables for the migrant workers to use and they charged RMB 2 for a game. Sometimes they could make as much as RMB 300 a day.

However, four months later, Gao and his partner fell out. His partner wanted to run the business himself and so Wenshu gave up his half share for a cash settlement. Being Wenshu, he was of course not about to give up. So he rented another shop next to the existing one that was now owned by his former partner, and set up another snooker business, but instead of RMB 2 a game, he charged only RMB 1. Unable to compete with Wenshu's cut-throat rate, his competitor's business went bankrupt. A year and a half later, Wenshu made RMB 30,000 and suddenly he became a well-known and respected figure, locally in Shantou and of course in Gao Village.

Wenshu's ambition by now went beyond the snooker tables in Shantou. Together with another entrepreneur, Wenshu went to Guangzhou, the capital of Guangdong Province, and set up a construction contracting company, each investing RMB 30,000. This again was very remarkable, as RMB 30,000 was a lot of money at that time for a Gao villager, and is equivalent to being a millionaire these days. It would have been tempting to take the money home, build a house and enjoy a comfortable and glorious life, but that was not Wenshu. He invested all the money that he had and employed a team, with sometimes as many as 300 people. He had a sharp eye for the real cost and profit margin of a project and he was also good at persuading people to agree with him.

For example, he would ask for RMB 3 million for a building contract. He would then pay the workers RMB 2 million and use RMB 500,000 as management fees, which included payments for gifts and banquets to relevant people, keeping a clear RMB 500,000 for himself. Despite his gift for making money, Wenshu had two weaknesses that proved costly to him. One was that he was virtually illiterate and the other was that he tended to trust the people around him whom he considered "mates," or whoever he thought he could trust.

Personal Trust and Business Deals

Gao villagers still tend to rely on personal trust for doing business, but Wenshu's reliance on personal trust would get him into trouble. Here is an instance that Wenshu told me about. Once, he got to know someone who was supposed to have the right network, a local person from Guangzhou. The man persuaded Wenshu to invest in a peanut oil factory. Being an outsider, Wenshu needed a local contact to get permission to invest in a project like this. The man said he could get everything else fixed, except that he had no money. Wenshu agreed to fund the project. Eventually, it emerged that it was a total scam and Wenshu managed to get only about RMB 45,000 back out of the 60,000 in cash that he had put up for the project, and the conman ran away with the rest.

Wenshu's trust of friends was of course not helped by his lack of ability to read and write. When his business got bigger and his ambition even bigger, Wenshu increasingly sensed his inadequacy. This is something he stressed to me many times during interviews, and gave this as an example. He had signed a contract for some construction materials with a mate. It was agreed that they each invest half and the profit should also be split fifty-fifty. Because he trusted his friend and because he could not read, he did not realize that on the written contract the split was seventy-thirty, in his friend's favor. Wenshu, of course, was furious and took the man to court. Not only did Wenshu not get back the RMB 20,000 that was owed to him, he also had to pay RMB 40,000 in legal fees as he had lost the fight, inevitably.

Despite some losses, Wenshu said that he had something like a few million in the bank in 2015. All the same, Wenshu did not use credit cards, as he did not seem to trust things that were not personal. Once, he took me, my two children, plus my two brothers' families, a total of about 20 people, to have dinner at a restaurant. At the end of this huge meal, he took a few notes from a huge wad of cash out of a black bag that he was carrying with him, and asked his wife to go pay the bill.

Wenshu as a Loan Shark

Nowadays, Wenshu mostly runs hotel businesses, which I will discuss in more detail in Chapters 6 and 7. Wenshu also makes money by being a "loan shark," a private money lender. There is a huge market for private lending in China, for the obvious reason that the Chinese state-owned banks do not lend money to private businesspeople, especially those from rural China. Until recently, there was a strong reluctance from the Chinese authorities to allow Chinese citizens to set up money exchanges, lending agencies, or financial institutions. The ideological logic was straightforward: a socialist country under the leadership of the Communist Party of China could not allow private capitalists to exist. However, foreigners were allowed to have loans from a Chinese bank, and to even open bank branches in China, though with some restrictions. This was acceptable within the ideological discourse because foreigners were supposed to be capitalists and China needed them to modernize. This has been changing, slowly, but it is still the case that financial services are underdeveloped and in many ways are very primitive in China.[2] Therefore, there is a huge market for private loans and illegal financial activities. Wenshu was one of those loan sharks who would

---

2   With various kinds of electronic payment systems in China and the most likely future a cashless market as articulated by the Alibaba boss Ma Yun, the financial situation in China has been changing rapidly. People like Wenshu will soon be out of the market.

charge something like 40 percent interest. He regularly lent a quarter of million to people and usually would get the principal sum back in a little more than two years. I asked him how to judge to whom he lent money and how to make sure that the interest would be paid in time or at all, since there was no legal resort to settle the issue if someone decided not to honor the debt.

Wenshu said there were two things that he would do to help him get his financial return. One was that he had to make sure the money was lent to someone whose business is profitable. If you lend money to someone who does not make money, then it is difficult to get the money back, let alone the interest. For instance, he knew that clothes shops didn't make money anymore and he would not lend money to any of those applicants. For a business that is likely to make money, he will do a careful investigation before he makes a decision. Wenshu gave me an example. He was once asked for a loan for a gas station, the kind of business that an outsider, i.e., those who have no local *hukou* like him, is not allowed to do in Guangzhou. Before he made a decision, Wenshu examined information about the wholesale price of gas and the retail price at a gas station. He then went to a couple of gas stations and secretly observed the business activities for a few days. He would count how many cars would stop at a gas station on any given day. He calculated that a gas station could make RMB 600–1,000 a day. Even if the operator had to pay 40 percent interest for a loan of half a million, the business could still make a lot of money, so he decided to lend the money. Now, every Sunday, he walks to the station and sits in the office, drinking tea, and waiting for the week's cash for the loan's interest. It is always paid on time.

Another thing he did was very unpleasant, to say the least. Wenshu inspired loyalty for the very reason that he placed importance on personal trust. Some people were very appreciative of his trust and, in turn, became very loyal. Therefore, he had loyal followers. Sometimes he would get a group of his followers, mostly from rural China, who would walk to the premises of the person who owed him money, and that itself was intimidating enough for some to hand over the money straightway, or else risk being beaten up. According to the ethics of this kind of underground culture, the victims of the bashing did not get any sympathy because they did not honor their word. In the area of construction contracts, Wenshu would not hesitate to employ very intimidating and unpleasant means to get contract business. He would employ his gang to do all kinds of harassment to frighten away other competitors, including staging protests in the street and paying journalists to write bad things about the competitors, even using explicit physical intimidation.

Wenshu now has a dozen small hotels and made something like RMB 50,000 a month before the 2008 global financial crisis hit. When I interviewed him in late 2009 and early 2010, he was only making about RMB 30,000 a month. Interestingly, the financial crisis had an impact on an individual like him in a relatively tiny city in China.

Wenshu the Person and His Values

What are Wenshu's vices? He said he never smoked, which was true. He also claimed that he never gambled. That was not strictly true, as I saw him play mahjong with family members and friends. The money involved in such games was usually RMB 10 a game, and one can lose several hundred RMB in a few hours. It is considered entertainment and is usually played among friends and family members. In other words, you win this time but may lose next time, all among your own people. It is just from one pocket to another and then comes back again. One day, while we were talking about how Wenshu enjoyed massage and sauna, his wife added that he liked *yeji* ("wild chickens") as well, meaning prostitutes. Despite this comment, Wenshu and his wife seemed openly affectionate to each other, touching and hugging, which was not very usual for rural people, including young ones, even these days. It was hard to say whether his wife was serious.

Wenshu's daughter and eldest son both studied in the city of Jingdezhen, where he was able to find the best possible school and where he had to pay about RMB 10,000 in annual fees for each of them. These days there are hardly any good schools in rural China. Not only has there been a lack of investment, but children of most of the rural elite, elite either because of money or because of official positions, go to schools in cities or nearby towns. Occasionally some of the best students from poor families are attracted to town or city schools through scholarships. The best performing teachers are also lured to town or city private schools by higher salaries and better living conditions. There is also a lack of incentive for students to work hard academically, because these days even a university graduate can end up being a migrant worker. Nonetheless, Wenshu, drawing from his own experience, wanted his children to have a good education and was willing to pay. Why did he not get his children to study in Guangzhou? He would like to but he did not have a Guangzhou *hukou*. Wenshu could pay for his children to attend school in Guangzhou where he and his wife worked and lived, but his children would not be able to register to take the national tertiary education entrance examination, therefore they needed to attend schools in Jiangxi because they could only participate in the examination in Jiangxi.

When I interviewed Wenshu in 2009, his parents were still in Gao Village, still working in the fields and raising pigs and chickens to support themselves. I asked why he did not bring his parents to Guangzhou to live with him. He said that they did come many times and at first they were very impressed and happy. Tap water was very convenient and they were amused that one could have hot water anytime. Back in the village, his parents had to fetch water from the well and heat water up in a wok. Despite this, they could not stay in Guangzhou any longer than one week. His father complained that staying in a hotel room (in one of the hotels that Wenshu runs) in Guangzhou was like being in prison and every day was torture. Wenshu's father complained that it was so painful that he felt as if someone was cutting his flesh every day.

As described elsewhere in this book, there has been a real estate boom not only in cities but all over the countryside throughout China. This has certainly been the case in the past 20 years in Gao Village.

Despite the boom, Wenshu, the richest son in Gao Village, had not built a house in Gao Village until 2011 and his parents lived in an old hut, which was cold in winter and hot in summer. He had been constantly pressured to build a house in Gao Village, not only by other villagers but also by his parents. Because of this dispute, he and his father were not on speaking terms for a long time. Of course it was not because Wenshu did not have the money, nor that he did not respect his parents and had no filial piety for his parents. In fact, Wenshu had signed a contract and paid a huge deposit for a flat in Guangzhou for his parents to move into, but his parents were so strongly against the idea that he had to give it up and lost the deposit.

His father was totally against buying a property in Guangzhou. Guangzhou was not home, his father would say. They speak a different language there. The Guangdong people were aliens to him. Guangzhou is too far away from home, and they did not want his offspring to be Guangdong people. To make his parents happy, Wenshu bought an apartment in Nanchang, the capital city of Jiangxi, and was going to purchase another apartment in the city of Jingdezhen.

Wenshu resisted for a long time, however, the idea of building a house in Gao Village, since he could not see the possibility of ever living there. Furthermore, the apartment he bought in Nanchang had already doubled its value and it did not make business sense to build a house in Gao Village. This is in conflict with the values still held dear by Gao villagers, who compete to build the best looking house. The bigger and the better looking the house is, the more "face" or honor you will gain for your parents and family. His parents wanted their grandchildren to get married in a house in Gao Village, even if they themselves did not live there. They wanted the grandest marriage banquet for thousands of people and the grandest marriage procession in the grandest house in the village. That would give them the most "face" and highest glory, befitting for the richest in the village, but Wenshu refused to see the point.

When I went to Gao village again in August 2011, I was surprised to find Wenshu there. I was even more surprised to hear that he had returned to Gao Village to supervise the building of a new house. I could see that the foundation was laid on the edge of the village pond and some huge concrete columns were standing on the foundation. What had made Wenshu change his mind? It emerged that it was due to the death of his father. Wenshu's father, Changshan, had been suddenly found to have lung cancer. Wenshu immediately returned to Gao Village and took his father to Nanchang, Jingdezhen, and even Guangzhou to seek the best medical treatment, but within a few months Gao Changshan had passed away, and his deathbed words to Wenshu were: "My son, you have to build a house in Gao Village. Promise me before I die." Wenshu made the promise.

I was very sad and surprised to hear the sad news of Changshan's death. Changshan and I had worked together during the Mao era and he was a high-spirited person, always healthy and strong. Now Wenshu seemed happy about building the house. He even had it designed by a proper architect in Guangzhou, at the cost of RMB 80,000. On the building site, Wenshu wore a helmet, a pair of rubber boots, and a vest, but what attracted my attention was the necklace, or more accurately the chain, that he was wearing around his neck. It must have weighed half a kilogram and was made of pure gold. Any other Gao villager would have feared that the gold chain might be a target of robbery, but Gao Wenshu's deportment suggested that the gold suited him perfectly and that nobody would ever dare to think of laying a finger on the gold chain. "When my son gets married, the marriage banquet and marriage procession have to be in Gao Village. Where do I do that, if I don't build a house?" he explained to me. In fact, Changshan's other four sons had each built a house in Gao Village, so it was not really necessary. "In any case, when I am old, I would prefer to return to Gao Village," Wenshu declared. He then asked me, "Why don't you build a house in Gao Village as well?"

In 2015, when I went to Gao Village again, Wenshu's house, the best in Gao Village and in fact, one of the best in the area, had been completed. It stood on the edge of the village pond and was strikingly good looking, as seen in the photo below.

Photo 5. Gao Wenshu's house. Taken by Pei Fei in 2015.

The house had a front yard fenced off from the street, with solar lights on the fence walls. Inside the house, there was an impressive wide staircase leading to the two stories upstairs. There was a chandelier in the sitting room, which was certainly the first in Gao Village, with a tiled floor, tiled walls and floodlights on the ceiling. The kitchen was bright and spacious with a lot of bench space, and the surfaces were topped with modern materials. The TV and sitting rooms were decorated with many artistic objects, as well as artificial flowers. The

TV room, which had a huge flat-screen TV and sound system, was used also as a dining room and had a hard wood table with a rotating tabletop. In the corner of the room were two bright big windows, one that looked out onto the pond and one onto the street. The decorations may look banal to some and the taste may be vulgar to others, but to many Gao villagers, the interior of Wenshu's house is impressive and appears to be the most modern, most fanciful, and certainly the most costly.

I thought the house would remain empty most days of the year, but I discovered that Wenshu has been going back to Gao Village more often since the house was built and he is more likely to travel from Guangzhou to Gao Village to spend the Chinese New Year in his new house. Houses, in many ways, seem a factor that pulls the Gao Villagers back, even though migrant working pushes them away.

Wenshu's eldest son planned to finish his twelfth year of school for the tertiary entry examination. If his son failed his tertiary examination in China Wenshu would send him to study in Australia. "You will have to look after him since you are my uncle," Wenshu said to me. Wenshu decided to choose Australia for his son's education because he knows a Gao villager there, so it is quite likely that Gao Village will have another migrant to Australia. One girl who has relatives in Gao Village completed her undergraduate degree in economics and accounting at the University of Adelaide in 2011 and has returned to work in the city of Nanjing. Another girl did a master degree at the University of Adelaide and now works at a South Australian government office, bought a house and married in Adelaide. They are both my sister's granddaughters.

Photo 6. The sitting room in Gao Wenshu's house.
Taken by the author in 2015.

Photo 7. The TV room in Gao Wenshu's house.
Taken by the author in 2015.

Conclusion

The story of Gao Wenshu illustrates and enlightens many aspects of contemporary life in China, in particular the change and continuity in Chinese society. It illustrates and explains the connections, links, and mutual dependence between rural and urban China. Wenshu worked in the modern urban setting thousands of miles away from his home and yet his values and identity were still shown very traditional. It illustrates and explains the resourcefulness and entrepreneurship of Chinese rural people, who have made the best use of the opportunities that government policies provide. One Gao Village man who was initially a failure has turned into a successful entrepreneur and the richest person in the village. Wenshu's story illustrates and explains how family values and traditional values manifest in economic activities and how they contribute to societal development in China. It demonstrates how rural Chinese are pushed forward and pulled backward by conflicting values, both modern and traditional. It demonstrates how the market economy has overthrown some aspects of traditional Chinese values. By traditional standards, Wenshu is not an outstanding person in any sense, as he was a failure in school and a troublemaker as a child. Previously, there was no such position as "entrepreneur" in the hierarchical status in traditional rural China. Now he is highly respected and considered the most successful person in Gao Village. Finally, his story illustrates subtly how a tiny village in China is related to the outside world, even to Australia, and how the Chinese can be so Chinese but at the same time, so global.

CHAPTER 6

Gao Changxian, Gao Mingxia, and the Background of Their Hotel Business

Gao Changxian and the Family Background

My mother gave birth to 14 children with only four surviving to this day, one of them being Gao Changxian, one of my younger brothers. He is tall, handsome, and intelligent, and has a natural talent of commanding an audience when he speaks. In Western terms, he can be said to be charismatic, though it is hard to translate that term into Chinese. In almost every aspect, this brother of mine could have succeeded better in life. However, in the eyes of some Gao villagers, I, the elder brother, lead a more successful life. I am a professor in one of the leading universities in Australia, who can make overseas trips almost like taking a bus down the road and who can afford anything in the villagers' imagination, and above all someone who does not have to do any physical labor in the rain or under the boiling sun. Very often when I go back to the village, some of them still ask me, "How come you are so dark and so thin?" According to them, I should look fair and well nourished, with some extra flesh around my chin, or better still, with a pot belly, which to them is a sign of leisure and good food. To them, it would therefore be utterly and totally pointless and stupid to do a workout in the gym, an opinion to which I more or less agree.

One of the main factors that initially made my life and that of Changxian so different might be that I liked reading more, a fact that

Changxian admits himself. I used to read whenever I could, while walking, eating, or even in the toilet. That was considered uncommon in Gao Village, and a factor universally considered by villagers there to have contributed to my doing well academically at school. But when I think about it, I doubt if that was a factor. Changxian thinks, and I think he is right, that circumstances have disadvantaged him in relation to me. If it were not for other factors beyond our control, I would have been a schoolteacher, or could have been a school principal locally and this brother of mine might have been who knows what. I really think he could have been anything he wanted. Now he and his wife Gao Mingxia manage a number of hotels. The development that has brought Changxian and Mingxia from Gao Village to Panyu District in Guangzhou can be usefully narrated to enlighten us about many aspects of the recent changes and developments in China.

I should start this narrative by talking about myself first. When I finished Year Six at a boarding school in 1966, the Cultural Revolution broke out. Normal schooling was interrupted and we did all kinds of exciting things, such as traveling free anywhere around the country (although we rural teenagers did not have the imagination to take advantage of that opportunity and mostly traveled only locally, if at all) and writing wall posters criticizing any officials and party leaders we wanted (except of course Mao himself). On the whole, my generation at that time had great fun, at least for some of us, but at the expense and misery of these party leaders and the intellectual elite. That kind of idealistic "fooling around" for me lasted for two years, and in 1968 I was considered to have nominally graduated from my junior middle school education. My formal education was terminated and I had to go back to be a "peasant" (*nongmin*) and I was then termed one of the "returned educated youth" (*huixiang zhiqing*).

This is the part in history that those who condemn the Cultural Revolution emphasize: the destruction of education by the Cultural Revolution and the deprival of the Chinese youth of the opportunities to have a good formal education. However, there are two important facts that the critics of the Cultural Revolution choose to ignore. Firstly, for rural Chinese like me, the continuation of formal education was beyond the means of my family anyway, even without the Cultural Revolution. There were only two senior high schools in the whole of Poyang County and both were located at the county town, more than a 100 kilometres from Gao Village. It was already financially too difficult for my widowed mother (by then my father had passed away) to send me to a boarding junior school in Youdunjie, about 15 kilometers from Gao Village, as described in *Gao Village*. For all the years prior to the Cultural Revolution, there was only one Gao Village family that could afford to send a boy to study at Poyang Town, and that was the family of the party secretary of Guantian Brigade, to which Gao Village belonged.

The second fact that critics of the Cultural Revolution ignore is the reconstruction of education soon after 1969. Precisely designed to address the issue of inequality between urban and rural China in terms of accessing education, a large-scale program of raising the standard of education in rural China started to take place. One of the measures was the pioneering of what was then called the "barefoot teacher" system, where basically peasants with little more than a middle school certificate were enlisted to teach classes. It was during the late 1960s and early 1970s that Gao Village, like almost all villages all over China, set up a school from Year One to Year Three and I was chosen to be the "barefoot," or non-professional, teacher. That was the first time in all of Gao Village's history that all school children went to school. The number of schools shot up in rural China, and consequently, junior and senior schools mushroomed locally. Children could now go to school without having to leave home for boarding, and the Youdunjie School where I had attended junior middle school had expanded to include a senior middle school component. What happened around Gao Village was not an isolated case, but a national development as a result of innovative Cultural Revolution policies (Pepper 2000).

My brother Changxian went through middle school during this period. It was true that there was a prevailing idea during this period that formal education was pointless, but Changxian did complete his middle school education and was sufficiently educated in terms of math and literacy. On the other hand, the stoppage of tertiary education was not meant to be for a long time and it was meant to keep the old way of education on hold so as to allow the establishment of a more idealistic revolutionary educational system. The innovation worked on two important areas: on the recruitment of students and on the curriculum. One important component of the curriculum innovation was to combine book knowledge with material production and with how society operated. An approach that was developed was called "open door schooling" (*kaimen banxue*), where students would spend some of their school time at a factory, in a village or at an army unit. When I was at Xiamen University studying English from 1973 to 1976, I did all these things, three months at a time. It was a requirement that my English textbooks had to include vocabulary and texts related to those activities.

Another innovative Cultural Revolution policy that profoundly affected me, and therefore my brother, was the new experimental recruitment policy in the early 1970s. The national tertiary entrance examination was then abolished and universities were commanded to recruit students who had to be recommended by "grassroots apparatus," or the local political unit, and the personal background of the candidates had to be one of the following three categories: workers, peasants, or soldiers. It is true, nonetheless, that many of those who gained entrance to university turned out to be from elite party and army official family backgrounds, but it is also true that some of those recruited did come from very poor and disadvantaged backgrounds as a result of this affirmative policy, and I was one of them.

Gao Village had no access to electricity until 1984, and my family found it hard to even afford to buy a piece of paper on which to write. There was no way that I could compete with those in urban China, if equal academic standards were applied, in terms of written examinations, even though I was always one of the best at school in terms of academic performance. It was the new affirmative policy that made it possible for me to enter one of the best universities in China and so, in this way, an ignorant peasant boy was assigned to study English.

However, the same affirmative policy and the same intention of giving the disadvantaged an equal opportunity actually disadvantaged my brother Changxian. The year after I entered Xiamen University, the local commune apparatus was considering making a recommendation for Gao Changxian to enter a college in Nanchang, the capital of Jiangxi Province. His general test results were good enough. He was healthy and so was considered to be an all-round person to be recommended, but opposition from one member of the local apparatus was enough to exclude him. The local apparatus, the commune in those days, consisted of representatives from different villages; otherwise it would be seen as unfair and unjust. One such villager, Jiang Minyue from Jiang Village, opposed my brother's candidature on the ground that it was not fair to other villages and other people to recommend Gao Changxian, since his brother was already studying at Xiamen University. In other words, the argument was that it was not fair for one family to have two university students while other families had none. This was a very fair and logical argument and as a result, Gao Changxian's name was dropped from the list of candidates.

Nonetheless, Changxian was one of the brightest young men in the Gao Village area, and he had been deprived of an opportunity to enter into tertiary education because of me. I was able then to study at Xiamen University, majoring in English at the full cost of the Chinese government. Though I did not need my family to support my studies, they had lost a source of income since I could not earn anything for the family. Changxian, still a teenager, had to bear the responsibility of being the main bread-winner for the family. My mother had bound feet, but despite this, she still had to work in the fields; however, it was mainly Changxian's work that sustained the family, including supporting our youngest brother Gao Changwen to go to school. By then, academic achievement at school was again considered very important, because that was one of the very few ways a rural person could succeed and aspire to have the kind of life an urban Chinese had. Changxian not only supported Changwen to finish senior high school, but also supported him to repeat Year Twelve three times, in the hopes that our little brother could succeed in passing the national tertiary entrance examinations. Unfortunately, Changwen never passed, although a couple of times his scores were only a few points short of the threshold. Changwen then went on to become a migrant worker in Xiamen and Changxian remained in Gao Village, looking after our mother until she passed away in 1998.

When I graduated in 1976, my starting salary was RMB 38.5 a month, which was actually more than enough to support myself but not enough to support my family back in Gao Village. As it happened, one event not only changed my life forever but also helped my family's financial situation. In 1977, I was chosen by the authorities to study in the UK for three years.

In order to make us more presentable, students were each given about RMB 1,000 to buy the necessary clothing to go overseas. I can still remember the exact amount I received, RMB 950. When I wrote to Changxian about it, he was shocked by the "astronomical" amount of money (his own words, in Chinese of course). A rural person would never dream of seeing so much cash at one time. With that money, I had a woolen Western suit and overcoat made, a couple of ties, a watch, and a pair of leather shoes, as well as some shirts and other things, all considered to be the best in China at the time, at a special shop called "the service department for those traveling overseas" (*chu guo renyuan fuwu bu*). The fortune that fell on me not only included a free trip to Europe, but also three years of study with all expenses paid by the Chinese government, including pocket money in the amount of 3.08 British pounds a month. I did not need that pocket money, because everything I spent I could claim from the Chinese embassy, including even a cup of coffee. I did not know how to spend money like that anyway.

The beauty about the arrangement for me was that my salary was still being paid back home in China. I had made arrangements for Xiamen University to send my monthly salary back home. At first it was kept by my elder sister, Gao Lingli, in a special bank account and later was handed over to Changxian. Though I did not care to keep the money for myself, I still owed a debt to Changxian for looking after the family so that I could study with no worries. My sense of debt was more keenly felt after I later learned about Changxian's missed opportunity to attend a tertiary institution. It was taken for granted then that within a family, individual gains and losses were both normal and necessary, and that every member of the family should do their best under the circumstances to contribute to the overall improvement of the family. The underlying assumption, of course, was that when I succeeded, all of my family would benefit. Later, as circumstances drew us apart, I began to develop a sense of guilt and started conscientiously to think of doing something to compensate Changxian. The only thing I could do was send him money from time to time, and the money that I sent did make a difference in his life, including him later turning into a hotel manager with the title of "Gao *laoban*" ("boss Gao"), as his staff would call him.

Gao Changxian: The Person

Before I discuss the circumstances that led to Changxian and his wife Gao Mingxia to become hotel managers, I need to talk a little more of their early life in Gao Village. Changxian had the reputation of having a lot of friends, in those days anyway, when he emerged as one of the most influential men in Gao Village. For some reason, Changxian had acquired a strong sense of brotherhood, known as *yiqi* in Chinese. He had formed a "sworn brotherhood" relationship with four other influential men in the Gao Village area: Cao Junxiu, once a party secretary of Cao Village; Jiang Huipeng, a retired PLA serviceman who was once the party secretary of Qinglin Village Committee (a local government body that covered about 10 villages in the Gao Village area at that time); Jiang Guode, the local doctor from Xifen Village; and Jiang Shuigui, one of the earliest self-made local entrepreneurs.

The brotherhood that Changxian formed with those influential local men was of course possible because Changxian was one of the power players himself in the area. Despite being self-taught, Changxian was one of the best abacus users in the area, and he could calculate complex numbers within a few seconds. Not surprisingly, Changxian was for many years the accountant of Gao Village. Very often, he would refuse to take up the position of village head or some more important position in the village government, partly because he tended to dread the responsibilities and partly because he wanted personal freedom and did not like dealing with all the bureaucracy. Changxian likes to chat, drink, and smoke, and nowadays to play mahjong. He thrives on little arguments and brawling among friends. He can go on and on for hours, doing this and chatting into the early morning—activities that are unbearable to me. Changxian does not seem to aim at developing friendships for personal ambition. If a friend needs help, he will do anything he can, as illustrated by the following example concerning a pig.

Pigs are greatly valued among the rural people of China, except the Hui ethnic groups.[1] To start with, pork has always been the main source of food in the Chinese diet. Every bit of a pig is made full use of for food: the blood, the intestines, the stomach, and everything inside the pig. The people in Gao Village have a tradition of making the tongue, the head, and the feet of a pig into a delicacy. Pork of course can be salted, smoked, or dried and therefore can last for a whole year. The pig is also such an ecological animal for the villagers. Their droppings are good fertilizer for crops and the pigs eat whatever food scraps are thrown out from the kitchen. Gao villagers used to grind rice husks into powder to feed pigs, although they don't do this anymore. One of the main tasks for children when I was small was to pick up whatever wild vegetables we could find to feed the pigs.

A pig raised in this traditional way was really a fantastic source of delicious food. Every bit of pig tasted good to me, at that time at least. This is not a matter of nostalgia of childhood memories. When I went to

---

1   The Hui is one of the 55 so-called national minorities in China, an ethnic people who may or may not be Muslims, but who may treat pigs differently from the majority Han nationality.

the UK, I discovered that pork did not taste the same as it did in China. When I first arrived in the UK, I thought it was wonderful because things like pig liver were so cheap and abundant. I would buy and cook the pig liver, which used to be my favorite dish in Gao Village, but it never tasted as good and was not the same. Very soon, I stopped eating pig feet and head, which were abundantly available at the local butchers for a very cheap price. I thought the reason why these things did not taste good anymore was that I was not starving as I used to be in Gao Village. But later I realized that was not the real reason. When I returned home from the UK, the food made from pig's parts that was cooked by my mother and the villagers still tasted great. Of course it was not "the West" that was the reason for the not so tasty pork, but the commercialization and industrialization of raising pigs that was the problem.

In those days in Gao Village, raising a pig from a piglet to a big, fat animal of a hundred or so kilograms usually took several months, sometimes even a year. My family was one of the poorest and therefore could not spare any grain to feed pigs. My family's pigs were always hungry and would never grow fat and big enough before they had to be slaughtered. I always admired other families who could raise huge, fat pigs and then slaughter them during the Chinese New Year. As well, pig fat was precious because it was used as oil. To have a big and fat pig in the family was not only a year-long aspiration, but also an indication of the family's wellbeing. One year during the late 1970s, when I was still studying in the UK, I got a letter from my brother that mother was seriously ill in bed. It turned out that what caused the illness was not some kind of bacteria or virus, but the shocking loss of all the money from the sale of the family pig. That year my mother had raised a big, fat pig; it was the first time in her life to have such a big pig. She was happy and sold the pig and got something like RMB 200 cash from the sale. She treasured her year's earnings so much that she dared not leave it in the house and carried it with her all the time. One day she went to the hill in front of the village to pick mushrooms and unfortunately lost the money while picking mushrooms. The shock of the loss resulted in a total physical collapse.

I have gone to so much length to talk about pigs because I want to show how important a pig was for a rural family in those days, the fact of which helps show how loyal and generous Changxian can be to a friend. One of Changxian's friends needed money for some venture and he came to him for help. Changxian didn't have any cash to lend, so instead he gave his friend the family pig, which weighed more than 150 kilograms! Sadly, he never got a cent back from his friend for that generosity.

I can think of another example. Changxian considered another villager, Gao Coudong, a friend so he lent him RMB 600 in 1997 so that he could repay a debt. My brother Changxian was an accountant of the village committee at that time and he earned an annual salary of about RMB 4,000. Gao Changxian agreed to take RMB 600 out of his salary to make up Gao Coudong's debt so that the latter did not have to pay the interest of the loan at the staggering 30 percent.

I have spent so much time describing Changxian and some aspects of his life in order to show a number of points. The first point is that one's success in life, whatever one may mean by success, in many ways can be so dependent on circumstances that one tends to conclude that life is in many ways accidental. That is why the Chinese tend to fall back on their belief in fate. Secondly, there are still so many traditional values in rural China. People help each other for no apparent or immediate return; loyalty and generosity are still treasured values. Finally, there is so much resilience and resourcefulness among the rural Chinese. All three points are actually related to my brother's starting and running of his hotel business.

Gao Mingxia: An Incredible Woman

Before I talk about their hotel business, I need to first present a brief description of the character of Changxian's wife, Gao Mingxia. In February 2015, I experienced a surprising outburst from Mingxia at the dinner table in their house in Gao Village. It was several days after their son Gao Wei's memorable wedding and my last night in the village, after which I would return to Australia and they would return to Panyu in Guangdong Province. It was a night of celebration and farewells, and we were drinking and eating some of the best local specialties. It all started when Mingxia wanted to stop Changxian from continuing drinking alcohol. Mingxia said that she wanted to take the opportunity in front of her, as well as in front of her son and new daughter-in-law, to say how much she had been working to contribute to the family. She said she wanted Changxian to be present so that he could deny anything she said about him if it was not true. She said that when Changxian was an accountant and village official, all he did was go to banquets and drink with local officials and his sworn brothers, and then he would often come home late at night, drunk. Not only did she have to look after the three children and the housework, but she also had to run the family shop (the one I described in *Gao Village*), like getting goods in and managing the counter, all by herself. Now, in Panyu, in order to protect Changxian's health, she took the night shift so that he could have a good night's sleep, though she has to look after the two grandchildren that lived with them and did the cooking and housework in the day-time. At one point as she told this story, Mingxia burst into tears.

Changxian could not really offer any evidence or argument to refute Mingxia, even though he was visibly disturbed and annoyed. A couple of times he stood up, about to burst into anger, but he managed to control himself in front of us. I then realized that what Mingxia had said must be true. At one point I did try to intervene by suggesting that perhaps Changxian did the kind of work that men were supposed to do, like moving heavy things or climbing up high to change a light bulb. But Changxian admitted that Mingxia even did things like that. I was somehow shocked by this revelation because I suddenly realized that I should have given more credit to Mingxia for the wellbeing of the family. The reason it took me so long to realize this is that Changxian was always the one who met with me whenever I went back and he was the one who provided me with information while I asked questions. Mingxia was always in the background, consciously being so, as she was required to do according to old traditions.

It was undeniable that Mingxia was the pillar of the family, as can be seen by the way the two of them ran the restaurant in Xiamen before they went to Panyu.

To retell the story of the restaurant in Xiamen, I need to start with my youngest brother, Gao Changwen. Changwen was in fact the first migrant worker from Gao Village. Having failed *gaokao* (the national-level tertiary entrance examination) three times, Changwen left Gao Village and worked in a cutlery factor in Xiamen owned by a Guangdong man, who himself had been a recent migrant to Hong Kong.[2] Changwen did not go to Shenzhen or Guangdong, where most migrant workers initially went, but to Xiamen, because Xiamen is where I used to study and work and where my ex-wife's family was living. Family ties would prove useful and be of potential assistance. As a high school graduate, Changwen was, in fact, among some of the most highly-educated migrant workers at that time. As a result, Changwen was given a job with some technological responsibilities and he therefore had some influence in the factory. It was through him that Xiamen became one of the main destinations for migrant workers from Gao Village. As the factory in which he worked started to expand, Changwen acted as guarantor to get more migrant workers from Gao Village. Naturally, Changwen would start by helping Gao villagers who were closest to him, like friends, then villagers related to his family, and eventually villagers that were even distantly related, a kind of "chain reaction of social networks," as I mentioned in *Gao Village*. As a result, many girls and boys of the lineage to which Changwen belonged went to Xiamen.

By the 1990s, running a family grocery shop in Gao Village was not enough to make a living for Mingxia and Changxian, so they decided to run a "makeshift restaurant" on the factory site in Xiamen where the Gao Village migrant workers were employed. I call it a "makeshift" restaurant because it was little more than just a shelter with a roof,

---

2   Because of his Hong Kong residence status, he was given all kinds of concessions to run a business in China in the early 1990s.

with some basic cooking facilities and a few cheap plastic tables and chairs scattered about. I would like to give a quick description of this little restaurant for migrant workers, which will show, hopefully, many insights into the lives of migrant workers, as well as into the lives of Changxian and Mingxia.

The restaurant provided lunch and an evening meal every day, seven days a week. The evening meal would usually start at 11pm for the night shift workers. Most of the customers would be from Gao Village and some were from its neighboring villages. For the same reason, migrant workers from Hunan Province, for instance, would eat in a restaurant run by a Hunan person. There would be about 200 customers every day in Changxian and Mingxia's restaurant. The restaurant provided 20 different dishes to choose from and each customer could choose four of the 20, together with rice. Rice was available without restriction but the four dishes were served by the restaurant staff in order to limit the quantity. Each male paid RMB 2.5 for a meal and each female worker paid RMB 2, on the rationale that a female worker would consume less rice. On average, each customer consumed about 0.4 *liang* (200g) of rice each meal. The food was basic with a lot of vegetables; in fact, most of the dishes were vegetables. I was told that there was no point in supplying better but more expensive food because migrant workers wanted to save as much money as possible. As there was only a one-hour break for the migrant workers, Mingxia and Changxian would work like fire fighters and afterwards the whole place looked like a robbery scene, with plates and bowls scattered everywhere. Palm oil, imported from Malaysia, was used for cooking because it was much cheaper than any other kind. Tea was provided for free and a huge barrel of tea was empty the second time when I was there just for the duration of lunch time, observing the business activities.

Of the 20 dishes, there was one made with pork belly and one with tofu. Some of these dishes had been pre-prepared, but Mingxia would also offer to fry ten kinds of fresh vegetables on the spot. Mingxia would be surrounded by workers, each with a dish of vegetables to be fried. She worked like mad, as if on a battle field, but on the surface she would always appear to be calm. Changxian and Mingxia would have to buy vegetables every day, but would leave it until late afternoon when the vegetable merchants were about to go home and the vegetables were cheaper to buy. That usually also meant that the vegetables were lower in quality, but also it meant more work to sort and wash them.

Changxian and Mingxia not only had to work hard, but they also had to economize as much as possible. One example of this was that after a dinner at a good restaurant to which I had invited them, Mingxia took home all the hand towels provided by the restaurant, saying she could use them to wash dishes. For them, the cost of tissues, disposable lunch boxes and disposable chopsticks amounted to RMB 3,000 a year—a big cost for such a venture.

It was possible to hire someone to help, but this basic restaurant could not afford other staff, so Mingxia and Changxian had to be very resourceful and quick moving, not only when preparing and serving food, but also to make sure those who had eaten paid before leaving. It happened from time to time that someone, not a Gao villager of course, would just walk off without paying. Sometimes Changxian and Mingxia would then ask one of the closest Gao villager migrant workers to go around to collect the bill.

While there, I counted eight such restaurants on the factory site, all next to each other and all with similar service, layout, and food. Each so-called room or compartment that was used as a restaurant was about 90 square meters in size, with the rent being RMB 1,100 a month. The landlord of the buildings was in fact the factory owner, who collected the rent each month.

Changxian and Mingxia worked tirelessly and had to do all the purchasing, cooking, washing, and cleaning, as well as serving all the customers. They could only sleep about four to five hours a day in order to get things ready, and despite all their hard work, they jointly earned only about RMB 3,000 a month. There was just too much work with too little return, so it was no wonder that Changxian and Mingxia decided to give up the restaurant business. All was not in vain, however, as their restaurant experience was a good lesson for them later when they started running hotels.

Panyu District in the City of Guangzhou

My extended family in Gao Village has a number of hotels in Panyu, so it is perhaps fitting to start with this place called Panyu, not only because the hotels that Mingxia and Changxian manage are located in Panyu, but also because what has happened in Panyu demonstrates China's rapid development. Panyu is located in the south of Guangdong Province, which is in the heart of the Pearl River Delta region and is at the center of the triangle of Guangzhou, Hong Kong, and Macau, spanning a total area of more than 786 square kilometers. It has an officially registered population of nearly two million people, but more than half are migrant workers like Changxian and Mingxia.[3] Panyu boasts a history of 2,200 years, starting in year 33 of the Qin Dynasty (221 to 206 BC). Now it has expressways, ferry routes, and railways to Hong Kong and the rest of Guangdong. South China's biggest railway station, the Guangzhou South railway station, is near Panyu and you can travel as far as Wuhan, Guiyang, and Nanning from Panyu. By 2013, the Guangzhou subway had also reached Panyu.

In 1978, there were only 84 individual commercial outlets in Panyu, like small street corner shops, but by 2004 the number had increased to 43,887, with the increase of employed people rising from 95 in 1978 to 84,102 in 2004. By 2011, there were nearly 200,000 industrial enterprises in Panyu District, of which 300 enterprises had assets valued at more than RMB 100 million; they were engaged in manufacturing all kinds of industrial commodities ranging from telecommunications equipment and motor parts to musical instruments and shoes and garments. Panyu is still engaged in agriculture but is gradually changing from growing grains, like rice, to other horticulture and aquatic products. The official available figure of total GDP for Panyu in 2011 was RMB 123.578 billion, of which RMB 8.26 billion was from the agricultural sector.

---

3   This information is from the website baike.baidu.com, the Chinese version of the Wikipedia, according to which about half of the permanent residents (anyone who resides one place for six months or more) are migrant workers like Changxian and Mingxia.

By 2011, the total value of imports and exports reached RMB 16.769 billion, of which imports consisted of RMB 6.75 billion and exports RMB 10 billion. However, the 2009 global financial crisis directly affected Panyu's economy, with exports and imports decreasing by 13.4 percent. As I will discuss later, this downturn had an impact on Changxian and Mingxia's hotel business.

The Hotel Business and Xu Congxi

It is necessary to introduce another important character, Xu Congxi, at this point, for a number of reasons. Firstly, Xu is related to Gao Village. Secondly, Xu's life and career is another mirror image of the changes and developments in China since the 1949 revolution. Above all, Xu was the pioneer of the hotel business for Gao villagers.

Xu was born and brought up in Xu Village, a much bigger neighboring village, about half a kilometer away from Gao Village. Xu and his sister were orphans, as their parents both died when they were little. Xu's relatives took over the care of the two children and the collective system in Xu Village bore the responsibilities of the cost of raising the two orphans, including sending them to school. Xu completed his high school education and succeeded in passing the national tertiary education examination in 1982, and then studied at the Jiangxi College of Technology. By any standard, his was an extraordinary success story and for that reason, Xu Congxi was listed in the Poyang County Gazette as an example of how the welfare system worked in the Mao era.[4]

After graduating from the Jiangxi College of Technology, Xu went back to Poyang and worked for the government of Poyang County (previously called "Boyang"). Xu was a hardworking, unassuming and very accommodating person. Because of his "politically correct"

---

4   Liu et al. 1989.

background (which meant he was poor and therefore loyal to the Party), Xu was soon invited to become a member of the Chinese Communist Party. Xu was more than courteous to his superiors but was also very well liked by his colleagues and the people with whom he worked. He was very popular and soon was promoted to the position of deputy director of the Bureau of Water and Electricity in Poyang County. It was at this point that Xu married my sister Lingli's daughter; in this way, Xu Congxi became the son-in-law of a Gao villager. Xu was not a man of many words, but he was competent and reliable. In those days, every time I went back to Gao Village I would always stop at Lingli's place, and I would see Xu always on call to help my sister, from buying something in the street to fixing something.

Though Xu appeared humble and modest, he was considered an important person in a county of a million people and in a place like Poyang, where water and electricity are important business. Apart from the Department of Organization which is under the secretary of the CCP's supervision, there are three other important departments in the hierarchy of a county governmental system—Bureau of Commerce, Bureau of Taxation, and Bureau of Water and Electricity. Water is important because Poyang is a large agricultural county bordering Poyang Lake, the largest fresh water lake in China, and where the growing of rice, a water-reliant crop, is the main industry. Therefore, water issues and irrigation have always been a priority in the running of government business in Poyang. In addition, because there is always a shortage of electricity, the Bureau of Water and Electricity has a crucial leverage in dealing with other departments. Although Xu was only the deputy director of this important bureau, he was young, very well liked and one of the most highly educated there at that time. Xu was expected to become the director whenever the current one was to be replaced or retired.

My sister Gao Lingli was proud of and excited about her son-in-law, and the Xu villagers were also proud and excited, until something went terribly wrong. Out of the blue one day, Xu was accused of embezzlement and corruption; he was then arrested and put into jail. My sister immediately telephoned me and asked me for help. I tried everything possible that I could, but there was nothing really that I could do, being a university lecturer in Australia. The whole story is too long to tell, but suffice it to say that there was evidence that Xu had accepted gifts that valued RMB 20,000. The real reason for his fall was internal factional politics, which was beyond Xu's control, and he just fell as a victim in the process. Eventually he was released without criminal charges being pressed, but in the meantime he had lost his official position and was out of a job.

Frustrated and disillusioned, Congxi decided to *xiahai*, or plunge into the sea of career uncertainty, so he left Poyang and went to Guangdong to seek work as a migrant worker. It was in Guangdong that his education proved useful, and he did not have to become a laborer or work on a factory floor. Previously, because at college he had studied electrical engineering, he got a job as an electrician, which was considered a white-collar job.

Because he was diligent, reliable, and hardworking, he quickly progressed in his career and he was given jobs with more responsibility, jobs that relied more on his brain than his hands. He was hired first to install lighting in houses and later to design lighting systems in new houses. His wage continued to increase until he was earning RMB 10,000 a month. That was a lot of money in the late 1990s for a migrant worker. Being a shrewd man, he saved money and kept having new ideas for making more money; one of these ideas was to run hotels.

At this point, I would like to spend some time discussing what I consider a very important sociological phenomenon in China, the "chain reaction of social networks" mentioned above. I described this phenomenon when I talked about how my brother Changwen helped so many other Gao villagers to become migrant workers in the factory where he worked in Xiamen. Changwen was the first Gao villager to be a migrant worker in the cutlery factory. As the factory expanded, more workers were required and Changwen introduced Gao villagers, one after another, into the factory. It was a win-win situation for both the villagers and the owner of the factory. The owner had a convenient way to recruit more reliable workers at no cost because Changwen acted as guarantor for the new migrant workers from Gao Village. Chang-wen also lent them money and assisted them with initially finding accommodation. The youngsters from Gao Village did not have to face the intimidation and uncertainty of trying to find work, and their parents felt relieved that there was someone to look after their children far away. As a result of this social network, in many a factory and assembly line, one may find that the workers are all from the same place. This gives a group of workers the benefit of mutual reliance and help, a strong sense of community, and a collective shield against discrimination when they are far from home.

Xu Congxi had the idea of running hotels because he was inspired by people from Poyang. For some reason, there is a group of people from Poyang who run hotels, a "chain reaction of social networks" phenomenon similar to what happened to the Gao villagers working in the cutlery factory. One Poyang person started to run a hotel business and then that person introduced another Poyang person into the business, who was usually a friend or relative. That person further introduced another into the business, again a friend or relative. Being from Poyang, Congxi got to mix with people from Poyang and made friends with them, and in this way was introduced to the business of running a hotel.

Congxi became very successful and gradually introduced his two uncles and one aunt into the hotel business. These people are of course my nephews and nieces. It was at this point that I started to get involved. I talked to my sister, my sister-in-law and Congxi, as well my nephews, and suggested that perhaps they should introduce my two brothers Changxian and Changwen into the hotel business as well, which was precisely what happened. It was this development that one day caused, to my total and pleasant surprise, a group of Gao villagers with four brand-new cars to meet my family and I when we visited Panyu from Hong Kong.

I had to intervene on behalf of my two brothers, because their lives had become desperate. First let me describe Changwen a little further. As the first migrant worker from Gao Village with a high school education, he earned good money and in turn, helped a lot of other Gao villagers, but then he thought the grass was greener on the other side of the fence and so he left his employer and went to another one. Unfortunately, it did not work out well this time and his first boss, understandably, did not want him back either. So Changwen had been drifting around Guangdong and Fujian trying to find a job that he liked and that would pay well enough, but without much success. He began to gamble by playing mahjong and he started to smoke heavily. His wife, meanwhile, who had left their son in Poyang with her parents in order to work in another factory, became increasingly unhappy with the situation and was talking of divorce.

Changxian had not been doing much better either. He had not left the village to become a migrant worker because by then he was the village accountant and a member of the village committee. With my help, he had built a house and the family was running a grocery shop. It was tolerable and he was well respected in the area, and in many ways he and Mingxia had quite a satisfying life. But gradually, their grocery shop began to make less and less money because there were more and more shops set up in the area with better stock. There was not much to do in the village either, as the governing of the village had become virtually non-existent. His son had gone to university in Wuhan, which meant he had to pay his son's tuition fees and living expenses. One of Changxian's daughters, upon completing a teaching degree, could not find employment because education in rural China has been on the decline (as described in Chapter 3). Changxian and Mingxia then went to Xiamen to run a makeshift restaurant, without much success, as described above. So Changxian and the family were also in a very difficult position.

I intervened on behalf of my two brothers in two ways. Firstly, I made a request to my sister, nephews, and Xu Congxi that they should help our two brothers by letting them buy shares in the hotel business. To their credit, I did not have to say much before they agreed to help, largely because traditional family values are still very important to them all. Secondly, I gave my two brothers some initial capital to buy some shares, and as a result both brothers are apparently doing very well.

In the words of my sister Lingli, they have turned over a new leaf. In Chinese, we would describe this as *fanshen*[5] ("to turn the body over"). One of the latest developments in 2014, which I heard from them, was that Changxian had bought a new car. Currently, to possess a new car is a sign of a good life in urban China, and in rural China, it is also a status symbol. How did Changxian managed to *fanshen*? What is his hotel business like? This will be discussed in the next chapter.

---

5   The title of William Hinton's successful documentary of land reform in Long Bow Village is *Fanshen: A Documentary of Revolution in a Chinese Village* (Hinton 1966). I expect his use of the word *fanshen* was to denote the same meaning.

CHAPTER 7

The Gao Family Clan and Its Hotel Businesses

In the previous chapter, I introduced the two main characters involved in the Gao family hotel business venture, its background, and the other people involved, the circumstances of how the venture started, and the location of most of the Gao Village clan hotels. In this chapter, I will present a picture of what the hotels are like, how the hotels are run, what the arrangements are between hotel shareholders, the profitability of the businesses, and the relationship between the businesses and local authorities. Finally, I will attempt to place the Gao villagers' hotel businesses within the overall situation in China.

The Gao Family Clan

In order to undertake research for this book, I took three trips to Panyu to examine the hotel business in action and to see my brothers' families. In 2009, I arrived at one of the hotels in Panyu run by one member of the Gao Village clan. I was led to a huge, air-conditioned room with a queen-sized bed with white sheets, two bedside tables, a couch, a desk, a color television set, and pendant lights. I was also surprised to find that I did not need the socket adapter that I had brought with me, as the power socket had two systems: a Chinese one with two pins and another one with three. There was a coat hook and a wardrobe, and a corner nook with a light. It also had a large bathroom of about eight square meters; the bathroom itself was bigger than the whole room in which I had stayed in Hong Kong for the previous two nights. In order to save money, I had booked the Hong Kong room through an online site recommended by the Blue Planet Guide. It was clean, near the central Kowloon area of Tsim Sha Tsui, a few meters away from Nathan Road, small and spartan; It cost HK$450 for Thursday and HK$500 for Friday. In Panyu, all three walls of the bathroom were tiled and the floor had porcelain tiles. The bathroom counter tops were made of marble, with one of the most fashionable kinds of design I have ever seen. Obviously this was the Presidential Suite reserved for my first visit.

The Gao family clan, consisting of my sister Gao Lingli's two sons, two daughters-in-law, two daughters, two sons-in-law, my two brothers Changwen and Changxian, and their wives, Mingxia and Xiongying, has been running hotels for several years now and they have been fairly successful. This can be confirmed by the fact that Changxian was able to renovate his house in Gao Village, inside and outside, in a way that was comfortable yet looked expensive. I was told by some other members of the family, not by himself, that he earned about RMB 10,000 a month from the shares of the four hotels that had invested in. To put that in perspective, it was about the monthly salary of a professor in a Beijing university. The average monthly salary for white-collar workers in Shenzhen, one of the highest earning cities in China, was about RMB 7,000 a month in 2011. Even Changwen, considered the least able in terms of making money, together with his wife Xiongying, had saved enough to buy a house in Poyang for RMB 200,000 and a piece of land for RMB 50,000. I guess that both my brothers had made the least money among the hotel business clan. This assumption is based on casual conversations with them when they commented on each other and on the fact that my sister's two daughters and her two sons' families had all bought cars, whereas neither of my two brothers had a car at that time as they claimed that they could not afford one. That was in 2009. In 2014, my brother Changxian also bought a new car.

The fact that Changwen made the least money, and that my sister's children made more and that Xu Congxi made the most, had in fact nothing to do with management skills or the way their businesses were run. All together they had several hotels in Panyu, and they also had hotels in Xiamen by 2015. In fact, the management style and the way the hotels were run was more or less the same in all of these hotels.

The Hotel Business Arrangement

What happens is this. When one person has an idea and finds a property, one or more of the clan may be invited to join the venture. Depending on what is available and on their agreement, they divide the shares of the investment; the investment being the money that is required to renovate the property into a hotel, set it up, and make it run. Once the hotel is in operation, the profit is divided according to the percentage of the initial input. Once the hotel is set up, one of the clan will be assigned as the manager of that hotel, usually the one who has the highest initial investment. All the managers will be paid a monthly salary, and the amount of the salary is decided by the family clan. The monthly salary for a manager of a hotel was RMB 600 in 2006, although this increased to RMB 800 in 2009 and in 2015 it was RMB 1,500 a month. It is a full-time job and involves living and working in the hotel 24 hours a day, seven days a week.

As a consequence of this arrangement, there are several important outcomes. Firstly, the profit of any specific hotel depends more on the location than on management skills. Secondly, whoever in the clan has the highest initial capital investment, of course, will take the highest percentage of profit. Thirdly, those who have the most capital available have the advantage of deciding where to set up a hotel, and more crucially, have the power of deciding who to invite to be shareholders. It is due to these factors that Changwen made the least, because he had the least capital invested and as a consequence, he had the fewest shares in the smallest number of hotels. Finally, one member of the clan might have shares in several of these hotels or have shares in all of them, though at different percentages.

It is also interesting to note two other relevant facts about this arrangement and its consequences. Xu Congxi obviously made the most money and called the shots. This was the case not only because he was the initiator of the hotel business for the whole Gao Village clan, but also because he had the highest percentage of capital due to having accumulated enough money while working as an electrician and earning more than RMB 10,000 a month. He was able to be a skilled worker because he had studied electrical engineering at college and that education gave him an advantageous start. For his share of the hotels, he earned about RMB 60,000 a month in 2009, without having to run or manage any of the hotels.

The difference between my sister's children and my brothers clearly shows a disparity between urban and rural people. Though my sister and her children live in a backwater county town (Poyang is listed as one of the poorest counties in the country), they are still considered to have urban household registration. Though my sister and her husband are ordinary people and both are retired, their children still have the advantage over my two brothers, who are registered as rural residents. My sister's children were somehow able to find enough initial capital for the hotel business, whereas my two brothers were not. Both of my brothers' initial capital is actually the money I managed to send them. My sister's children only let my brothers into the hotel business because of my intervention. Otherwise, Changxian would still be in Gao Village and Changwen would still be a migrant worker earning RMB 1,500 or thereabouts if he were lucky, if they were not granted shares in these hotels.

The gap between the origins of migration, one urban and one rural, was already manifest in 2009: the best room available to cater for my family was in the hotel run by one of my sister's younger sons, Qiao Zhanping. His hotels were already a grade higher than those run by my rural brothers. The latest news is that Zhanping has bought a BMW.

The Hotel in Shiji Village

The hotel that Changxian manages is located in Shiji in the Panyu District of Guangzhou. Shiji used to be a village and it is still so called, but now it is mostly urbanized, though one can still see some vegetable plots on the edge of the village, worked on by farmers who are migrant workers hired by the locals.

At the center of the town, there is an imposing town hall. Shops and restaurants are lined along the streets, with branch offices of all the major Chinese banks: the Bank of China, the Agricultural Bank, and the Commercial Bank. There are also thriving local markets where the nearby farmers bring all kinds of produce and animals like live fish, chickens and ducks.

The main street was renovated because of the Asian Games held in Guangzhou, to such an extent that it is not different from any modern road in any major city, with trees lining both sides and a corridor of trees and plants in the middle dividing two-way traffic, with three lanes on each side. There are not too many cars yet, but there are many taxis.

When I got off at the bus station in May 2011 to take a taxi, my brother had come to meet me. He negotiated with a taxi driver, bargaining the price of the fare from RMB 35 to 30, even though it was for quite a distance. I asked the driver why he did not use the meter, since I could see a meter installed. The driver said he could make more money without having to use the meter. Though there were traffic lights in perfect working order, the taxi driver just drove through the red lights when he saw there was no traffic in his way, and I saw other cars and motorbikes doing the same.

When I went to a bank with a wallet in my hand, my brother warned me that I should not do that because I risked being robbed. His daughter Gao Yan had been robbed when she had taken her daughter to the nursery one day; a motorbike rider had just snatched her bag from her shoulder before speeding away. When I got onto the train from Guangzhou to Beijing, my brother sent me a text message: "Look after your things. There are many bad people in China." It is in this kind of environment that the hotel is operated.

The Hotel and Its Employees

During my fieldwork in 2009, 2010, and 2011, I stayed in one hotel that Changxian managed. In this hotel, Changxian and Changwen both had shares and Changxian and his wife Mingxia were the managers and lived in the hotel. In order to maximize occupancy, they chose the smallest and darkest room for themselves to live in. They also made the storerooms under the stairs into rooms for the hired receptionist and their daughter, who was staying there during a number of my visits, to live in. On the other hand, they allocated the best rooms for me to stay in, which were spacious and had broadband internet access.

This hotel in Panyu has about 40 guest rooms in a three-story building. The rooms on the third floor had free broadband in 2009 and the tariff was RMB 120 a night, but in 2011 it was actually reduced to RMB 118 a night, due to the decrease of customers, which was in turn supposedly due to the global financial crisis, I was told. The Gao family clan started this hotel in 2006 when they rented it from a local resident for ten years; the rent they paid was RMB 8,000 a month in 2009 and RMB 10,000 a month in 2011. The running cost, including salary payments, was about RMB 10,000 a month.

The building they rented used to be just a shell, with concrete walls and concrete floors. Changxian and his fellow business partners spent about half a million RMB to make the place into a hotel, by wallpapering the rooms, painting the ceilings, tiling the floors, installing a bathroom in each room, and filling each room with simple but adequate furniture. I was very surprised to hear that they managed to pay off their debt in two years. I was surprised partly because when I was there in 2009, business was not that good. On October 21, 2009, the day I asked Changxian about the business, the daily turnover was only RMB 900. I could see that many rooms remained empty. They did not seem desperate though. Changxian said, half-jokingly: "Big Brother, I might need to borrow money from you for a new investment."

It was also during this time that I asked Congxi whether he wanted to buy a house in Australia. I proposed to him that it would be a good investment, since property prices had been rising steadily. As his daughter Mimi had been studying at the University of Adelaide, the added benefit of buying a house in Adelaide would be that Mimi would not have to pay the very expensive rent. Furthermore, Mimi could rent some rooms to have some income. But Congxi did not seem interested in the proposal. His response was that he would have a higher rate of return by investing that kind of money in China, in a hotel business for instance. I assume therefore, the hotel business they run must make good money. But how? A description of the hotel below may provide us with some idea.

For an average room there was a bathroom of about two square meters, with a squat toilet and a showerhead over the toilet, as in the bathrooms of many Chinese homes. There was a sink and a mirror, and a gas heated water supply unit. Possibly because the house was not originally designed for the purpose of being a hotel, or for some other reason that was not apparent to me, the toilet was on a platform that was higher than the floor of the room. As a result, water was likely to flow out into the room when one had a shower. In any case, the bathroom got completely wet after a shower, so one needed to wear a pair of slippers, a couple of which were supplied. The trouble was that once you walked out of the bathroom you made the bedroom floor wet and dirty. This was one of the most annoying things for me when I stayed there.

Apparently in order to attract customers, there was a print of a completely naked young woman in each bathroom, and for some reason, the naked women, either Western or Chinese, all had big breasts. Surprisingly, for a hotel like this, there were also a couple of toothbrushes and a small tube of toothpaste, which were supplied for free. There was also small bar of soap, shampoo, and two towels, although these were much smaller than standard Western bath towels.

In the room, there was a table, a chair, a TV set, bottled water on top of a hot plate for boiling water, and a cupboard; they were all of reasonable quality. There was no bed lamp, but the room light could be turned off by a switch on the bedside table. There was even an air-conditioner, which was important since it was very hot in summer in Panyu.

Most rooms were fitted with twin beds and there were some rooms with a queen-sized bed. The sheets and pillowcases were washed every day. There was a cleaner who serviced the room every day, mostly changing the sheets and mopping the floor. For a room like this, the cheapest price was RMB 48 a night. The best room was RMB 120 a night when I was there.

The hotels were required to install a CCTV to monitor the corridors, but not individual rooms (I specifically asked about this). The CCTV tapes had to be kept for a month for any potential public security police inspection. It was also a requirement of the public security authority that every customer had to register using an identity card when checking into a room; however, I was aware that many people did not present their IDs. Sometimes the hotel might let them stay, but they ran the risk of being penalized by the police if they carried out a random check. According to Changxian, the ID requirement was not good for business.

During my first visit, the receptionist was a girl from Guangxi, who was said to be 19 years old, but looked like she was 12. She lived in the hotel but did not eat with the family. Mingxia cooked one or two meals a day for the family, but not for customers. There were only instant noodles and soft drinks on sale in the hotel. This was not a problem as there were so many food stalls and cheap restaurants around the area, and even the Gao family bought breakfast and sometimes lunch from these places.

The receptionist lodged in the hotel for free, and earned RMB 800 a month in 2009 and RMB 1,500 a month in 2011, with a top-up commission of 0.5 percent of the daily turnover. The arrangement of the commission was obviously an attempt to give the receptionist an incentive to lure in more customers. The cleaner was an elderly woman from Sichuan who changed the sheets and towels every day. The washing would then be collected by a laundry company van in the morning and clean ones would be delivered in the afternoon. The laundry fees were RMB 0.8 for a sheet and RMB 0.4 for a towel or pillowcase, which was not cheap by Chinese standards. The cleaner earned RMB 900 a month in 2009, working about eight hours a day, seven days a week. This was a much worse deal than for the receptionist, who had some education and computer skills. In March 2011, when I visited the hotel again, the elderly woman cleaner was gone and instead, Mingxia had taken over the job herself. In answer to my query, I was told that it was very difficult to find a cleaner who did not demand too much money. Changxian complained that nowadays it was too expensive even to hire a street sweeper. There was also a security guard in every hotel; the security guard in Panyu was Changxian's son-in-law, who earned RMB 1,200 a month. In 2014, I found out that Mingxia still did the cleaning for the hotel that she managed, as she wanted to earn that money herself, for the family, rather than paying someone else to do the job.

The Customers and Taxation

What kind of people are the customers of hotels like this? Certainly not migrant workers, even though RMB 48 a night does not sound like a lot and it is good value for a simple but clean and quite comfortable room. For a long time, since the 1980s up to the late 1990s, the average monthly salary for a migrant worker remained at about RMB 600–800. For instance, the average monthly salary for migrant workers in 1990 in Shenzhen was only RMB 400–500, and it was not until 2010 that it reached RMB 2,000–2,500 a month (Li Changping 2011).

According to Changxian, most of the customers consist of two groups. One group of customers is business people from other parts of China who come to seek business opportunities, or to buy or sell something. The second group of people is mostly men who come to have "fun." The second group again can be divided into two subgroups. One subgroup is lower- and middle-class Party and government officials from other parts of China, who use business or conferences as an excuse to come to the south to study the "experiences of development." The second subgroup consists of local people, people within Guangdong Province, even within Panyu, who may call an escort agency for a prostitute to stay the night. Occasionally, there could be two or more men with one woman, although they may not stay the whole night. It is perhaps for this reason, according to Changxian, that from April to September the season is busy, but the hotel has fewer customers from

October to March. It has more customers during warmer months because during those times the locals spend time outside, including call girls. Changxian and Changwen also informed me that many factories had started to move inland and that had affected their hotel business.

The hotels pay very little tax—a few hundred RMB a month at most. Fake accounts can be made to avoid tax auditing, although there is a risk of penalty if they are caught not paying tax. From my interviews with businesses around the area, I found that the local government did not make an effort to collect tax. Upon closer investigation, it can be seen that there is not much incentive for the local taxation bureau to bother about those who run small businesses. There are several reasons for this. First of all, in a place like Panyu, where commerce and business have been expanding and the place is quickly developing from a local town into a city-like urban center, the government bureaucracy simply cannot cope with the increasing demand for skills and personnel that are required to collect tax from small businesses. Secondly, the local government makes a lot of money out of land taxes and big business and it is not short of money. Therefore, it does not pay for the bureaucracy to spend time and energy to collect a small amount of tax from small businesses. Finally, a hotel business like this one run by Changxian made good use of unoccupied properties, and was considered a good deed by the local government.

That is one of the main reasons why, as I found out from my interviews, the local people and outsiders like Changxian do get on well and the Gao family clan does not feel discriminated against in Panyu, a finding that was slightly surprising to me. The tax bureau personnel may know that fake accounts can be provided (any way who does not do that in China?), but arrangements can be made to make both sides happy. For instance, if you pay RMB 600–1,000 a month to the younger brother of the director of the local tax bureau, everything should be fine. Finally, according to Changwen, some tax collectors are just too lazy; if you go visit them any time, you can see all they do in the office is play mahjong and drink tea, all the time.

However, that does not mean hotel ventures like this one, or indeed any other businesses run by migrant workers, are left in peace. It seems that the fewer state regulations there are and the less explicit the state rules are, the more there are opportunities for local government officials and relevant government personnel to make money by exploiting the situation. The local security personnel *chengguan* who would frequently visit the Gao Village clan's hotels for inspections. They may want to examine one day's CCTV footage, and the inspection is always in the name of finding a violation of regulations, such as whether the guest has registered with a proper ID, whether drugs are being used, or whether there is gambling or prostitution; these are the so-called "three inspections" (drug inspections, gambling inspections and prostitution inspections). A far as I know, there is never any drug use or gambling involved in these kinds of hotels; even a mahjong table is not provided in the hotel for customers, although the Gao Village clan themselves play mahjong all the time. However, prostitution may be the reason for some clients to stay in this kind of hotel. The police and local authorities know that, and that is why many clients do not want to register with their real ID when they check in. These *chengguan* from the City Urban Administrative and Law Enforcement Bureau usually come to inspect once a month, and then they leave their telephone numbers for the hotel to contact them about the inspection results. The hotel management then phones them to invite them to a meal to talk about it. During the meal, a red envelope containing RMB 600 (current practice) for each of the *chengguan* who come around is delivered discreetly. Following this, there will be no news about the hotel for a month. Once, Changwen gave RMB 600 each to the three who came, but a reply came back that there was a need for another person. Sometimes, they may suddenly explicitly demand a payment of RMB 1,000 and then leave their numbers for you to make arrangements. If you do not cooperate in this kind of deal, they will come to announce that such and such regulations have been violated and the hotel has to close down for one month for "rectification." This happened once to one of the Gao villager's hotels and the hotel stopped running for six weeks. I was also informed that this was not an isolated case but was quite common; however, it was pointed out that since the ascendance of President Xi Jinping, the police were less arrogant in this kind of extortion.

A Little Incident

In what follows I will describe a little incident as an illustration of how informal business management is and how dispute settlements can be made. Changxian, Changwen, one of my sister's daughter's Guiping, and Guiping's sister-in-law all had equal shares of a hotel in Xiamen, which was doing good business. Guiping's sister-in-law and her husband (this is an example of how the family chain expands) were managers of that hotel. One day, something very unfortunate happened. The sister-in-law's husband, that is, the male manager of the hotel, tried to climb through a window to get into a room to open the door, because the key of that room had been locked inside by a customer who had just left.

This is a good example of how small business owners in China cut corners to save costs. They should have called a locksmith to open the door. In any case, the male manager of the hotel, in his effort to climb in, fell from the window and was killed instantly. The family of the man wanted compensation for his death from the other three shareholders, since they claimed that the man died in the process of running the hotel. One can somehow understand this, since surely the man did die on duty. Unfortunately, they could not demand compensation from anyone else, since the business was not insured—another practice to save and make quick money. There was a dispute and a dilemma.

The four shareholders were family related: One shareholder, Guiping, is the daughter of Lingli, who is the sister of the other two shareholders, Changxian and Changwen, and the fourth shareholder is Guiping's sister-in-law, whose husband died in the fall. After the accident, her husband's family demanded compensation. However, because the four shareholders were related to the man who died, none of them wanted a fight in court. Eventually, a settlement was reached without legal intervention, with the result that the four shareholders would share the death compensation payment of RMB 600,000, which meant each shareholder paid RMB 150,000. Changxian and Changwen did not want to pay cash and so handed over their share of the hotel to the family of the dead man as settlement.

Problems in Management

There are a number of problems in managing this hotel. Firstly, there is no advertising of any kind; there is not even a website for the business. Whether there are clients or not depends entirely on luck or on people passing by, it would seem. Secondly, the hotel has no business plan or policies and procedures, which are essential for any reputable or sustainable business. Instead the management is ad hoc and tends to cut corners to save cost. I could observe, for instance, dirty carpets with damage due to burn marks by cigarettes everywhere. This kind of cheap budget business, on the run for quick profits, means that smoking rules are not enforced for fear of losing customers and carpets are not professionally shampooed, as it is too costly. Even this type of low-budget hotel can prove to be too expensive in some areas. Changwen and Wenshu, who is mentioned in another chapter of this book, had to close down a hotel business in an area where the people were too poor even to afford this kind of service and as a result, both made substantial losses from that failed venture.

There is a new development of rental properties that compete for the market of this kind of low-end accommodation. According to Changwen, in the area where he runs a hotel, some customers are taken away by those who run rental properties. For the same kind of accommodation, the rental business can afford to offer customers even lower prices because, firstly, they do not have to cope with more than half a dozen of bureaucratic fees, such as the very expensive fire safety certificate, permit for commercial activities, contract filing fees, and a special permit for land use, the total cost of which can be as much as RMB 100,000. Currently, rental properties are not required to pay these costs because they are considered residential, not commercial. Secondly, because these rental properties are supposed to be residential, the price for electricity is almost half that of commercial use buildings. Electricity is one of the largest operating costs, since air conditioning is required for a long time of the year in Guangdong. Thirdly, the police are less intrusive to residential rental activities.

Another problem is inherent in the way the clan arranges the hotel's management. Profits are distributed on the basis of shares in the investment and that seems fair enough. However, management staff is inadequately remunerated. Changxian and Mingxia had to manage two hotels and they were paid around RMB 1,500 a month. This is not a salary for a professional manager. On the other hand, Xu Congxi, working as a full-time electrician, did not manage any of the 10 or so hotels in which he had shares. In the actual sense of the word, Xu has been exploiting the labor of his relatives. Of course, because they were family members, they did not quarrel over the issue. In any case, for Gao villagers like Changxian, his payment as manager, however unfair, is already a huge improvement in terms of status and income. Why would he complain? But I did hear from their conversation hints that there were complaints that my sister's children tended to gang together to gain advantage over my brothers, and that some members of the clan had been seen taking cash from the hotel register. Who could blame them if they take out some cash for daily use, given that their income was so low?

Conclusion

To summarize this chapter on the Gao family hotel businesses, the first point is that for villagers like Changxian and Mingxia, life is infinitely better than it used to be. In spite of the reduction of income since 2013, Changxian and Mingxia, I was told, could make a combined income of something like RMB 200,000 a year from their shares in the five hotels, including their wages for being managers of the hotels and Mingxia being a cleaner. They have a decent house back in their home village, though it would not be considered the best these days. However, most days of the year the house remains empty, as it is only occupied a few days a year when they go back to spend Chinese New Year. Sometimes they do not even go back to for Chinese New Year these days. With a new China made Toyota vehicle they purchased recently, the family drove home in February 2015 for Chinese New Year. The drive from Guangzhou to Gao Village took 17 hours. The family went back this year because they wanted the wedding of their son, the youngest of three children, to take place in Gao Village. The wedding was huge and very successful. With three children all properly married, one daughter married to a man from Yingtan, a city in Jiangxi but far away from Gao Village, the other daughter married to a man from a village not far from Gao Village, and their son married to a girl from Youdunjie, about 15 kilometers from Gao Village, Changxian said that now he was content, because there was nothing else to worry about in his life. To connect this with the big picture, like my descriptions of other Gao villagers in this book, the rural people, in contrast to the discontent expressed on various websites by urban dwellers, are actually content. For most of them, this is the best time they can ever remember.

The second point that can be identified from the Gao family's hotel businesses is that everything seems to be done on the run, to make a quick profit. To make a quick turnover, the businesses tend to cut corners. For example, there is no insurance policy for the businesses, and there is no legally identified or legally enforced taxation system. The authorities do not seem to have a policy to enable migrants like Changxian and Mingxia to settle down as Panyu residents. The total number of officially registered residents of Panyu is only a little more than half its nearly two million people. The whole place is in a permanent state of change. Everything is temporary, with uncertainty and restlessness.

The third point that can be made is that there is a strong family or clan concentration in terms of both location and occupation. For certain reasons, some of which are listed below and are quite obvious, migrants from rural villages tend to stick together to do the same kind of business in the same location, as is the case of the hotel businesses run by Poyang people in Guangdong described here. This is entirely rational: Given that there is no public or government services or administrative help, village people feel insecure, alien and intimidated by the unfamiliar urban environment. In any case, there is not a lot of information about jobs and opportunities, not for them anyway. Furthermore, they do not feel they could trust either the local government or the local residents. It is for this reason that they acquire information from home from members of the family or friends.

The same logic applies to the further extension of their network, from family to fellow villagers, from fellow villagers to hometowns of the same area, and from hometowns of the same area to the same county, and even to the same province. The further the distance, the less trust and reliability there is. But two rural migrant workers from Jiangxi Province would feel a closer identity than if one of the two is from Hunan Province and another from Heilongjiang Province. This kind of place of origin identity is gradually breaking down as a result of migration, but the idea still exerts influence on rural Chinese. Changxian and Changxian's son, Gao Wei, who works on Hainan Island as a landscape designer, met a girl from Chongqing and they got on very well. Nonetheless, his mother Mingxia worked very hard and succeeded in breaking up that relationship. Eventually Gao Wei, through an introduction, married a girl from nearby Youdunjie Town in 2014.

As a result of this rationale of place of origin identity, we witness all over China that a group of rural migrants from the same place of origin are engaged in one urban center in the same kind of business venture. For instance, there is a group of vegetable businesses run by migrants from Ji'an in Jiangxi Province, a group of car-washing businesses managed by migrant workers from Yaoyu in Shenzhen, and ground digging and demolition ventures by migrants from Guangfeng in Shanghai (Cheng 2011).

What led Xu Congxi to initiate the hotel business for the Gao family clan was that when he worked in Guangdong, he made friends with other people who are also from Poyang, the county seat of Poyang County. The people from Poyang Town are known as a group that runs small hotels in Guangdong. It was from these Poyang people that Xu Congxi acquired the information about running hotels, and it was these "hometown" people that inspired and helped him. In turn, he introduced a group of his relatives who were migrants to run hotels in Guangdong.

Another point is that, in the big picture of China, the market has visibly affected the income of the Gao clan's hotel business. The 2008 global financial crisis impacted Changxian and Mingxia only slightly, in that they have to pay higher wages to their employees. The impact was not huge, probably because of the government's economic stimulus package. However, the impact of the Chinese economic downturn itself is more visible. According to my interview with Changxian, there has been a reduction in income by 30 percent in their hotel business since 2013. Recently, the situation has been getting worse: a group WeChat conversation among the clan seems to suggest that there is a growing consensus among the Gao Village hotel managers that the business is unlikely to be sustainable if the current business climate continues.

Finally, the hotel business run by the Gao Village clan not only shows the migration and occupational patterns in contemporary China, but also the rural-to-urban transformation taking place in front of our eyes. It shows how the rural sector connects with the urban sector, such as in Panyu itself, which is in the process of changing from a rural town into an urban center, and in the fact that some Gao villagers are running businesses in Guangzhou. It demonstrates how Gao Village links with the outside world, with Gao Village as an emotional anchor for the villagers to return to after they go out all over the country to make money so that they can fulfill their traditional ideals of building houses and getting their children married. Modern economic developments have pushed Gao villagers away and traditional values pull them back. They are being pulled and pushed, in the middle of China's unprecedented transformation, without any certain sense of destination. What enables them to survive is their sense of home and their place of origin.

One might ask: what is the purpose or meaning of these hustling ventures except for making money? There does not seem to be any certainty or destination for people. Everything seems transitional to something else. For Gao villagers, their only certainty and purpose seem to be to build houses back in the village for their families, competing for the better-looking ones, and to get their children properly married. In recent years, there seems to be another purpose, which is purchasing a car, and of course, competing for the most expensive ones.

CHAPTER 8

The Poor in Gao Village: Gao Lati

Introduction

What poor is can only be defined relatively. For the period between 2008 and 2015, the poverty line was set at US$1.25 per day by the World Bank, and was updated to US$1.90 as of October 2015, whereas the Chinese official poverty line has been calculated and updated since 2011 on the basis of 2,300 RMB in 2010 constant price, which is about RMB 6.3 a day. If we use the exchange rate at the time I am writing (2017), that comes to a little more than one US dollar per day, and this is why the Chinese government still holds that there are 200 million Chinese living below the poverty line (*The Economist* 2014). Given the purchasing power parity (PPP), especially in rural China, the value of RMB 6.3 is probably close to two or even more US dollars. The Chinese authorities want the world to know that China is still a poor country, and definitely it is. What is also definite is that most of the poor in China are from rural families, including those who are begging for a living, as seen in urban centers.

China has performed remarkably well in terms of reduction of absolute poverty, as the chart below shows. In other words, China's reduction curve of absolute poverty is dramatic, from the far above the world average to below the world average. This improvement is certainly reflected in Gao Village. When I started my inquiry about poverty in Gao Village in the post-Mao era and wanted to identify the poorest Gao villager to interview, my brother Changxian said to me without any hesitation: "What do you mean by poor? If you are talking about food, housing, and clothing, there are no poor people in Gao Village nowadays." It is true that no Gao villager would complain about hunger and there are no homeless people. They all seem well-fed, well-clothed and well-sheltered. Every child in Gao Village can afford to go to school, at least for the first years of school age, though some parents struggle when their children leave home to board at a high school. The officially reported poverty example of the ten-year-old Jiao Qiang picking up rubbish is without doubt, poor (He et al. 2011). But no Gao Village child has to live like that now. I have never seen a child living like that in all the years that I have traveled in the Gao Village area and other places in Poyang County, a county considered poor by Chinese standards.

Chart 2. China's poverty headcount ratio compared to the world's from 1987 to 2013.

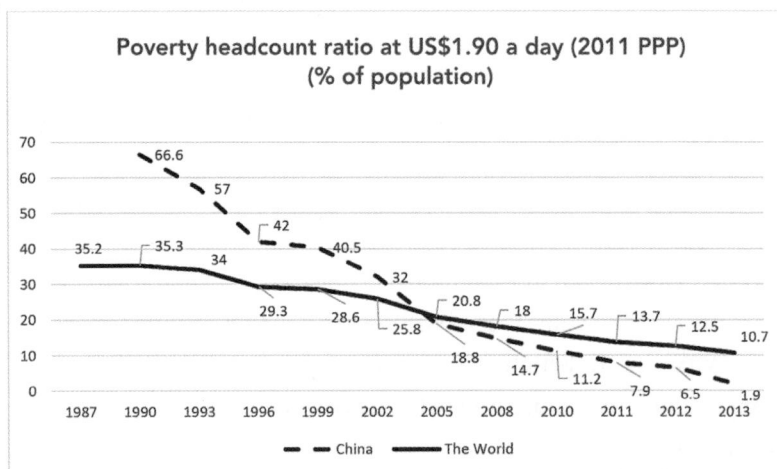

Poverty headcount ratio at US$1.90 a day (2011 PPP) (% of population)

Source: World Bank, Development Research Group.

Chart 3. China's official poverty line from 2007 to 2016.

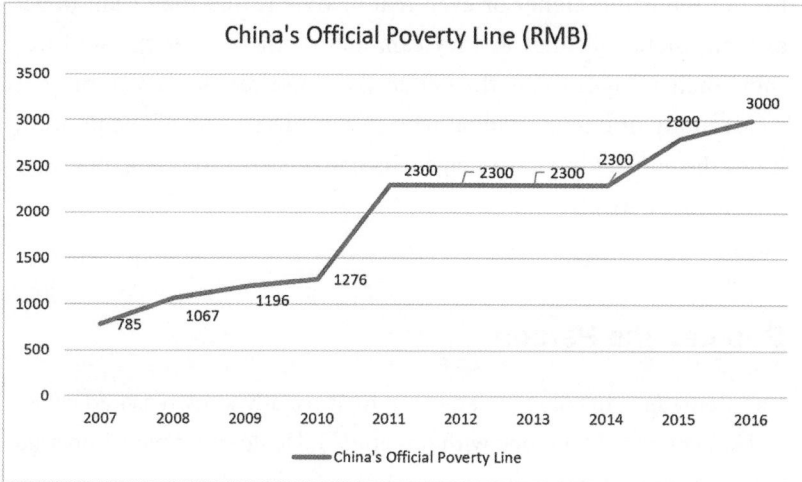

China's Official Poverty Line (RMB)

3500		
3000		3000
2500	2800	
2000	2300 2300 2300 2300	
1500		
1000	1276	
500	1196	
0	785 1067	

2007 2008 2009 2010 2011 2012 2013 2014 2015 2016

China's Official Poverty Line

Source: The State Council Leading Group Office of Poverty Alleviation and Development.

Who are the poor in Gao Village? How poor are they? Why are they poor? This is what I have set myself to answer in this chapter. It is difficult to talk about these issues regarding the whole village. To start with, there is no institutional set-up to regularly record household or personal incomes. There are no taxes and no tax returns. Agricultural subsidies are distributed to the villagers, not according to income, but on the basis of per unit of farming land. Secondly, most Gao Village income is from migrant workers, but hometown authorities have no knowledge of what migrant workers earn far away, all over the country. Local authorities will come up with some guesstimates if and when they are required to provide some statistics for government authorities. Finally, while there is a motivation for the provincial and even county authorities to present an average income figure as high as possible, because that can be a performance index for promotion, there is a motivation for the authorities at the village and village committee level to present the average income figure as low as possible. There are two main reasons for this behavior. Village and village committee officials do not have a promotion issue because they are villagers themselves and will never get promoted anywhere. Another reason for not reporting higher or even real income is that they want to get as many state subsidies as they can, and so the poorer the statistics show their villages to be, the better. For those reasons, I will present a case study of one individual who is considered one of the poorest, if not *the* poorest in Gao Village. His name is Gao Renfang, but he is nicknamed Lati.

Gao Lati the Person

Gao Renfang is his official name, but he is usually known as and called by Gao villagers Lati ("one with impetigo"). He does not have impetigo anymore, but he did when he was little. As described in *Gao Village*, impetigo used to be a common contagious skin infection in the area and many Gao villagers had it, especially men. One Gao villager is simply called *cou lati* ("an additional person with impetigo"). Another one is even called *lantou* ("rotten head") because his head is full of scars. Like many other contagious diseases in Gao Village, this kind of skin disease was eliminated due to improvements in hygiene and health in the general population in the Mao era.

Lati is one of two sons of my mother's elder sister, Jiang Xianhua. The other son, Gao Shihua, usually known as Baoshui, was not born a Gao villager but came to Gao Village from Wan Village with his mother when she married a Gao villager, after her former husband had passed away. Baoshui was a village barefoot doctor, and, as described in *Gao Village*, was the one who influenced me to become involved in Gao Village clan politics during the Cultural Revolution. Baoshui died of lung cancer in the early 1990s, but is survived by his wife and three children.

Lati was 65 years old in 2015 and married with three children, and his wife Yuangui is from Wan Village, where Lati's mother had her first family. In fact Lati and Yuangui are cousins, a blood relationship so close that their children were born with lower than average health and intelligence. Marriages arranged between cousins were not uncommon in those days, partly because of the lack of knowledge of the risks involved, but also partly because of economic considerations. When two families of relatives arrange a marriage, it is not necessary to have a go-between to carry out sometimes complex and costly negotiations. As the two families know each other well, matters such as the dowry and gifts of this and that kind can be less difficult to manage. Furthermore, the relationship between the two families can be made closer with a marriage. This is called *qin shang jia qin*, meaning to cement old ties by adding a new relative.

One of their sons, Zhimin, developed epilepsy early on during childhood and died in his late 20s in 2006. Their daughter Pingping was born with some defect on her face and was considered unmarriageable. My family helped Pingping get a job as a maid to look after my ex-wife's parents in Xiamen for some years. My ex-wife's parents, two retired professors at Xiamen University, liked the honest, hardworking, and unassuming Pingping and even helped her to have an operation, which made her look much better. She left Xiamen when she married a man in Xiangshuitan, not very far from Gao Village. Pingping has a son and a daughter now; a very good ending, apparently. The two retired professors have fond memories of Pingping to this day. Lati's son Zhihua works as a migrant worker in Xiamen.

Lati is considered by the villagers a *laoshi ren* ("simple and honest person"). The term *laoshi ren* is difficult to render in English, though the name of Voltaire's innocent and naive Candide, when translated into Chinese by Fu Lai, was rendered *laoshi ren*. Lati can be described as a person who is the opposite of "slick and sly," and is a person who is inarticulate and timid, but hard working. I will give an example as illustration, which not only shows what kind of person Gao Lati is, but also what kind of interactions are possible among the three parties of local governance: the State, the government agent, and the villagers.

An Issue of *Dibao* for Lati

There are several Gao villagers who are in the category of what is called *dibao*, which literally translates as "low guarantee" and means the minimum living standard guarantee, a kind of social welfare. Those who are categorized as *dibao* persons are considered to be poor enough to receive annual government support in cash, the amount of which in 2013 was RMB 1,350. Lati is one of the Gao villagers belonging to the *dibao* category. In 2013, Lati went to the Yinbaohu Township administration to get his allowance, using his household registration card. For some reason, Lati was given RMB 2,700, two people's entitlement. Lati did not ask why he was given that amount, or whether he was given too much by mistake or whether he should pass half of that money to someone else, but he took the money, probably happily. A few weeks later, the then-chairman of the Qinglin Village Committee, a person from Jiang Village, paid Lati a visit, during which he demanded Lati give back RMB 2,000. Naturally Lati would not agree, as it meant he would only retain RMB 700. Chairman Jiang told Lati in no uncertain terms that if Lati did not give him RMB 2,000, he would exclude Lati from *dibao* in 2014. Confused by the situation and frightened by the threat, Lati complied and Chairman Jiang took the money. During our chat I asked Lati why he gave in like that. Lati said he was afraid of being excluded from *dibao* and that RMB 700 was better than nothing. Lati did not even dare to ask for a receipt, though I assume even if he did ask he would not get one anyway. In the end, Lati was 650 short of his due, the money that Chairman Jiang took remained unaccountable, and Lati did not receive any payment in 2014. For some reason I was more angry than Lati after I was retold the story. I immediately asked my brother Changxian to telephone Xu Congchang, who worked as a social work officer in the Yinbaohu Township government, to see if I could pay him a visit. In fact, I had met Congchang the night before when he came to a celebration dinner for my nephew's wedding. Congchang and I were good friends back when I was in Gao Village, and we slept near each other on bunk beds when we participated in local militia training together. Later,

Congchang joined the Chinese navy and we kept correspondence for some years before I left Gao Village. I walked to Xu Village and talked to Congchang about Lati's case. Congchang was sympathetic and promised to look into the matter when he returned to work from the Chinese New Year holiday. Before I left Gao Village, I also asked Changxian to telephone Congchang to make sure that the matter had been dealt with. The latest I heard is that Lati is getting paid as a *dibao* person for the year, 2015. As for 2014, the issue is too murky to clarify, I was told. The party secretary of the township government had actually paid Lati a visit to tell him to keep the matter quiet.

Work, Income, and Life

Lati is in bad health, is weak, often coughs due to bronchitis, and has stomach complaints all the time. He hates the cold weather because that makes his cough worse. We used to be next-door neighbors and one thing I remember of Lati as a child is that he was known to have an irresistible desire to eat charcoal, though I had never seen him doing it myself. He used to be a migrant in Guangdong working as a simple mechanic at construction sites. He taught himself how to work on engines during the Mao era, when Gao Village bought an engine pump to pump water from the river to irrigate rice fields. The pump engine would usually run day and night during summer, and Lati was one of those who would stay at the pump station on night duty. Even this kind of simple skill proved useful when he went to Guangdong in the late 1980s. However, as his son Zhimin's illness got worse, he had to give up his work in Guangdong to go back to Gao Village, with great regret. For one thing, he preferred the warm weather in Guangdong where he felt much healthier, he told me.

Now Lati is too old and weak to be a migrant worker. He and his wife Yuangui work on a little more than six *mu* of land. Because Lati is weak and in poor health, most of the physically strenuous work is actually done by Yuangui, who is stronger and healthier. Based on the price index in 2014, what Lati and Yuangui produced was priced about RMB 15,000. Supposing that both of them spent 200 days in a year working in the field, each would earn only RMB 37.5 a day. They probably spend less than 200 days a year working on a little more than six *mu* of land, but their daily earning would not be more than RMB 50 a day.

However, this income is considerably higher than the official poverty line of RMB 2,300 a year, which is set by the Chinese government. Lati and Yuangui have an income of RMB 15,000 a year, which does not include the hidden income that is not calculated. First of all, this income does not include the pigs and chickens that they raise at home. Nor does it include the vegetables they grow for their own consumption. Secondly, they do occasionally earn cash from work in and around Gao Village. For instance, starting in 2015, Lati earned RMB 1,500 a year by collecting rubbish along the main road running through Gao Village. In 2011 when I visited Gao Village, Lati was still fit enough to work at Gao Wenshu's construction site for about RMB 100 a day plus a pack of cigarettes. Nowadays, Lati is too weak to do that but Yuangui actually still earns some money from this kind of work in Gao Village, as there is always some construction going on in the village.

Lati's son Zhihua is a migrant worker in Xiamen and now earns RMB 4,000 a month. According to Lati, his son only gives him a few hundred RMB a year. During the 2015 Chinese New Year, Zhihua came home for the festival and left RMB 600 for his parents before he left again for Xiamen. For Lati and Yuangui, this was not only disappointing but worrying. They thought, Zhihua earns a lot, so where is the money? If Zhihua could save up to build a house or for his own marriage, that would be great. But who knows what young people do these days?

When I visited Lati a couple of times in 2015, there was no evidence of lack of food. In fact, the leftovers on the dinner table were good food, like pork, fish, and tofu. When we sat down in the sun in front of Lati's house, other villagers came along and we were treated with peanuts and tea. The peanuts tasted nice but were commercial ones they had bought from a shop. Lati ran around on an electric motorbike, which was very convenient and easy to use. His clothes—leather shoes, wool-like lined trousers, and an imitation leather jacket, which all appeared new—were more fashionable than those that Yuangui wore. Lati was proud to show me the lining of his trousers, but I guessed it was not real wool, although it still seemed to be warm enough. On the other hand, Yuangui's shoes, trousers, and jacket were obviously made by herself. Lati told me that his jacket, trousers, and shoes were gifts from his daughter Pingping.

What Does It Mean to be Poor?

During one of those many informal chats when Gao villagers came to see me, one after another, my brother Changxian loudly proclaimed that there were no poor people in Gao Village, a statement concurred with by the other villagers present, including Lati, who said that life was infinitely better now in terms of food and clothing. There were only those who were better off versus those worse off, Changxian further commented, worse off either due to illness or laziness. Changxian gave an example of one young Gao villager who could earn a few thousand a month and thus save up to start a family. It turned out that the young man would stop work after a couple of months and spend all the money on who knows what, before he would have to look for work again. I did try to talk to this young man but he was reticent and the only relevant information I got out of him was that work was too boring. All the same, this young man was an exception in Gao Village and even he left for Guangdong to look for work a couple of weeks after the Chinese New Year. He said goodbye to me, and added that it was too boring to stay any longer in Gao Village.

How poor is Lati then? For the Gao villagers, the fact that you are not poor is indicated by two accomplishments: that you have built a house that is up to the current standard, and that your son or sons are properly married. Girls are never an issue in rural China these days, for they can always get married. One of the consequences of the post-Mao family planning policies is that there is a huge imbalance between genders, with males far outnumbering females. In other words, the circumstances are such that almost any woman has the luxury of choice when it comes to choosing a husband.

In contrast, in urban China there is a sociological phenomenon called *shengnü* ("leftover women"), meaning women who remain unmarried after the age of 27.[1] The fact that there are women who remain unmarried in urban China can be explained in a number of ways. One is that there is in general no gender imbalance in urban China. In fact, it is possible that, if anything, there might be more females than males in the cities. This is the case because there is virtually no gender discrimination in urban centers like Beijing or Shanghai, where people would not even think of aborting a child because it is a girl. This lack of discrimination in urban centers has nothing to do with them having a higher quality of people (the so-called *suzhi*), as some Chinese intellectual elite would like to claim, but can be attributed to two main facts. The first fact is that away from clan villages and lineage traditions, urbanites don't have the peer pressure or traditional value of having the male to carry on the family line. The second fact, which is more powerful in influencing changing mentality, is that urban people have had a better welfare system for a long time, ever since the Mao era. Parents do not need, as rural people do, a son to stay with them and look after them when they are old, since they are looked after by the State.

Another reason why more urban women remain unmarried is that women, for reasons that are too complex to discuss here, are not supposed to marry men whose social status is lower than theirs. A female university graduate would not marry a non-tertiary educated male; a woman with a doctorate degree would not likely seek a man without a post-graduate degree. Most of all, and most definitely, an urban woman

---

1   There are always a couple of *shengnü* appearing on the hot dating television program *Feicheng wurao* ("don' t bother if you are not sincere"). The program, translated as *If You Are the One*, has been running on the Australian television station SBS (the Special Broadcasting Service). The subtitled show has proven to be quite popular and is claimed to be the longest-running foreign TV series in Australia.

would not marry a migrant worker from rural China. The wall that has divided the urban and rural has never been higher. In many ways it is like a caste system.

In any case, Lati and Yuangui have not accomplished either of the two achievements that is evidence of success and symbolic of not being poor. Even though their daughter has married, their surviving son Zhihua is still single at the age of 37. Every year, one of the main reasons that Lati and Yuangui want their son to come back to Gao Village during the Chinese New Year is to help him find a marriage partner. In 2015 when I was there, Zhihua was arranged to meet two women in nearby villages; however, Zhihua failed in securing a partner. They had wasted RMB 400 on the go-between, Lati complained. I was curious to know why Zhihua had failed in getting a marriage partner, as he was reasonably good looking and earned RMB 4,000 a month, which was not too bad for a rural villager in current China. Several reasons were offered. One was that the Lati family did not have an impressive house to show, and this was of course known around the area. They had started to build a house but the project was stopped due to lack of money, as a result of Zhimin's illness and Lati not being an earning migrant worker in Guangdong anymore. The second floor of the house has been left unfinished and they do not have the money to decorate either the interior or the exterior of the house. Compared to the other beautifully decorated and imposingly big houses in Gao Village, the description of which is in the next chapter, this decent and adequate, though not luxurious, house looks an eyesore.

Another reason offered was that Zhihua is another *laoshi ren*, like his father: inarticulate, timid, and simple. Zhihua would not know how to start a conversation, especially among strangers. He would appear nervous in this kind of situation. This weak point was especially damaging in Zhihua's prospect of looking for a female partner, because these days even rural young women would have had a few years of education and would have "seen the world" as they are also migrant workers. They would not start a relationship with a man if they were not attracted to him in the first instance.

This lack of attractive personality is made worse in regard to Zhihua's prospect of finding a marriage partner by the fact that there are so many men looking for female partners. Lati could see the situation clearly. The second woman that Zhihua met during the 2015 Chinese New Year actually was a divorced woman with a child. For Lati and Zhihua, to agree to meet a woman of these circumstances was already a concession on their part. For a long time in Gao Village, according to traditional values, a divorced women was considered to be second rate for marriage, and in the mind of some even today, a breakdown of marriage is always the fault of women, just as it is considered to be the fault of the wife if she does not give birth to a son. Of course, that kind of attitude and value is eroding in China, but Lati indicated that he had lowered his standard in agreeing that his son meet a divorced woman with a child. Alas, the problem was his; on the day when Zhihua met that woman, five other men were lining up to meet her, as Chinese New Year is the time when young migrant workers return to their home villages to get married or to look for marriage partners.

Why Is Lati's Family Poor?

Apart from the fact that he is weak and always sick, which reduces the chance of making more income on the one hand and incurs a considerable medical cost on the other, another reason is that his son Zhimin's epilepsy meant that not only could he not make an income like other young men in the village, but he also incurred significant medical costs also. Furthermore, Zhimin's illness meant that Lati, who could have made some money as a migrant worker for a few more years, was unable to do so. Yet another reason why the family was poor, Lati pointed out to me, was that as Zhihua was single, the family had lost income from another able person. If he had a daughter-in-law, she would work as a migrant worker earning something like RMB 3,000–4,000 a month for the family. According to Lati, his family was caught in a conundrum: unless he has a good house ready, no girl will marry his son, but he is not able to build a house unless there is additional income.

Underlining all these reasons is the fact that farming does not make enough income; not enough to get married, not enough to build a house. All the successful households in the Gao Village area are successful because of additional income from sources and work other than farming. Farming can yield you enough to eat, maybe to clothe oneself, but not enough to build the best house possible.

Conclusion

In this chapter, I have discussed the life of an individual, Gao Lati, and his family, to illustrate what it is to be poor in Gao Village. There are several conclusions that can be drawn from the personal life of Lati. The first one is that, in terms of income, the poor in Gao Village are still considered to be above both the World Bank's and the Chinese government's official poverty line. From what I can observe, this seems to be the case in the Gao Village area and in the whole of Poyang County, which is classified as one of the poor counties by the provincial authorities of Jiangxi, which itself is considered a second-tier and backward agricultural province without much industry.

There is also some anecdotal evidence that Gao Village is certainly not among the poorest in China. During the 2015 Chinese New Year, I encountered a very pretty and articulate young mother of a six-year-old child, a daughter-in-law of a Gao villager, who looked like a university student. She was from Hubei Province and worked in Hainan, but traveled back to Gao Village every Chinese New Year to see her child, who had been left behind with the grandparents. She said she liked Gao Village, much better than her home village in Hubei. She spoke perfect Mandarin and, of course, her hometown language, but also the Gao Village dialect. When she heard that I was living in Australia, she said the company where she worked produced massage armchairs that were even exported to Australia. The fact that such an able woman finds Gao Village better than her hometown is an indication that Gao Village is certainly not the poorest in China. Furthermore, two Gao Village women divorced their husbands after they had visited their husbands' hometowns. One man was from Hubei and the other from Sichuan. Why did the two Gao Village women want to divorce them? *"Tamen tiaojian tai cha"* ("their conditions are too bad"), they told me.

The second conclusion is that the rural sector is still at the bottom end of Chinese society and farming, or at least household farming, is at the very end of the bottom. Gao Villagers have only recently started to enjoy some kind of welfare in terms of education, health care, and retirement, which the urban sector has taken for granted since the Mao era. The fact that there are no longer any taxes on agriculture, and that instead there are subsidies, is a great improvement for rural people. However, the cessation of taxes and introduction of subsidies are still not enough for farmers to make a living. The villagers have to rely on earnings from migrant workers.

Further evidence of the rural sector being at the very bottom end of Chinese society is the fact that even the urban unemployed would not be willing to work as a migrant worker. These days, migrant workers from rural China do not just work in foreign-owned companies such as Apple or Foxconn. State-owned Chinese firms and enterprises employ migrant workers from rural China to do the most strenuous work with the lowest pay, keeping better pay and better conditions for the urban registered workers.

The third conclusion is that the conceptualization of poverty is not something that can be taken for granted. For Gao villagers, currently what is poor is defined by the inability to build a house that is up to the current standard, and to get the family's son or sons properly married. China may still be considered a developing country, but daily necessities such as basic food and shelter are no longer the main and only aims and purpose of life for most people, even the poorest in Gao Village.

Finally, the story of Gao Lati is relevant to the issue of the GDP in China. There have long been debates of whether China's GDP is overestimated or under-reported. In scientific terms, there are certainly inaccuracies in the Chinese government statistics. This case study of Gao Village suggests there is no systematic record of incomes or GDP at the grass roots level in the rural sector. The evidence from my study here seems to suggest that the GDP in the rural sector is under-reported. To what extent and in what way this has an effect on the aggregated county, and then provincial statistics, is beyond the inquiry of this book.

CHAPTER 9

The Real Estate Boom and Gao Changqi, the Entrepreneur Rubbish Collector

In this chapter, I will deal with the phenomenon of the real estate boom that has been taking place in the post-Mao era Gao Village, which is parallel with but entirely different from the real estate boom in urban areas. As is well known in the field of international trade and economics, the real estate boom in China, which has been on an unprecedented scale, enabled countries like Australia, a resource-rich country and one of China's major sources of iron and ore imports, to escape from the 2008 global financial crisis.[1] What have been the causes of this real estate boom in Gao Village? Who are building the houses and from where do they get the money? Is there a bubble that is about to burst? This chapter aims to answer these questions. I will describe and discuss one Gao villager, Gao Changqi, to serve as an illustration to address these questions. Before I proceed to do that, I need to present the reader with some background.

---

1   During the height of this energy resource boom, Wayne Swan, the Treasurer of the then Labour Government, was once hailed the world's greatest treasurer.

Traditional Dwellings and the Era of Mao Zedong

In *Gao Village*, I spent a fair amount of time on housing in Gao Village during the Mao era. Even by the end of the Mao era, i.e., the end of the late 1970s, there were still some traditional-style dwellings, which were a less elaborate variation of the Hui architecture style associated with the Huizhou region. The construction of the walls of these buildings is ingenious in that the walls consist of little boxes formed by bricks and filled in with soil on the construction site. It is an environmentally-friendly and resource-saving way to have well-insulated walls that make the house warm in winter and cool in summer. However, in spite of an opening in the middle of the roof, called *tianjing* (literally "sky well"), to let light into the house as well as rain into a square well in the middle of the house, these houses are dark and wet inside because the opening also lets in rain, especially during early spring, and lets in cold air in winter, which cancels out some of the walls' insulating effect. This kind of full traditional-style, well-built house was the best in the area at that time, but not every villager was able to live in those houses. It is interesting to note that almost all the householders who lived in those houses, both before and after the 1949 revolution, were middle-income peasants. Poor peasant families like my parents lived in much simpler and cheaper houses before and after the 1949 revolution, like the one in the Photo 8, below.

No traditional-style house like this was built during or after the Mao era. To start with, building houses like these required many tall wooden pillars made from big, tall trees, which were—and are more so now—difficult to find and too expensive to afford. By the 1970s, the consequences of the twofold increase in population since 1949 in Gao Village was such that a quick way of building cheap dwellings was the best way to house the villagers. For this reason, a couple of traditional houses were dismantled and the materials were used to build small but cheaper houses to cater for the increasing number of households, increasing because adult sons of a family needed to establish their own families. The remaining traditional-style houses were either dismantled during the late 1990s, thanks largely to the policies of the strong man, then-premier Zhu Rongji, a point to which I will come later, or fell out of repair.

In the collective period, building a new house still required two dozen pillars made from smaller trees, and the walls were not made of baked bricks forming boxes, but from only one layer of baked bricks or just dried mud bricks. There was no "sky well" in the middle of the house anymore, as the new houses were not big enough for that. To build a simpler and cheaper house than the traditional one still cost something like RMB 3,000 at that time. That does not sound like a lot these days, but in those days the currency had a lot more value, roughly something like a hundred times more value, judging by purchasing power. That is the same as the average cost of building a house in Gao Village now, which is something like RMB 300,000. But there is one crucial difference: these days all the houses are huge and multistoried, what they call *yang fang*, or Western-style houses. The most expensive one in Gao Village cost around one million RMB.

Photo 8. The kind of house that my family had before and after 1949 and until the late 1990s. Taken by the author in 2010. This disappeared in 2015.

Photo 9. A traditional-style wall, with the baked bricks that form little boxes filled in with soil. Taken by the author in 2010. This was gone in 2015.

Photo 10. The remains of a traditional house in 2010, but by the author's last visit in 2015 it was gone. Taken by the author in 2010.

Photo 11. The front yard of a much simpler and cheaper version of a traditional house. Note that the walls are not formed by boxes filled in with soil but by a single layer of bricks, which are thicker but smaller. Also note that a modern-style window was installed to address the darkness problem of traditional houses.
Taken by the author in 2010.

Photo 12. These buildings were no longer there when the author visited the village in 2015. Taken by the author in 2010.

Photo 13. The wood in these walls shows how much is required
for even a simpler version of a traditional Hui style house.
Taken by the author at a friend's house in Xu Village in 2015.

The Urban Real Estate Boom

Having outlined the background in Gao Village, I need to spend a little
time on the urban real estate boom so as to give a wider context. If one
travels in China, one can see high-rise residential buildings everywhere.

We constantly read headline news about property speculation and "ghost houses" where tens of thousands of apartments remain unoccupied. When I travel to places like Shandong, Beijing, or Nanchang, the capital of Jiangxi Province, I find that those sometimes referred to as middle-class people in China, like taxi drivers, staff members at tertiary institutions, or journalists aged 40–50 years or even some in their 30s, all seem to own more than one apartment. This was something of a shock to me, since their nominal salaries are only within the range of RMB 3,000–10,000 a month. These apartments are not cheap, either. A colleague at the Chinese Academy of Social Sciences was only in his 40s and owned three apartments with his wife, and one such apartment could fetch more than RMB 10,000,000 at today's market price. This makes one feel rich, especially in contrast to how poor one was in the Mao era, to the extent that one tends to think that the so-called *gaige kaifang* ("opening and reform") period was a miracle that made everyone rich overnight.[2] However, we need to be reminded that at least one, and for some, even two apartments are inherited from socialist China: the first apartment one owns is usually the one allocated and sold to them at a symbolic price. The second apartment is most likely purchased at heavily subsidized prices, because it is built by the person's socialist *danwei*, or work unit. In fact, in some cases, if the husband and wife work at two different *danwei*, they each would have purchased a subsidized apartment. Only the third or the fourth one is bought at market price for speculation. Capitalism has turned Chinese citizens into millionaires not because there is any miracle that has created new wealth overnight, but because socialist accumulated assets have been

---

2   For instance, Norman Webster (2013: 2), former editor-in-chief of the Canadian *Globe and Mail*, declared, "At a stroke, it ['to get rich is glorious,' a saying dubiously attributed to Deng Xiaoping] set loose the formidable talents of the Chinese people and this desperately poor country, now a billion or so strong, was launched into the modern world." Yes, the miserable and poor Cinderella Chinese were rescued by the capitalist prince. The only thing missing in this story is a discussion of where the prince gets his wealth from.

divided up and are given the commercial prices at market value. A crucial point that has not been discussed as it deserves is that in this process of "grabbing the state assets," the process in which the families and friends of Party and army officials have grabbed the lion's share, the rural people—who have contributed the most to the accumulation of assets—were excluded.

The First Real Estate Boom in Gao Village

In 1998, one year after *Gao Village* left off, one of the severest floods in Gao Village history occurred. All the houses in the village were underwater. The Chinese authorities, under the leadership of Zhu Rongji, took very strong measures to do what they thought would solve the problem once and for all, and that was to get all the houses surrounding Poyang Lake, especially counties like Poyang, moved to higher ground. In the case of Gao Village, all the houses were to be moved to the hill in front of the existing village. As an incentive, the Central Government allocated a special fund through which each household was given a subsidy of RMB 10,000, a substantial amount at that time. Some villagers took this with great pleasure since their houses were falling down, or were too small anyway. This subsidy gave them a good opportunity to build something anew. However, for most of the old houses it was not a matter of moving. It involved dismantling the old; in most cases, there was not much left that was useful once the house was dismantled because they were too old. Therefore, a substantial amount of investment was required on top of the government handout. Some households just did not have the money available for such a project. There was something else that was also an important reason for some villagers' unwillingness to move: they would be further away from the fields where they worked and grew crops. The distance might well be a little more than 500 meters, but when wheelbarrow and shoulder poles were transportation, to carry the harvest from the fields to the storage building uphill was not a small matter.

In any case, there was not much choice and all the households were commanded to move. Some resisted, which resulted in their houses' roofs being smashed by men employed by the Village Committee. In 1999, when I visited the village, I could see the damage to some houses. My brother Changxian also resisted the move, mostly because of the fact that his was a house newly built with concrete. For a house built with concrete, once it is dismantled not much material can be rescued, unlike a brick and wood house. Although my brother used me as an excuse by saying that the house was actually built by me (in fact, it was the money that I sent him that enabled him to build his second "modern" house) and therefore it was the property of an overseas Chinese, but that did not stop them making a hole in the roof of my brother's house. The rest of the house, however, remained intact. This was basically true of other houses that were not moved, a symbolic destruction to show that authority was exercised for the sake of the superior bureaucracy. The local authorities were of course actually sympathetic with those who resisted, but on the other hand, if they did not do something it would be unfair to those who had complied. In any case, the money was a special payment and could not be used or handed out for anything else.

As a result, some households built simple one-story houses on the hills by using the government subsidy, while keeping their existing house on the lower ground. My youngest brother Changwen, who did not have a house in the village, was also given the money and he built an unfinished shell that was not meant to be livable, like Photo 14, below. In this way, the first real estate boom started after 1998, as a result of government subsidies. In the first phase of the real estate boom, 72 houses were built in Gao Village. As indicated above, some households took the opportunity and built much more comfortable or bigger houses on hills. Some households built a one-story house and then gradually added on to it in subsequent years to make more desirable dwellings.

Photo 14. An abandoned attempt at building a house.
Taken by the author in 2010.

The Second Real Estate Boom

The second real estate boom in Gao Village started at about the same time as the global financial crisis of 2007–2008. This is interesting because it shows that the Chinese economy, though connected with the global economy, has its own internal dynamics. Although the global financial crisis eventually did have ripple effects on China a few years later, it did not affect Gao Village that much, if at all. Not only has the real estate boom continued unabated in the Gao Village area, there has been a car purchasing boom in the past few years. In 2010, there was only one Gao villager who owned a car. By 2015, there was one car for every ten Gao villagers.

To analyze the reasons for this "prosperity" that was seemingly unaffected by the global financial crisis requires a lengthy macroeconomic discussion that cannot be done here. I will just outline a couple of general points that are backed up by examples from the era. One point is that the global financial crisis may have affected the first-tier areas in China, like the Yangtze River Delta and the Pearl River Delta, from where China's connection with the global economy first started. Some of the enterprises in these areas might have moved to countries like Vietnam or Bangladesh, but some have moved to second-tier areas like Sichuan, Chongqing, and Jiangxi, where labor is cheaper and labor conditions are more likely to be more favorable for the employer. For instance, a large shoe-making factory in Panyu, where Changxian's hotel is, has moved to Henan in 2015.

The second point is that there is an emerging, indigenous entrepreneur class who have copied the first-tier area development and started their ventures in their hometowns in second-tier areas. There is already a quilt-making factory in Zhangtiandu, which is only one kilometer from Gao Village, and is run by a local entrepreneur who employs only workers from Zhangtiandu. Youdunjie, 15 kilometers from Gao Village, was a little town with only one street when I attended middle school there, but is now a busy and bustling town where there are three-star hotels and even a glitzy jewelry shop that is open late at night. It looks more modern and more prosperous than the county town of Poyang did in the 1980s. In Tianfanjie, a town 35 kilometers from Gao Village, there are dozens of factories and business establishments that employ tens of thousands of local and migrant workers, including several Gao villagers.

Guiping, one of my sister's daughters who was mentioned in Chapter 7, runs a karaoke bar in Tianfanjie. Guiping, with her husband Zhou, is one of the most entrepreneurial people in the family. As early as the 1980s, she started a soy sauce factory in Poyang and then she shifted to making soft drinks to adjust to market demand. Then again sensing a new market demand, she and her husband closed the factory down and built a set of apartments on the factory land, which they are now able to rent out for tens of thousands of RMB every month. Guiping and her husband also run hotels with the Gao Village clan. They were able to build then one of the best houses in Poyang Town, and after a new renovation the house is still one of the best in the middle of fast-developing Poyang. She was, with my help, able to send one of her daughters, who failed in the Chinese national tertiary entrance examinations, first to attend high school in Tasmania and then to earn a bachelor's degree at the University of Adelaide.

With every step of China's economic development, Guiping has changed her strategy and runs enterprises that are most likely to be profitable at any particular time. Then she had the good sense to know that the little town of Tianfanjie was on the rise, so she opened a karaoke bar. In 2015, I paid a visit to the establishment, which was named East Number One. It had 17 rooms and on a good day Guiping could earn as much as RMB 10,000 a day. Guiping employs young girls to serve guests, for example to set up the equipment and get them drinks. After questioning her further, Guiping admitted that guests could take the girls to hotel rooms upstairs on the sixth floor in the building, but she added that she did not own or run the hotel upstairs.

Photo 15. The inside of a karaoke room, decorated with 3D computer printed copies of European masterpieces. Taken by the author in 2015.

Photo 16. One of the two corridors to various rooms in the karaoke establishment in Tianfanjie. Taken by the author in 2015.

It appears that the global financial crisis has provided opportunities for development in central and central-west second-tier areas like Henan, Anhui, Sichuan, and Jiangxi, and there has been a rise of a range of small to medium urban centers like Youdunjie and Tianfanjie, which used to be rural towns. There is little wonder, therefore, that in this context we have seen a second real estate boom in Gao Village.

There is another context combining government policies, traditional values and economic rationalism that underlines the real estate boom in Gao Village. Two of the Chinese government policies are directly related to this development. One is that no conditions are created for migrant workers to settle where they work. The other is that all of the land of a village is collectively owned by all the villagers. The consequence of the first policy is that migrant workers want to build houses back in their home villages so that they can return to settle there when they are too old to work in urban centers, where they do not belong. The implication of the second policy is that for those who do settle in urban centers far away from Gao Village, they are still able to build houses in the village from where they come because by doing that, they can continue to claim their share of the collectively-owned Gao Village land. For instance, Gao Huanxi bought a house and settled in Hainan Island, but he still built a house in Gao Village and is counted as a Gao villager for the purposes of the land share. Gao Xiangxi, who settled in Leping, did the same. The richest Gao Village entrepreneur, Gao Wenshu, to whom a chapter is devoted in this book,[3] bought an apartment in Nanchang but still built the best house in Gao Village and identifies himself as a Gao villager, and as a result, he not only has his share of land but also has been able to lease the village pond to cultivate fish.

The economic rationale behind migrant workers' hard work is to save money for the three big projects in one's life: 1) to build a house, 2) to get one's son married (usually you only have one son), and 3) to get one's children educated. Without project number one, you cannot complete project number two, because no girl will marry your son if you do not have a house, so almost every important milestone in life starts with buying or building a house. There are two other important factors to be considered: that a house has to be a *yangfang* (Western-style house), and that to gain *mianzi*, or reputation and prestige, for the family, the villagers compete to build the best house possible in the village, or even better, the best in the area. If you build the best house in the area, you not only win respect and reputation for your family but also for your village. Gao villagers compete with each other to build houses like the one in Photo 17, below.

---

3   See Chapter 5, "Gao Wenshu: From Troublemaker to Entrepreneur."

Photo 17. This is a standard Western-style house, the type popular with Gao villagers. Note the attached traditional dwelling on the right, which is used as a kitchen. Taken by the author in 2015.

Photo 18. A construction site in Gao Village.
Taken by the author in 2015.

Photo 19. The newly-built house of Gao Changqi, the rubbish collector.
Taken by the author in 2010.

Gao Changqi, the Entrepreneur Rubbish Collector

Having described and discussed the background, context, and phenomenon of the real estate boom in China in general, and Gao Village in particular, in what follows I will present a case study of Gao Changqi, the rubbish collector who until 2015 enjoyed the reputation of having built the best house (pictured in Photo 19, on the left) in Gao Village, to show how a villager can build a house of this kind.

From Jingdezhen Then Back to Gao Village

In *Gao Village*, Gao Changqi's father was discussed in relation to my father. When the Nationalist KMT government was in power (1925–1948), my father was coerced into being a *jia zhang* (head of one or more villages, like village committee heads these days), and one of his responsibilities at that time was to recruit a villager to be a soldier in the Nationalist army. The way to recruit a solider then was to pay them. The first recruit ran away after the payment was made, so my father had to pay out of his own pocket to recruit a replacement; but the second one also ran away with the payment. My father sold everything the family had, but still could not secure a recruit. Out of despair he offered himself but was rejected on the grounds that his health was not up to standard. Eventually, Gao Changqi's father, Gao Renchang, agreed to be recruited, in return for very little payment from my father. However, Gao Renchang did not intend to serve in the Nationalist army either and he also ran away, but at least he was registered in the Nationalist army before he ran away. My father was finally relieved of his responsibilities and Gao Renchang served the purpose of filling in the time gap when the KMT government collapsed.

Gao Renchang was obviously a restless young man at that time because, soon after he quit the Nationalist Army, he registered himself as a recruit for a local militia army, which called themselves the Ninth Route Army. This army had only a few men, but it was ready to be on the side of the KMT when its opponents, the Communists, were about to win. Renchang of course could not have anticipated that this episode of his life would greatly impact him and his family later. When the Great Leap Forward started in 1958, there was a great expansion of industry and the restless Gao Renchang, together with a couple of others and their families from Gao Village, migrated to Jingdezhen, the once famous capital of porcelain, as a porcelain factory worker. Gao Renchang seemed to have done well in life and he would sometimes return to Gao Village in what was considered well-cut clothes, looking well-nourished and clean compared with the weathered and dirty-looking peasants.

However, in 1962, following the failure of the Great Leap Forward, some of these migrants were ordered to return to their own villages. Some refused to leave and succeeded in the cities, but others were not so lucky. While Gao Changming and his family was not forcefully repatriated, Gao Renchang was one of the unlucky ones because he was bullied by the authorities for his record of being a soldier in the "reactionary" Ninth Route Army. Gao Village accepted Gao Renchang, his wife, and three children, without a question because they were considered Gao villagers. Nonetheless, Gao Renchang and his family kept up their hopes of returning to Jingdezhen for many years. Even as a child, I remember not only how the family looked different—not just in clothing but also in manners—and how the family was trying to fight for their case. But the good news never came and Gao Changqi, like his elder brother, though he spoke the Jingdezhen dialect and was still able to wear clothes of superior quality and style and had the air of an urban kid, suddenly became a Gao villager, or *nongmin* (peasant).

Gao Changqi the Rubbish Collector

By the time I left Gao Village to attend Xiamen University, Gao Changqi (who was nicknamed Tiansende) was totally and thoroughly a peasant, speaking like a Gao villager without a hint of Jingdezhen accent. The family was poor, though Tiansende did manage to get married. The marriage was no worse than others, but better than some, like most married couples those days—Tiansende and his wife Yu Lanfen just muddled along. They were hugely disappointed, however, that their three children were all girls. Who would look after them when they became old and when all three daughters were married away? They needed a male to carry on the family line, so they decided to let one of the daughters marry a Gao villager. This arrangement would make sure that at least one daughter would be with them when they were old. Eventually, the arrangement with another Gao villager family was that the man would move to live in the woman's family and bear the bride's family name. This is called *zhaozhui*, a case of which is discussed in *Gao Village*. The son-in-law is one of the three sons of Gao Chaozhu, who had a stroke when he was only 50, and his family was worried that they would not have enough resources to build houses for three sons. So one son was rented out, so to speak, which was not a good outcome but the best to be expected in the circumstances.

Photo 20. Some rubbish collected by Changqi that had not been sold yet. Taken by the author in 2015.

This arrangement, together with the money made from rubbish collection and the contribution from another daughter, enabled Changqi to build his house. Changqi used to go around Gao Village and neighboring villages with a pushcart. He would visit one household after another and ask if they had anything to throw away. Sometimes, and over time increasingly more often, he would pay the household for the items, the price of which would be low enough for him to make a profit when he sold it to the recyclers. Changqi has a truck now and he pays a network of local rubbish collectors to get the discarded items for him and drives his truck to pick them up. He then takes a load, when ready, to sell to a large recycling enterprise. In this way, Changqi can earn on average around RMB 10,000 a year.

His youngest daughter Gao Youxiang was a migrant worker and earned about RMB 1,000 every month in the late 1990s and early 2010s, and she has also been saving money for the construction of the house. One development that was also crucial for the family's savings was when the second daughter learned the business of selling hot pot food on street corners. She learned this from her husband, who is from Zhangtiandu. Like Poyang people, who are known for running hotels in Guangzhou, the Zhantiandu people are known for selling hot pots on street corners in Fujian. As a part of the Zhangtiandu clan, Changqi's son-in-law opened a small food stall at the gate of Fuzhou University, selling hot pots (rice with spare ribs or pig's intestines), which was popular with students, and in this way she and her husband could earn around RMB 70,000–80,000 a year. The idea, experience, and management skills from running a hot pot stall with her husband were passed on to her Gao Village sister, Gao Chouxiang, who was married to a Gao villager, as described above. Together with the earnings from this development, Changqi's extended family made enough money to build such an elaborate house.

The Real Estate Boom and the Lifestyle of Gao Villagers

As the real estate boom charged ahead, one of the things the villagers tried to do to outdo each other was to pay more attention to the comfort and decor of the house. The house had flush toilets, running tap water, and even air-conditioning. They managed to have running tap water by digging a well in the house or beside the house, and the water was electrically pumped into a tank that was installed on the roof of the house. An underground tank was built to collect the sewage flushed from the toilet, and the waste was often collected as fertilizer for the field.

Houses built in the 1960s, 1970s, 1980s, and even the 1990s in Gao Village tended to have a pigsty inside the house, not only for convenience but also for preventing potential theft. One consequence of this arrangement was that it smelled in the house. But in those days pragmatic considerations took priority in buildings. One other result of being practical was that the villagers might or might not have decorated the house inside, but the outside appearance was always ignored. That has been changing in recent times. Take the example of Changxian's house: When it was built in the 1980s, it was concrete and bare, however in 2009 it was thoroughly renovated. Now the villagers are not just competing to build bigger houses, they are also competing for their houses to be more decorative inside and out.

In 1999, the cost of building a brick or concrete house was about RMB 15,000. Since then, the cost has been increasing and in 2015 it would cost more than RMB 20,000 just to build a shell and another RMB 10,000–12,000 to make it livable. Most of the Gao village households have to save for many years from their earnings as migrant workers to build a house. There are a few who have made more money more quickly. One was Gao Chaobing, who was able to obtain the contract to build a cement road through Gao Village, the funding of which was from the Central Government allocated to the village as part of the program of building a New Socialist Countryside. He made RMB 60,000 from that project. Another Gao villager, Gao Dongsheng, who was a little child when *Gao Village* was published, earned his money not as a factory worker but first as bricklayer and then as a small contractor at various building sites. Still another Gao villager Gao Chaoliang made good money by driving a medium-sized truck, mostly transporting building materials for the villagers who built houses.

The houses built in recent years were all built on the lower ground on both sides of the road that goes through the village, a road that connects the local areas to Poyang county town and the cities of Jiujiang, Jingdezhen, and Nanchang. Now there are households that have two houses, one on the hill and one on the lower ground. As a result, many of the houses on the hill are not lived in, and in 2011 there were 14 empty houses in Gao Village. Nonetheless, the villagers keep on building more.

Gao Changtao, the elder brother of Changqi, is known in the village as Liu Zhide ("six fingers") because he has an extra finger on one hand. He has two sons; one went to college but could not find a job, or a job that suited what he had studied in college, so he went to Shanghai and delivered bottled water with a three-wheeler. After a couple of years of hard work and hard saving, he managed to buy a small one-bedroom house in Poyang County, and for that reason he was in a position to find a girlfriend there and marry her. In a sense, this son of "Six Fingers" was successful in getting educated and out of lower-class rural population in China. However, Gao Changtao was not entirely happy with how his son turned out. He complained to me that he had invested a lot in this son, but his son did not get a job good enough (like a state bureaucrat) or earn enough to build a house that could give his family "face."

His other son, however, did much better. This second son actually did not even succeed in getting a tertiary education, but he was clever and energetic. When all the Gao villagers of his age left the village and traveled everywhere to look for work, he stayed behind. Because of his talent and because there was hardly any competition, he became the village head for many years. For many reasons, he managed to make enough money and in 2011 built one of the biggest and best-looking houses in the village (the one on the right-hand side next to Changqi's house in Photo 19). The house is a three-story house that has seven rooms, two of which have an en-suite bathroom. There are large balconies on each floor and the rooftop has railings around it. The ground floor is tiled with marble.

Photo 21. The interior of a Gao Village house.
Taken by the author in 2015.

Conclusion

The first point that can be made from the above discussion is that building a house or houses, depending on how many male children there are in the family, is the top priority for Gao villagers. This priority is based on a combination of factors, such as one of the necessary conditions for the male to get married, future security, traditional values, and government policies.

By examining the details of how Gao villagers have accumulated enough to compete to build the best houses, we can further conclude that there is not going to be a real estate bubble, because the villagers do not have any debt as they do not borrow money from banks or financial institutions, although they may borrow from their friends or relatives at any particular time.

The real estate boom as a result of competition among the villagers seems to have brought them a new lifestyle . They appear to want more comfort and a more hygienic environment. I was struck by the fact that on my visit there in 2015, it was the first time I had not seen people spitting everywhere, a habit that I had previously found very disgusting. Nonetheless, traditional habits persist in some ways. When I was in Gao Village in February 2015, the water heating system had broken down in Changxian's house, where I was staying. As a result, all the family members washed themselves by the traditional way of using a bucket of water. Changxian arranged for me to have a shower at Changqi's house. When I went to the house, Changqi's wife, Yu Lanfen, was watching TV. Upon my query of what programs she liked to watch, she said she liked Chinese traditional shows such as Peking Opera and especially *Ganju* (Jiangxi-style opera). The reason was, as I was very surprised to hear, that when she was young during the Cultural Revolution, she had played the heroine role of Li Tiemei in one of the model revolutionary operas called *Hongdeng ji* (*The Legend of the Red Lantern*). Here was an old, humble, and unassuming rural woman who used to be on stage. Old habits persist, and though she had a perfect shower system in the house, she never used it. She even did not know how to turn it on.

Finally, to conclude, the competition for the construction of houses may have implications for the question of whether Gao Village will disappear in the process of industrialization, modernization, and urbanization, which has been rapid in China. A tentative conclusion, given the current government policies on land and the divide between the rural and urban, is that Gao Village is not going to disappear anytime soon. Gao villagers want to go back home to retire and spend the last days of their lives. More on this will be discussed in the final chapter.

CHAPTER 10

Change and Continuity: Conflicts of Values

Introduction: Tradition and Change

In Chapters 6 and 7, I have discussed aspects of Changxian's life, one of which shows that personal loyalty, wrapped in the term *yiqi* (a sense of brotherhood with fellow villagers), still exerts influence over the behavior of Gao Villagers, and offers of assistance and generosity are still valued in Gao Village. I experienced generosity in Gao Village when I visited the village in August 2011. As I was walking around the village, I bumped into Tanxiang, a woman I knew very well when I was a Gao Village teenager. She was coming back from her vegetable plot and was carrying a basket. I looked at the basket and yelled with excitement when I saw a local sweet melon among her harvest. For some reason, the sight reminded me of my childhood days, when we would steal melons in the field during the collective period. She immediately took out the melon and gave it to me, in spite of my continuous refusal. This kind of generosity occurred again when I commented to another villager, whose name I did not even know, that the bitter melon in front of her house was growing well. She went over without saying a word and picked up a couple and placed them in my hands.

However, at the same time, there has been a profound change in values taking place in the minds of villagers. Commercialism has reached the village and modern business based on economic rationalism has been taking root among the villagers. I use the term "modern business based on economic rationalism" in order to anticipate a very often patronizing attitude among the Chinese intellectual elite that the rural people are backward and often irrational. In what follows, I will present a couple of examples of the change in values that have taken root among the villagers.

I will start with Cao Junwen, who is from a neighboring village and is the younger brother of Cao Junxiu, one of Changxian's "sworn brothers." Cao Junwen had gone to college and considers himself well-educated. He is now a very successful entrepreneur settled in Shenzhen, and is married to a daughter of the former vice chancellor of a university. Cao Junwen was a teenage boy when I returned from the UK in the 1980s. At that time, he was still in Cao Village, which was one of the three villages under what was called the Guantian Village Committee that governed Xu Village, Cao Village, and Gao Village. Cao Junwen is a big boss now and has been overseeing a housing estate project in Changsha, the capital of Hunan Province. Cao travels back to Shenzhen once a month to see his wife and his young son. Cao contacted me when he heard that I had come back from Australia. He said that people like him in China now would like to make friends with people like me, because overseas connections were valued and because his son could practice speaking English with my children. I was a little surprised by his frankness and the way he put the matter to me, as it is not very traditional among Chinese to be so direct, and certainly not among rural people.

Economic Rationalism Versus Human Worth

Cao Junwen had bought some land in Changsha and had been overseeing contracts worth RMB 200 million to build a residential complex, consisting of seven buildings, each of which was to be 27 stories high. When I was doing field work with my brothers in Panyu, Cao came to see us. Changxian took us and some others to a restaurant.

During the conversations, Wenshu (see Chapter 5) and Changwen, my youngest brother, requested that Cao give some construction contracts to them so that they could make some money out of his building project, which is big in the eyes of Gao Villagers. They said they could supply his buildings with all the nails. Cao said to them, "Why would I give you contracts since you do not have any experience or expertise in doing this kind of work?" This was, to me, a very legitimate question. But I was still a little surprised by his straightforwardness. Changwen, however, replied to this question without a second's thought: "You don't know how to help us people from the same hometown" (*tong xiang ren*). Cao was speechless for a while, but eventually managed to reply by saying that he could not give them the contract to supply all the nails because there was no guarantee that the nails could be supplied in time, and would be of good enough quality. Changwen and Wenshu told him that the very fact that they were fellow villagers and knew each other was a good enough guarantee of work quality.

Cao Junwen, naturally, refused to budge. From his point of view, no human relationship could guarantee quality and one could only rely on expertise and proven record. I tend to agree with Cao Junwen; how can you contract business to someone who has nothing to do with that business to start with? However, from Changwen and Wenshu's point of view, with the help of Cao Junwen, they could gain experience and get into the business. They also argued that precisely because they were from the same hometown, they would not let Cao down with poor quality goods and it was a matter of finding the right manufacturer. When I thought about it, Changwen and Wenshu did have a point. Doesn't everyone have to start somewhere? After Cao Junwen left, Wenshu commented that Cao Junwen was not a good person. He further elaborated that Cao's younger brother was still poor, but Cao, already a millionaire, did not even want to help his brother and therefore had no *jiaxiang qing* ("hometown compassion"). (I found out later, in fact, that Cao Junwen did help his younger brother). Many rural people still have this traditional value of helping each other just out of having a close relationship, such as being from the same village. For people like

Cao Junwen, who was from rural China but was educated at an urban university, however, these traditional rural values are out of date. It just does not make any rational sense in business.

What to Invest In:
Human Relationships or Financial Returns?

This conflict of values between business-based economic rationalism and human compassion can be seen in the argument between Cao Junwen and his elder brother, Cao Junxiu. It was Cao Junxiu who worked hard to provide enough resources for Cao Junwen to finish his university education. Their father had already passed away when Junwen was young, and Junxiu was like a father in supporting the family.

Now Cao Junxiu is still in Cao Village while his younger brother is a high-flying businessman, the envy of everybody. In the middle of the real estate boom in the area, Cao Junxiu wanted Cao Junwen to spare some money to build a house in Cao Village. Cao Junxiu did have a comfortable house of his own and did not really want to live in a modern house himself. It was just that he would not have a "face" to show (*lian shang wu guang*) among the local people if his family, which meant the three brothers, did not have a modern new house in the village. Everyone had or was building a house, one better than another, but his household had not built one, even though Cao Junwen had the reputation of being the richest in Cao Village.

But Cao Junwen had very good economic rational logic for refusing to listen to his elder brother. If he were to build a house for RMB 200,000–300,000, that would be considered too ordinary, and therefore would not serve the purpose of gaining "face" for the family. If he were to build a house that is worth one million RMB or more, it would not be worth the money in any sense. What is the point of building a house like that if nobody is going to live there? They had settled down comfortably in Shenzhen, in an apartment that was worth a few million RMB. His wife had a good job in Shenzhen and his son was doing well and was easily one of the best students in a prestigious school. This little boy, whom I had met and who was confident and articulate, was planning to study overseas and aimed to be a world-famous scientist. Cao Village for them now means very little. On the other hand, a couple of million RMB in investment on something else will get Cao Junwen a good return.

My two brothers Changxian and Changwen, as well as Gao Wenshu, did not agree with Cao Junwen's rationality. What my brother's wife Mingxia said was very revealing: She questioned what was worthwhile and what was not. If Cao Junwen's family felt proud to have a grand new house and if the family got "face," then that itself was worthwhile. If Cao Junwen's mother could live in that grand house for the rest of her life, then that itself would be worth the money. What is life for anyway?

Cao Junwen replied that he could invest the million and make more money to send his son to study in Australia, for instance. Gao villagers retorted (and this was all in front of me): "Your mother and your elder brother worked so hard to raise you. Don't you think you should make them happy just for the sake of that?" "They could come live with us in Shenzhen." But, the Gao villagers argued, Cao Junwen's mother did not want to stay in Shenzhen. She was not used to that kind of life. For her, a high rise-flat was like a cage, with nobody to talk to, and was alien. Cao Junwen, as a way out of losing the argument, said: "If I had that kind of money I might just donate it to build a school or set up a scholarship for the poor." The Gao villagers retorted that you could not even look after your own parent, so stop talking about a donation. Cao Junwen left visibly disturbed, with everyone feeling very unhappy.

As I have discussed in Chapter 5 on Gao Wenshu, the richest Gao villager did not want to build a house back home either. Just like Cao Junwen, Wenshu also thought that it did not make any economic sense to build a house in a village that was left empty, simply for the sake of gaining face. But the pressure is on people like them, as the villagers work hard and save hard to compete to build the grandest house in their home village, so as to *rong zong yao zu* ("make the family shine and ancestors glorious"). It is so ironic and in many ways baffling for modern and business rationalists that Gao villagers, like other villagers in the area, would work and save so hard, and would abstain from consumption all year long far from home for so many years, just so they could build a house that they may or may not live in eventually, in order to obtain glory for the family and ancestors.

When I visited Gao Village in August 2011, Gao Wenshu was actually there on site, building a house. He had even paid RMB 80,000 for an architect to draw up the design for the building, a practice that was rare in the Gao Village area. Usually, the builder just gets some ideas from the future owner and the house will take shape as the building work progresses. The builder can change a bit here and add a little there if the owner makes suggestions or if there is a shortage of money. There is usually no paperwork involved. But Wenshu had the money and had seen how things were done in urban areas, so he wanted to do things properly.

Why and how did he change his mind? As described in Chapter 5, he actually had a fight with his father over refusing to build a house in Gao Village, and subsequently they were not on speaking terms for a long time. This tug of war continued until one day when Wenshu received the sad news that his father was dying. Wenshu, of course, rushed home from Guangdong and took his father to various places, including Nanchang and Guangzhou, to try to find a cure, sparing no expense, but sadly his father died only three months after he was diagnosed with lung cancer. On his deathbed, Wenshu's father said he wanted his son to build a house in Gao Village, and Wenshu promised to carry out his father's death wish.

One cannot help think of the Chinese gold rush in the 19th century in America, or the Chinese migrants to Canada, New Zealand, and Australia. Unlike the European settlers in these continents, the Chinese were perceived as temporary residents and were accused of being opportunists who did not want to contribute to their migration destination, but just wanted to make quick money to send back home (Petty 2009; Gao 2017c). They too wanted (and many of them did) bring glory to their families and ancestors by building grand houses back home. Many of these houses, in places like Taishan and Kaiping in

Guangdong Province, hometown of most early Chinese migrants to the new colonies during the Gold Rush remain intact, but unoccupied, they became historical heritage because the people who built them did not return, having settled somewhere else.

In Taishan and Kaiping, there are also traces of evidence that Chinese migrants to the new colonies donated money to build bridges, schools, and hospitals in their hometowns. This was not only because they felt they wanted to make some contribution for the improvement of the life of their fellow villagers—of course they did want to do that—but also because their hometown could accord them the honor and prestige that they could not dream of getting in their migration destination, where discrimination against them was rampant. Likewise, Gao villagers wanted me to donate, for instance, to the building of an irrigation channel. Because of the income and labor cost difference between China and Australia, it was affordable for me to donate something to make a difference, whereas it is not in Australia. To obtain that kind of honor and prestige in Australia, you would have to be a multimillionaire or even a billionaire. It is therefore not only interesting, but also ironic, that the same pattern is being repeated 200 years later, although not internationally but domestically.

Family Planning and a New Generation of Migrant Workers

Another profound change that has been taking place in rural China is that people do not want more children anymore. In the olden days, there was a motto on everyone's mind, *duo zi duo fu*, meaning the more children you have, the more happiness you have. The Chinese word *zi* can be ambiguous in that it can mean children, but it also can mean just male children. For a long time in rural China, male children have been the preference by parents. This was so ingrained in the minds of villagers for so long that even women propagated it without thinking whether it was to their advantage or disadvantage. It was almost second nature to them that one needed to have a son, otherwise there would be nobody to carry on the family line and there would be nobody to burn incense on the family's graves. Once there was a group of women surrounding me (a father of three daughters), each trying to talk louder than the other, to convince me of the importance of having a son and carrying on the family line.

However, there has been a visible change. To start with, once you become urbanized, the influence of these traditional values seems to lessen and even disappear. One important reason is that once you lead an urban life, your lifestyle changes and the people you come into contact with have no idea about clan villages or lineage identity. Together with that— and perhaps because of that—you don't have any connection with the discourse of the continuation of family lineage. Another important factor has something to do with the economic circumstances. Once you lead an urban life, there is such a thing as social security for the elderly and you don't have to depend on your children to look after you when one get old. In rural China, there is no prospect of being looked after when you become old, since daughters do not live with their parents after they get married.

Therefore, it is reasonable to expect that young people from rural China who live and work in urban areas, because of being educated in this modern, business, or industrial discourse, tend to be less burdened with the traditional value of preferring male children. This kind of change seems visible in Gao Village. The feedback I've received and interviews I've done seem to confirm this trend, which means that it is now not very hard work for local Party and government apparatuses to enforce the government's family planning policy. In the Gao Village area, there is no longer any practice of forced abortions. Villagers have told me that they didn't want to have more children anyway. Two were enough and three were the most. The reasons seem obvious: young people are too busy working as migrant workers in urban areas. More importantly, it is just too expensive to have children these days. In other words, with the rise of living standards, the upbringing of children is also more expensive.

More importantly, young Gao villagers are less likely to have any prejudice against female children. There are several factors contributing to this value and attitude change. One factor is that most young Gao villagers are more educated. Another factor is that at their workplaces they are exposed to different values, values that are different or even alien to clan and lineage traditions. Another factor is that girls not only earn as much as sons when they are migrant workers, but also contribute more to the family, for the very fact that girls don't get any share of the family wealth when they are married out (*chu jia*) of the family. Finally, underlining all these factors is the improvement in security, security in the sense that children do not die young as they used to and therefore there is no need to have more children. There is another improvement of security, which is that there is the development of social security, medical insurance and even aged care facilities, as discussed in Chapter 11 on local governance and the reach of the State.

Where Is Home for the Younger Generation?

Another change is that the cohort of migrant workers is different. In China, this is being talked about as a new generation of migrant workers. A typical new generation migrant worker was born after the 1980s, is unmarried, usually with either 12 years or at least nine years of education. These days they do not look different from the urban youth: they wear blue jeans and very often a t-shirt with English, maybe incorrect English, on it. Unlike the old generation of migrant workers, who would carry their belongs in a huge plastic bag (*she pi dai*, or snake skin bag) that was tightened up with string, the new generation migrant worker pulls a wheeled traveling bag, either talking or writing text messages on a mobile phone. Finally, after 20 years of wage stagnation, they are getting better pay. From the late 1980s to the late 1990s, the average migrant worker earned about RMB 600–800 a month, whereas in 2010 the average new migrant worker would not agree to work unless their basic monthly wage was about RMB 1,500 (Wang Zhongyuan 2011). By 2015, the average pay had risen to RMB 2,000–3,000. According to one study (Ye Yu 2011b), hardly any older generation migrants in the late 1990s and early 2000s wanted to settle down in an urban center. Of the group aged between 40 and 50, only 21 percent wanted to live in a city permanently, whereas 37 percent of migrant workers between the ages of 30 and 40, and 45 percent of those aged between 20 and 30, wanted to stay in an urban center, and 61 percent of migrant workers of under the age of 20 wanted to settle in a city permanently. This largely fits the situation of the new generation of migrant workers from Gao Village, in that they are more highly educated, less pressured by economic circumstances at home, and can spend more money on themselves. Their manner and appearances are not much different from the urban young, unlike their parents.

I have talked about villagers competing to build better-looking houses to gain face and glory. But there is also an underlining economic reason for the real estate boom in rural China, that is, the migrant workers somehow feel they will have to go back to their village eventually unless they are successful enough to be accepted by the urban sector, like Cao Junwen. That kind of success is really rare. When I was visiting Gao Village in August 2011, a young Gao village migrant worker happened to return from Wuhan, with his wife. They had built a house where his parents were then staying. It was a two-story house, with a small shed attached to it as a kitchen. It was clean and bright, in a position that was cool in the hot summer days when I was there. The breeze going through from the front door to the back door took the heat away and we felt nice and cool. There was a pond at the back of the house with steps to it from the doorstep, for washing. Surrounding the pond there were various kinds of vegetables. In the front garden there were fruit trees, cucumber, eggplant, and pumpkin plants. There were chickens around the house clucking about. Even my 10-year-old daughter, who had been living in Shenzhen for more than a year, and who had been complaining about how dirty China was, commented that that was a nice house. I sat with them chatting about life. The young couple said they would like to return home eventually. The young man said: "City life is too noisy, too dirty. Look at it here, the air is clean and it is beautiful." And it was.

I was really surprised that it was a young, articulate migrant worker who said that. While I was in Gao Village, I had been asked several times by the older residents or the elderly when I would return home. They even asked me to build a house in Gao Village so that I could have a house to return to. A couple of villagers suggested that the village could give me a piece of land free for the purpose. I asked them, in fact quite seriously, why I should return to Gao Village. They replied without even thinking, "Because you are a Gao Village person." I have been thinking, but still cannot work out why, there is such a strong feeling of belonging in one's birth place and why the villagers take it for granted that a Gao villager should finally return to Gao Village.

A Festival Occasion in a Tradition Way

Gao Anneng is my brother Changxian's wife's brother. Gao Anneng's son succeeded in passing the national tertiary entrance examination and was accepted by Chang'an University in Xi'an. As is now the normal practice in the area, the family decided to host a big banquet to celebrate the occasion. A big banquet for an occasion like this is important for two reasons. One reason is to recoup some money back for the family, which over the years has given money as gifts to friends or relatives for occasions like this. The other reason is to show off their success and gain glory for the family. My brother Changxian especially traveled from Guangzhou to Gao Village to organize the banquet. As it is the traditional practice for occasions like this, whether it is a wedding ceremony or a funeral, one person from each family in Gao Village was invited, and guests of course included the relatives of the family, in this case, relatives from Guangzhou, Jiujiang, Jingdezhen, Nanchang, and Poyang Town, as Gao Anneng has four brothers who have settled in different places. Of course, local notables like officials from the township government, village committee governments, and teachers of local schools were also invited. Local teachers were invited because Gao Anneng is a teacher.

As expected, each guest gave a present for the occasion, mostly RMB 100, 200, or 500, and some even gave RMB 1,000. I was also invited and therefore also had to give a *hongbao*, money in a red paper envelope. Just before midday, when the banquet was about to start, I noticed a procession of a group of villagers, with a woman and a man each holding a huge plastic bag. They paraded to Gao Anneng's house and then set off a huge string of firecrackers in front of Anneng's house before they were received by Anneng, his wife, and their son. It turned out that each person in the procession represented one family and each family contributed RMB 20; with that, they together bought two woolen blankets for the boy to take to university. I later noticed a booklet that recorded in detail how much was given by whom. The amount of money given depended on the distance of the relationship: the closer, the more money, and the more distant, the less. It also depended on the gift-giving family's past obligations to the host. It also depended on the reputation and wealth of both the givers and receivers. The wealthier and higher the reputation of the families, the higher amount of money they gave; otherwise, it was considered a loss of face. The families that gave the two blankets were the most peripheral in relationship. I did a quick calculation and the amount of money that was collected that day was RMB 22,300. Changxian gave the most, RMB 1,200. Firecrackers were also bought as part of the gifts. Towards the end of the day, Anneng's front yard was covered with debris from the firecrackers.

To arrange a banquet for nearly 200 people that included 22 courses, ranging from pigs' trotters, eel, and noodles to steamed pork, was a huge effort, but the villagers made this happen without incurring much cost in terms of manpower. What happened on that occasion, as has been traditionally the case, was that different tasks were distributed to the family's relatives and the most closely-related village members, usually offspring of the same lineage of the village clans. On the banquet day, there were more than 20 cooks working in different houses in the village. They used cooking utensils and furniture like tables, spoons, chopsticks, bowls, and plates from their own houses. There were different cooks for different dishes spread across the village.

When the banquet was finished, the families that contributed items took home the leftover food so there was no waste, and all the work of washing up was divided up among the villagers. For an outsider, it looked like everything happened smoothly and effortlessly, quickly and in an orderly way.

It is also interesting to observe in this connection that when I visited the newly-built houses, I always noticed that in the fairly modern and even Western-style kitchens, though invariably they had no ovens, some actually had marble top benches and gas cookers. Every kitchen was also equipped with a traditional *zao*, consisting a big wok fixed on top of a stove with a chimney. This kind of *zao* requires firewood to cook. In everyday cooking, hardly anyone uses *zao*, but when building houses they still have a *zao* together with modern cooking facilities for cooking banquets and ceremonial dinners at Chinese New Year. For example, a pig's head is usually cooked and then offered to the ancestors before it is cut up for consumption. A *zao* is big and can cook a vast amount of food quickly and at a high temperature. Other traditions are still in place as well, such as the traditional music band, as Photo 22, below, shows. The instruments are traditional and the music notes are traditional without anything on paper, all passed on from one generation to the next through practice. Other traditions are not only in place, but have seemingly re-emerged in greater force. One of these is the clan system. As described in *Gao Village*, in this area every village has its own lineage and all the people, with few exceptions, have the same surname. As socialist values and collective identity are being abandoned in the post-Mao era, rural villagers are struggling with their identity to cope with rapid modernization. For these reasons, villagers use their newly-gained financial ability to build impressive clan temples (described in Chapter 11), temples they did not have even in the pre-1949 period. The tradition of praying to the Buddha for good luck is also thriving. In the politically radical times of the Mao era, this was considered superstition and was held in contempt by the young people. But now, as seen in the photos below, younger villagers are praying just as much, if not more than the old.

Photo 22. A traditional band in Gao Village.
Taken by the author in 2015.

Photo 23. Inside the Buddhist temple in the Gao Village area, restored and visited
often by young migrant workers, where the young are praying.
Taken by the author in 2015.

Photo 24. In front of the temple.
Taken by the author in 2015.

Change in Poyang County Town

Poyang Town is the capital of Poyang County, where Gao Village is located. Poyang County is the largest county in Jiangxi Province in terms of population, which had a population of 1.5 million by 2017. Poyang is an agricultural area with hardly any industry, but Poyang County Town is the nearest to urban life that Gao villagers usually get. It was certainly where I had my first taste of urban life as a child when I visited my sister, who had married a mechanic in the town. It used to have only one narrow street, unevenly paved with slate rocks, with a few bare bulbs to light at night. There was one cinema and one opera house. There was never a car in sight, because there were only two official cars for the county officials, which were used only when long-distance travel was required.

By the late 1990s, there was already a mall about one kilometer long, called *buxingjie*, meaning "the street for walking," lined with sleek lights and modern-looking shops. Now there are traffic lights and also taxis, though a lot of rickshaws are still around. The county government sold land that was in the middle of the town to a commercial real estate agent and moved to what used to be the outskirts of the town. As symbols of power, grand and imposing-looking buildings for the government and the law court were built. To my pleasant surprise, there was also a large and very good-looking public library built nearby.

One of my relatives started a garage shop, called a *meiche dian* ("auto beauty shop"). They installed a very modern car wash, but this is hardly used and most of the washing is done by hand, because the customers not only want their cars washed but also dried, and they want the footpads washed with towels and the inside of the car vacuumed. For all these services, the bill is only RMB 15. I witnessed the service done to one car, involving two boys working for half an hour. The charge was not enough to cover their wages, but the owner of the shop said that it was reasonable to lose money in this way in order to initially attract customers. He thought the garage was going to be a big business, as already half of the families in Poyang County owned a car at that time.

There was sign of a huge construction boom in the town when I was there in 2011 and 2015. On a short drive around the edge of the town, I witnessed more than 30 high-rise blocks being built. In 2009 the price was RMB 1,000 per square meter and in 2011 when I was there it was 3,000. I was told that of all the new houses, 30 percent had been bought by Poyang residents, 20 percent by rich people from the rural areas, and 20 percent by the real estate people themselves.

Two Weddings

In February 2015, I was obliged to attend two weddings, one for the marriage of my nephew, Gao Wei, and the other for my sister Lingli's grandson. I was urgently invited to go because the presence of an uncle or great uncle from a foreign country would give them more face. In any case, I was happy to go because it was part of my research. Gao Wei's wedding was an interesting combination of East and West, tradition and modernity. The bride was collected from her home with a parade of cars and appeared in Gao Village in a beautiful Western-style white dress, holding hands with the groom who was wearing a Western suit. They were followed by two flower girls and walked on a red carpet through an arch to the groom's house, amid the tremendous thunder of firecrackers and thick layers of smoke. Photos were taken with bride and groom kissing each other, which is not traditional in China.

About half an hour later, the bride and groom reappeared from their wedding chamber upstairs. A Chinese wedding tradition called *baitang,* meaning to pay respect to one's ancestors, started and went on for more than an hour in the hall downstairs. The bride wore a red dress and the groom was dressed in a Chinese jacket. There was an MC named Gao Huobao, who was one of the sons of a former rich peasant in Gao Village and officiated at the ceremony, speaking in the local dialect. Both the bride and groom had to kneel down on a quilt, which was used as a cushion, and lowered their heads to the ground to bow down, or kowtow, three times as a way of paying respect. The couple had to kowtow three times first to Heaven and Earth (*tiandi*), then three times to the ancestors of the family. After that, they had to kowtow to the groom's parents (the bride's parents were not to be seen on occasions like this). As Gao Wei's grandfather and grandmother had both passed away, the young couple kowtowed three times to the portraits on the altar called a *xiangtan,* which was placed along the wall that faces the front door. They had to repeat this ritual of three kowtows to every relative of the family, from the eldest to the youngest, and from the closest to the most distant. The relatives who in turn sat in front of the bride and groom were supposedly proud to be invited and were obliged to leave a *hongbao* as a gift. The gift or money in the little red envelope on this occasion was RMB 200 minimum, but the more the money in the *hongbao,* the more honor there was on both sides of the family.

Gao Wei and his bride had to do a lot of kowtows on this occasion before they were allowed to be alone in their wedding chamber. Following this, there was the wedding lunch, when hundreds of guests, including one representative from every family in the village and all the members of the families who were closest to the groom, took part in the wedding banquet. The banquet, all prepared by the family and relatives in the village, included traditional dishes such as *hongshao rou* (slow fried pork in brown sauce) as well as exotic food such a fish called *yinyu* ("silver fish"), a specialty from Poyang Lake that is a tiny fish like whitebait but thinner and smaller. The banquet lasted a long time because it consisted of more than 20 dishes, with plenty of alcohol, the local specialty being *si te* ("four specialties"). What made the banquet more expensive for the family was the prevailing practice in the area in which the host of the wedding gives each guest a packet of cigarettes. Of course, like everything else now, the more expensive the cigarettes the more honor and face the wedding family gains. At Gao Wei's wedding banquet, each guest was given (irrespective of whether they smoked, both adults and children), Zhonghua (China) brand cigarettes that cost RMB 45 per box.

In contrast, the wedding of Lingli's grandson, Qiao Zhu, was not traditional. Qiao Zhu is from Poyang Town but could not find a job, so he went to Guangdong to look for work and eventually was employed as contracted security officer in Guangzhou. His bride was a girl from Lianhu, a district close to Poyang Town. Qiao Zhu's immediate boss, and two of his colleagues, drove all the way from Guangdong to Poyang in their security car for less than the normal 17 hours because they could speed. There was no *baitang* and it was not a family affair for the groom. Guests were invited to the wedding banquet, during which no cigarettes were given out. The MC spoke Mandarin because there were guests from all over the place, all speaking different dialects. It was all loud music and a lot of speeches.

Like the Gao Village wedding, guests at the Poyang Town wedding were obliged to give *hongbao*, but what was strikingly different was that the banquet was prepared commercially, with the food less interesting but more expensive at the cost of RMB 1,000 a table. Also in contrast to the wedding in Gao Village, the wedding in Poyang was held in the Raozhou Hotel, the only five-star hotel (according to the hotel itself) in the whole of Poyang. The hotel was built by a local man called Wu Xingwang, who was from Youdunjie where I went for my secondary school education. It was widely rumored in 2011 that there was gambling and prostitution in the hotel, all illegal, and that Wu was so powerful and influential that even the police could not enter the hotel without his permission.[1] However, in 2015, when I stayed there for two nights, I did not see any sign that could confirm these rumors. Thinking about it, 2015 was the year when every government official and army officer was scared of the anticorruption campaign under the leadership of Xi Jinping, which would explain the lack of any illegal activities at the hotel.

Conclusion

In this tremendous transformation of contemporary China, we can see not only the change in values, but also the conflicts that occur in the process. Changes in material conditions and economic circumstances inevitably have led to a change in values and behavior. Some villagers

---

1   According to local media and interview information that I have gathered, Wu Xingwang is a national figure because of an incident in 2003. It was reported that the nightclub that Wu ran in Zhuhai not only arranged hundreds of Chinese women for a group of Japanese tourists, but also for them to have sex with these women on September 18, the day in 1931 when the Japanese started their invasion of the northeastern three provinces of China (the Chinese call September 18 "Humiliation Day"). How Wu became so apparently rich is still a myth. One version is that when he was a contracted security guard, like Qiao Zhu, in Xiamen he became friends with someone surnamed Zeng, who was apparently the nephew of a powerful Chinese official in Beijing. It was this nephew Zeng who introduced Wu to the city authorities of Zhuhai, and it was with this connection that Wu could manage to build a nightclub where 1,000 girls were employed as prostitutes (Zhao 2003). Wu Xingwang's way of showing his wealth is legendary. For his mother's 70th birthday celebration, Wu had dinner banquets prepared free for anyone who cared to come. Not only could one go without having to present a gift, but also one could also get a hongbao in return. It is reported that he has built a house for each of his family members in his hometown village.

have tended to hang on to the traditional end of the value spectrum, while others have tended to move towards the opposite direction. Gao Mingxia, for instance, tends to be more traditional in values. She practically broke up her son's relationship with a girl from Chongqing and more or less arranged for her son to marry a girl not only from a rural background but also near Gao Village. On the other hand, Cao Junwen is more of a modern middle-class urbanite, who cannot see why he should spend money to build a house in his hometown village that he and his family have nothing to do with. His eyes are set on business expansion and his son's education in countries like Australia. In 2016, Junwen traveled to Australia the first time and is planning to purchase properties in Australia.

Clearly, the villagers are torn between rural and urban, between tradition and modernity. Gao Wenshu, discussed in Chapter 5, is a good example. He holds similar views as Cao Junwen in terms of investment, in that it does not make sense to build a house in his hometown village where he does not live, just for the sake of gaining face and glory for the family. But Gao Wenshu eventually gave in to his father's wishes and built a house in Gao Village. How do we explain the different choices the two successful entrepreneurs of rural backgrounds have made? Maybe the very fact that Gao Wenshu is not as successful as Cao Junwen in business is the reason. Wenshu may be a millionaire, but Junwen is a multimillionaire. Perhaps it is also because Junwen is more urban and more highly educated. Junwen married a woman from a middle-class urban family, whereas Wenshu married a village girl. Junwen was tertiary educated, whereas Wenshu was expelled from school in his third year. It is also possible that Wenshu moved further to the traditional end of the value spectrum because he was persuaded by his father to build a house, whereas Junwen's father died when he was a child. Had Junwen's father lived to this day, he might have been able to pull his son towards the more traditional end of the value spectrum.

What also seems clear is that the more one is supposed to be urban, the more one is likely to be more modern and less traditional. Qiao Zhu, for instance, is less educated and has a lower social status in terms of work and money than Gao Wei. Gao Wei graduated from a good university in Wuhan and is now a landscape designer earning more than RMB 10,000 a month, whereas Qiao Zhu did not even finish high school and earns only two to three thousand RMB a month as a contracted security guard. But Qiao Zhu's wedding was more "modern" and cost more than that of Gao Wei. Apparently, the only reason for this difference is that Qiao Zhu is from Poyang Town, whereas Gao Wei is from Gao Village.

Gao Wei's wedding also shows that a hybrid of tradition with modernity, East and West, is possible. White used to be the color of mourning in China and still is. For instance, a funeral wreath is made of white flowers and mourners wear white hair bands. However, the bride's Western-style white dress was not only accepted in Gao Village, but also considered very beautiful. When *baitang* was taking place, I could see some sign of boredom on the face of the bride when it went on too long. The MC also had to teach the bride and groom how to kowtow. Nonetheless, it was done and the villagers thoroughly enjoyed it, and for many young Gao villagers it was the first time for them to see such a thing.

What happened to another Gao villager also illustrates the enormous change of attitude in the area. In *Gao Village,* I recounted the story of Gao Chaolin, who was put into prison for stealing a briefcase containing sunglasses while riding on a bus. I found out from his father Gao Changdian that he was sentenced to six years and imprisoned for five years at what is called the Zhuhu Farm Detention Centre. He was released one year early for good behavior, at which time Gao Chaolin left Gao Village for Shanghai where he worked at a company that made models for toys, a company owned by a Taiwan businessman. After only a couple of years of working there, Gao Chaolin knew enough about the business and earned enough to start his own business. Now, he runs his own toy model factory. He is well off enough to own a car, his father told me, not without pride. This is a villager who has a criminal record but there is no stigma against him, and he has turned himself into a new man that the Gao villagers respect.

CHAPTER 11

The Reach of the State in Gao Village[1]

Introduction

For roughly 15 years since the dismantling of the collective system, the post-Mao state returned the freedom of production to rural households, a kind of freedom that the rural residents could not have in the Mao era, but still the state remained more intrusive in many areas. At the same time, the state retreated from providing public goods for rural residents. The first 15 years of the post-Mao era roughly corresponds to when the first Gao Village book (Gao 1999) left off. The intrusive approach by the state, such as ferocious taxes, levies, and the brutal implementation of family planning policies, as well as hands-off approaches such as the almost total withdrawal of the provision of public goods, are described in that book. The first Gao Village book concludes with a not only uncertain but a dark note on the post-Mao state. What has the state been like since then? Has the retreat of the state in public services continued? Or has its reach returned? Has the state been continually intrusive? In this chapter, I will answer these questions by tackling the issues of the reach of the state in the Gao Village area.

---

1   Some information contained in this and the next chapter is published in Gao 2017a, 547–559, and Gao 2017b, 23–43.

The Changing Reach of the State in Gao Village

Before the discussion of these issues in Gao Village, I need to provide some background as context, with a brief outline of the history of the reach of the state in rural China. The reach of the PRC state in rural China, such as in Gao Village, can generally be described in terms of three periods: the Mao era, the first 15 years after the Mao era, and the second 15 years after the Mao era.

The Reach of the State in the Mao Era

The Mao era was the period when the state reached Gao Village the most, very often too intrusively and sometimes too brutally. But it was the first time in China's history that the villagers were treated like citizens of a state. Under the system of *sanji suoyou dui wei jichu,* ("three levels of ownership with the team as the foundation"), the Production Team (*shengchan xiaodui*) was the basic unit, while the two levels of local governance, the Commune (*gongshe*) and the Production Brigade (*shengchan dadui*), were run by state agents. The lowest level of governance, the Production Team, was run by the villagers themselves. Land within a commune was collectively owned by the commune in theory, but owned in practice by the villagers. The state agents not only supervised production activities (usually through the Production Brigade) and the distribution of salaries, but also organized education and health care (usually by the Commune).

It was also during this period that public spaces began to appear; there was a sports ground in the middle of Gao Village, and sports meets and theatrical performances were organized. Young people got together to perform in the theatre, basing their performances on Peking Operas, and to play sports and participate in local militia training. It was also during this period that substantive grass roots democracy was experimented with: every member of a production team participated in the evaluation of every member's labor contribution to the collective in terms of work points, taking into account physical ability and work attitude. It should be pointed out that it was during the two most radical periods, the Great Leap Forward and the Cultural Revolution, that the state reached the areas of education and health care the most. A primary school in the Gao Village area was established during the Great Leap Forward, and a middle school campus was established during the Cultural Revolution.

There were, of course, serious problems caused by excessively brutal state intervention, such as those during the years of the Great Leap Forward that caused hunger and starvation, and when the system of management of a production team was yet to be established. For any changes of such a nature to take place in a country that has such long and entrenched traditions, and a country where the population and land ratio is so precarious, it would be surprising if there had been no ups and downs. When the system finally got settled with stable rules and regulations, life started to improve and the serious starvation during the Great Leap Forward was the first and the last in the entire history of the PRC. However, just as Gao villagers were about to get used to the system, in the early 1980s the regime in Beijing, and hence the policies, changed.

The Reach of the State during the First 15 Years of the Post-Mao Period

The irony is that for the first 15 years of the post-Mao era, the retreat of the state from rural China in terms of providing public goods did not mean a less intrusive governance. The state had village officials to collect taxes for the government and to levy the villagers to pay for their education and health care, in addition to paying the salaries of the state agents; worse still, village officials had to implement the sometimes brutal and sometimes violent family planning policy. The three layers of governance still remained, but under different names: There was the *xiang* government, which was the new name for the Commune, the *cun weihui* ("village committee"), which was the new name for the Production Brigade, and the *cun xiaozu* ("village team"), the new name for the Production Team. This intrusive and sometimes ruthless governance—which was interested only in extracting from but not investing in the rural sector— was typical of the first 15 years of the post-Mao reform period. The villagers still remember these years as the period of "the three forceful demands" (*yaoliang, yaoqian, yaoming*),[2] meaning the forceful demand for grain, for money and for life, the last referring to forced abortion.

The Reach of the State during the Second 15 Years of the Post-Mao Reform Period

Within the context of these policies, the disparity between urban and rural people increased rapidly in those years, in spite of the extra income added to the rural sector from migrant workers. To address the issue of the rural and urban divide, the OECD Rural Policy Review on China in 2009 argues that:

> In order to bridge rural-urban divides the current policy approach needs to go beyond agriculture and that food-security targets need to be balanced with wider rural development objectives. This will entail a greater focus on investment rather than redistributive measures. (OECD 2009)

We do not know if the Chinese state actually took advice from the suggestions made in the report quoted above, but the Chinese state has come a long way to invest in the rural sector. To the credit of President Hu Jintao and Premier Wen Jiabao,[3] as of the beginning of the 21st century, the Chinese government had experimented and eventually abolished all agricultural taxes and levies on the rural sector. This was the first time in China's more than 2,000 years of recorded history that there was no agricultural tax. Furthermore, the state has gradually introduced agricultural subsidies in Gao Village since 2004. Currently, the subsidies, paid directly to the households to prevent state agents

---

2   The Chinese characters for this are 要糧，要錢，要命.

3   For a critical assessment of the Hu-Wen leadership, see Gao 2012, 175–192.

from charging rent, are RMB 40 per *mu* of dry-crop land and RMB 188 per mu of rice paddy. The return of the state's provision of public goods also included medical care and other social services, the details of which are discussed below to demonstrate how the state reaches Gao Village.

Family Planning and the State

It is fair to say that "the three forceful demands" by the state has become history. Several factors contributed to the disappearance of tension between the state and Gao villagers in the matter of birth control. Even before the change of policy to two children per family was announced in 2015, relaxation had already been in place for several years. Moreover, young migrant workers, with a higher standard of education and an increasing living standard, do not want to have more than two children anyway, unlike their parents and grandparents. Therefore, family planning is more or less a non-issue for the state.

Medical Care and the State

Having outlined a brief history of the reach of the state, let me now discuss how this has changed in Gao Village in practice. I will start with medical insurance, which is one of the social insurance policies in China. The head of Gao Village in 2015 when I conducted an interview with him was Gao Chaojiang, who used to be a teacher at the local school but later retired. One of the few tasks for Gao Chaojiang was the annual collection of social and medical insurance payments from the villagers. The fees set for medical insurance for 2013, when the program was initiated in the Gao Village area, was RMB 50 per person per year; for 2014 it was RMB 70 and for 2015 it was RMB 90 per year. The policy was such that the villagers could not claim medical expenses when they saw a local doctor—or any doctor—for long-term illnesses or for everyday complaints such as the flu or a cough. They could only claim about 70% of the cost when they were hospitalized, such as for surgery or if they were in an accident, and it had to be at a designated hospital, the nearest being in Youdunjie, about 15 kilometers away. The cynical villagers complaint that doctors inflated the cost if you tried to claim a medical insurance.

In 2015, when I accompanied Gao Chaojiang to visit households from door to door while he collected the fees, I was convinced that most villagers were willing to pay. The villagers, gradually, came to see the benefits after witnessing the consequences of a couple of motor accidents, and also the cost of another villager who had to have surgery. If it were not for the medical insurance, these villagers would have had to spend out of pocket RMB 40,000–50,000, which meant bankruptcy for the family.

Social Insurance and the State

Social insurance has started only in recent years for the rural sector and is different from that for the urban sector. Payment for a social insurance policy for urban township residents is higher, and the benefits are also higher, varying from place to place and time to time. Here is an example: One Gao villager was lucky and clever enough to use the name of a distant relative who had Poyang town resident status, which is considered urban, but did not have enough money to purchase a policy entitled to him. This Gao villager paid the policy in the name of this town person, which costed RMB 40,000 in 2013, as a one-payment policy. Two years after the policy was taken up, when this Gao villager turned 60, he started to receive a monthly payment of RMB 950. This Gao villager had already collected more than RMB 20,000 from a RMB 40,000 insurance premium. This person was lucky to have the cash at that time and clever enough to take up this insurance opportunity designed for urban residents, an opportunity that was usually not available for rural residents.

For rural residents, the threshold set for social insurance premiums was low, and was only RMB 100 per person per year during the early 2010s. The benefits, of course, are also low: RMB 55 a month in 2011 when it was started, increased to RMB 70 a month in 2015. Men can start receiving payments at the age of 60 and women at 55. For the Gao villagers who are young, their benefits will be much higher if they start to purchase the policy when they are still young. A couple of young Gao villagers that I interviewed did not want to be bothered with social insurance payments. Their rationale was that 30 years from now was too uncertain. This is a totally understandable position to take given the uncertainty and unstableness of Chinese governance in the past, but may be difficult for readers in developed Western societies to understand, who may not realize how turbulent modern Chinese history has been.

Once every year the village head has to visit all the households from door to door to collect the fees, and he has to do it during the Chinese New Year period when most migrant workers come home. Gao Chaojiang had two spreadsheets when I was there: one for medical insurance and one for the social insurance, and he would fill in the name of the household when the pay was collected. After Chinese New Year, all the young villagers would disperse to their work destinations and the village would be quiet again, with only the elderly and children around. If it happened that Gao Chaojiang could not find the person he was looking for, then the fee was not collected, even though the family might be willing and had the money to pay. There was no meeting called and no letter or notice from the state to explain the policies. There was no form to fill in and the village head did not even write a receipt for the payment.

On the one hand, the policies designed by the state are really a huge step forward for rural people like Gao villagers. It is sign that the rural people are citizens of the state, as well as an indication that the state admits its responsibilities to look after them when they are old or in a desperate situation. On the other hand, both the policy content and the ad hoc collection process illustrate how limited the state's reach is for rural people these days. Though the fact that there are different policies between the urban and rural residents is discriminatory enough by the standard of a modern state, but to have social insurance for rural residents at all is a step forward. However, the state still has a long way to go, for not only an effective social insurance policy for migrant workers at their working destinations is not ensured,[4] the ad hoc procedure at their place of origin also fails to cover them even for a very elementary medical care.

The Environment and the State

One of the major and most serious environmental issues that has not been addressed by the state at all, or not taken seriously so far, is the water and soil pollution that is getting worse because of the chemicals used for agriculture. There are no fish to be caught in local creeks or ponds in Gao Village, whereas catching fish used to be a great pastime for children and fish a nutritious source of food. Another distressing phenomenon that one cannot fail to notice when traveling in rural China is the rubbish everywhere. Used plastic bags and bottles of chemicals are abandoned in the rice paddies, and all kinds of industrial and commercial waste is littered along the roads, paths and in corners.

However, in 2014 this started to change. The villagers were told of the problem and the *xiang* government, urged by the higher authorities, started to do something. There are two rubbish sites in Gao Village, though they are just simple square enclosures, with three sides made of concrete walls, only one meter high. Each household is allocated a rubbish bin to collect rubbish and the two poorest Gao villagers are paid to collect the rubbish. One is Gao Lati (see Chapter 8), who collects rubbish along the one and only main street that runs through Gao Village for a salary of RMB 1,500 a year. The other is Gao Xianggui, who is paid to collect all the household rubbish and move it to the rubbish dump

---

4   For a detailed discussion of the problems and issues of social insurance for migrant workers at their work destinations, see Han 2014.

sites, from where, at the *xiang* government level, a truck is arranged to regularly transport the village rubbish to a designated rubbish dumping site. Xianggui is also paid RMB 1,500 a year, a pittance of a payment considering the amount of work she has to do. The budget for their salaries comes from a levy collected from each household. According to new regulations that were set up when all taxes were abolished, a levy may be imposed if it is for a special project that is proposed by, discussed among, and agreed upon by the villagers for the collective good of the village. A levy to pay for the care of the village environment is such a special project. The villagers are not told to sort rubbish into categories for recycling. However, that does not seem to be a big problem because there is a vibrant rubbish collecting industry by local individual entrepreneurs who collect the recyclable rubbish to sell, one of whom is Gao Changqi, discussed in Chapter 9.

The initiative by the state to deal with the rubbish is again a welcome step in the right direction. It is a good arrangement also because the two poorest villagers get some employment and payment. One could argue that generally two factors play an important role in environmental protection: One is technology and the other is awareness. In current rural China in particular, and China in general, it requires the state to bring two factors into play. What is good and what is bad for the environment has to be explained and promoted to Gao villagers. What technology is required to deal what environmental problems has to be on the agenda. All of this requires effort and even intervention from the state. The next big challenge is for the state to take the initiative in both raising awareness and in providing the technological guidance to tackle the overuse of chemicals, which pollute the soil and water.

The Elderly and the State

Traditionally, Chinese people look after the elderly in their family, and for the most part this is still true today in Gao Village. In the Mao era there was what was called a *wubao hu* ("five guarantee households"), a program designed to look after the childless elderly, with resources, however meager, from the state for food, clothing, shelter, medical care, and burial. However, that program was gone with the retreat of the state following the dismantling of the collective system. Recently, the state has resumed, to a certain extent, looking after the elderly. Not far from Gao Village, the Yinbaohu Xiang Jinglao Yuan (Yinbaohu Township Old People's Home) was set up. As of 2015, any Yinbaohu resident at the age of 70 or above was entitled to live in the home at the cost of RMB 1,800 a year.

This old people's home set up by the state has not seemed to have had much of a positive impact yet on Gao villagers. On the one hand, those who may need the program most cannot afford it. For those who can afford to be in the home—which very spacious and quite comfortable, as I found out when I went to visit my brother's mother-in-law there—the choice is not really open to them. When the young and able Gao village migrant workers leave Gao Village to work far from home, they mostly have to leave the family's elderly and small children behind. That means that the elderly have to stay in the family home to look after the young, and therefore cannot go live in the old people's home. As of 2015, my brother's mother-in-law was the only Gao villager in the home, though she is one of the Gao villagers who needs the least from the state, as her sons and a daughter are all well off.

Upon further inquiry, I found that some Gao villagers seem to be reluctant to send their elders to live in the home. They feel that by having their parents or grandparents in an old people's home they will lose face, as the situation will be understood either as a lack of ability to look after the elderly or as a person who does not hold the morality of filial piety. The elderly themselves do not like the idea either, as they do not want their children to lose face and they want to stay among the villagers for social reasons.

Clearly, two developments of the reach of the state during the second 15 years of the post-Mao era have greatly benefitted Gao villagers: 1) the retreat of an intrusive state in terms of the abolition of all kinds of taxes and levies and the relaxed family planning policy, and 2) the return of the state investment in public goods. Gao villagers are happier and there is a visible reduction of tension between them and the state. However, this is not to say that local governance is already very good. On the contrary, local governance is far from being modern in the sense of being transparent and accountable, even though village elections are genuinely implemented. One of the main reasons for local governance problems has to do with the continuity of the traditional value of lineage identity. This issue and its related problems are discussed in the next chapter.

CHAPTER 12

The Reinvention of Tradition and the Impact of Lineage Identity on Local Governance

Introduction

In the first Gao Village book (Gao 1999), local tradition is discussed in chapter 12 titled "Change and Continuity," which reflects the tensions between changing modernity and well-established tradition. One of the clear tensions between the modern and past narrated in detail is lineage identity. In fact I was a victim, albeit a minor one, of that tension. Though I was only a teenager, I was detained for two weeks for tearing a few pages out of the Gao Village Lineage Records or Genealogy Book[1] for the purpose of practicing calligraphy (as paper was rare and precious in Gao Village at that time), accused of attempting to preserve the old and backward feudalist practice of lineage identity. On the other hand, I could also be considered a beneficiary of lineage identity, as narrated in the first Gao Village book. The person in overall charge of recommending students to tertiary institutions was at that time a person from another Gao Village, Gao Changyan, to which my Gao Village is related. According to what Gao Changyan himself told me, I was able to enter Xiamen University because of his recommendation. The perception among Gao villagers was that he recommended me

---

1   The Chinese for this is 宗譜 (*zongpu*).

strongly because I was a fellow Gao villager of his, even though I was from a different Gao Village.[2]

That was during the Mao era, when lineage identity was considered something un-modern that needed to be weakened, if there was a tolerance of its existence at all. In this chapter, I will first show that lineage identity is thriving and that tradition is being reinvented in order to strengthen lineage village identity, even though most of the younger generation of villagers don't have much time for it. The chapter will then examine how lineage identity impacts on local governance. It is in this connection and this context that local village elections are discussed. Village elections were only mentioned in the first Gao Village book in passing because there were not significant. What has been the case since then? In the Mao era, lineage identity played its role in local politics implicitly, and sometimes explicitly even though it was officially

---

2   When the Chinese state started experimenting the recruitment of tertiary education students from the grassroots by a method that combined local official recommendation with examination results, termed as the recruitment of Worker-Peasant-Soldier students, the education section of the local government in rural China was put in charge of the recruitment process. In 1973, the head of the education section of the Yinbaohu Commune happened to be Gao Changyan from another Gao Village, to which my Gao Village is related. I was one of the three candidates recommended. A Xu villager candidate Xu Xianqi was recruited straightway by a Nanchang railway engineering college because of his excellent political credential: a member of the CCP and had served in the People's Liberation Army. I was recruited to Xiamen University to study English whereas the third candidate, a Jin villager failed to get a place. The reason why I had been recruited by Xiamen University was not known for certain even today. It was years later when Gao Changyan wanted me to help his daughter to find a good job that he told me that it was upon his strong recommendation that I got accepted by Xiamen University. I did not and still do not doubt his words. That is one side of the story, and I wrote it in *Gao Village*. Another version is that a teacher from Xiamen University who was recruiting students in Jiangxi really liked what he saw of me. What I did not point out specifically in *Gao Village* is that of the three candidates I was the strongest academically: I was teaching high school students of my age mathematics and Chinese in a local school. I did not point this out because the marks of the entrance examinations had not been made public, partly as the result of the Zhang Tiesheng Incident after which academic achievements were downplayed officially. Academic results were claimed to be less important than political credential but the teacher from any Xiamen University had the right to choose any candidates presented to him and therefore could make a decision on the basis of academic achievements.

politically incorrect. How does lineage interact with local politics and local governance when genuine village elections are attempted?

Good Governance and the Social Environment[3]

Before we examine the precise situation of Gao Village, we need to explore a couple of theoretical issues related to governance and local governance. One issue is how to measure good governance and another is how to ensure good governance. Only a few years after his famous declaration of "the end of history" following the collapse of the former Soviet Union—with the advantage of hindsight of what has happened in the Middle East and some notable failures of the Obama presidency—Francis Fukuyama proposed three requirements for a good government model: good governance, accountability, and the rule of law (Fukuyama 2014). In this proposal for a three-dimensional government, Fukuyama maintains the importance of democracy, since democracy is generally considered the best way to hold a government accountable. However, Fukuyama realizes that democracy by and of itself does not guarantee good governance. There could be bad governance in democracies and good governance in non-democracies, at least in democracies in the conventional sense that are being practiced in the West.

China is not considered a democracy by Western tradition, but it has been practicing elections at the village level for many years, as documented and discussed by an extensive literature (He 2002, 2007; Oi and Rozelle 2000; Lu 2015; Teets and Hurst 2014). For the purpose of discussing local governance[4] in Gao Village, there is therefore the

---

3   Some of the information and descriptions here are also used in Gao 2017a and Gao 2017b.

4   For one of the new approaches to discussing governance in China, see Heilmann and Perry 2011. One chapter in this volume by the seasoned China watcher Joseph Fewsmith, "The Elusive Search for Effective Sub-Country Governance," has some relevance to my discussion here.

issue of whether village elections contribute to good governance. Many scholars conclude that village elections in China are conducive to good local governance, whereas other scholars argue that there is an issue of what social environmental factors are required to be in existence for village elections to be conducive to good local governance (Zhang et al. 2002). One of the important social environment factors for villages like Gao Village is lineage or clan identity.

Tsai (2002) argues that village elections promote accountability, but she also argues that lineage identity affects local governance. By comparing two sets of four villages of comparable economic conditions in Jiangxi and Fujian provinces,[5] Tsai suggests that two of the villages are better at raising resources for public goods, not because they have democracy while the other two do not, nor because one is wealthier than the other. They are better at raising funds for public good because they have a strong sense of lineage identity.

As O'Brien and Li (1999) point out, for many years after the post-Mao reforms, there was no incentive for the local state agents to provide public goods for the villages because their governing performance were not judged by whether they provided public goods for the community or not. Therefore, public goods have to be organized by villagers themselves and funding has to be raised locally. If, a good indication of good governance is the availability of public goods to residents, then

---

5   Tsai first does a comparative study of two villages in Jiangxi and discovers that the village with a single lineage organizes activities, such as fundraising for public goods, whereas in the multi-lineage villages there is an absence of such activities because there is distrust between the villagers and village cadres. Tsai then presents a comparison of two village committees, the River Bridge and West Gate village committees in Fujian. While both village committees represent multi-lineage villages, one of them, the River Bridge, consists of several small villages of different surnames (or "hamlets," as Tsai calls them). On the other hand, the West Gate village committee, though also representing villages of several different surnames, has the Wu surnamed villagers as the majority, who comprise about 80 percent of the households. West Gate has more solidarity and organizes more activities and was able to raise funds for public goods.

this study by Tsai shows that a more solid clan identity results in better governance.

A conclusion that can be drawn from this comparison of two pairs of four villages is that lineage identity is a social environmental factor in local governance. A lineage village with a single surname has an unambiguous identity, and as a result it is easier for it to organize activities than for a village of different lineages. A community, in this case, one village committee, with one dominant lineage, has more solid clan identity and is easier to organize than a committee of different lineages of equal influence. A governance institution can perform effectively if it can produce collective action and accountability, but as Lu argues, the relative effectiveness of that institution is contingent upon the social environment (Lu 2015). Just as the situation as presented by Tsai's study of four villages in Jiangxi and Fujian shows, one of the most important factors of the social environment in the Gao Village area is lineage identity.

Village Lineage Identity and the Reinvention of Tradition

In the Gao Village area, all the villages are lineage villages. There have always tension, disputes, and even physical fighting between neighboring lineage villages over land and water resources. Usually the bigger lineage villages exercise bullying and can sometimes get away with murder.[6] In the Mao era, the fight against entrenched lineage influence was hard but it was attempted. In the post-Mao era, lineage identity related activities and values are on the rise. One example from Xu Village is a good illustration. Xu Congxi, who was introduced in Chapters 6 and 7, does not belong to Xu Village anymore for all

---

6   For an example of how a big village got away with murder in the post-Mao era, see Gao 1999, 116.

practical purposes, since he has urban resident status and has four houses in Poyang Town, and his only child now lives in Australia. Nonetheless, Xu requested a large piece of land of around 1,500 square meters to build a house (planned to have a swimming pool, the first in the area) in Xu Village. The influential lineage members decided to allocate the land as requested. When the Xu Village head objected to this idea on the basis that such a large allotment had never been allocated to anyone—let alone to someone who practically was no longer a Xu villager—the village head was vetoed by the influential lineage members. Thus, the head of the village, who was an elected "governor" of the village and a state representative at the grassroots level, was denied a say in important matters such as land allocation, when in theory rural land in China was collectively owned. This would never have happened in the Mao era.

That Xu Congxi had such support from the Xu Village lineage power-holders has to do with two facts. The first fact is that Xu is perceived to be a successful son of the village, a person who went from being an orphan to becoming a self-made businessman,[7] with a daughter who is not only university educated, and overseas educated, but also a *huaqiao*,[8] very rare in the area. Congxi thus brings prestige to Xu Village. The second fact is that Congxi has donated RMB 50,000 for the construction of the Xu Clan Hall. That was the highest individual donation it has received, so his name has been carved into a stone tablet in the hall entrance.

There are several interesting and important points about the Xu Village Lineage Hall and other halls around the area that were built in recent years. Xu Village did not have a lineage hall in the pre-1949 years. These buildings are not a restoration after its destruction in the Cultural Revolution, as might be assumed. The second point is that this

---

7 Xu Congxi's life is briefly described in Gao 1999, as he is the son-in-law of my sister Gao Lingli.

8 *Huaqiao* refers to Chinese people who have immigrated and live abroad. In this case, she immigrated to Australia, which is considered a thing of honor and prestige in China.

Photo 25. The front entrance of the Xu Village Lineage Hall.
Taken by the author in 2015.

reinventing of tradition has been done in a China that is run by the supposed Communists, and some influential members of the lineage committee that planned and supervised the building of the hall are members of the CCP. The fact that activities to strengthen lineage identity are thriving is precisely because of the support of the influential members of the CCP. One such influential member in Xu Village was a former head teacher of the local high school who has since retired. Finally, the tradition has a modern embellishment: The names of both the Xu Village Lineage Hall and the Cultural Activity Center are engraved above the entrance door of the hall.

For all intents and purposes, the hall seems to be able to play an important role for the community, as it provides a public space for cultural activities, traditional or modern. Upon the opening of the hall, the Xu Village lineage committee hired a theatrical company to put on performances for five days and five nights. It was open and free to anyone. Sometimes the hall was packed with people and sometimes there were just a few people in the audience. The show went on, irrespective of whether there was an audience. It was a performance to show the glory of the Xu clan, a show to be remembered for generations to come and to consolidate lineage identity.

In February 2015, the neighboring Jiang Village had just completed its lineage hall, which was larger and taller than the Xu Village Hall, obviously to outdo the latter, whose village is half the size of the former in terms of population. The theatrical performance by a company invited from Lianyu in Poyang went on for seven days and seven nights, again to outdo Xu Village, to gain face and glory and to be remembered for generations to come.

I watched one of the performances and examined the program. I noticed that the themes and stories were mostly traditional repertoire, consisting of *diwang jiangxiang caizi jiaren* (emperors, generals, ministers, scholar gentries, and beautiful women), themes that were criticized by Mao for being out of touch with contemporary life and for

Photo 26. A celebratory performance in the Jiang Village Lineage Hall.
Taken by Pei Fei in 2015.

Photo 27. Some elderly villagers in the audience at the Jiang Village Lineage Hall. Taken by Pei Fei in 2015.

having nothing to do with the lives of ordinary people. Whatever one might think of these themes and stories of ancient China, the musical tune was local, from Jiangxi Province, called *Ganju* (one of the four great operatic traditions in China). However, the spoken language used was Mandarin, which was not surprising but it was unusual, because one is supposed to use the *Gan* dialect when one performs *Ganju*. It was not surprising because the *Gan* dialect has so many sub-dialects (Gao 2000) that it is hard for the performers to decide on which one to use if they travel around to perform in different dialect areas; therefore, Mandarin is chosen as a lingua franca.

Another instance of lineage activity was the 100th anniversary celebration in 2015 of the Gao lineage of another Gao Village, a much bigger village to which my little Gao Village is related, but which is located about ten kilometers away. Apparently the anniversary celebration was one of the largest and most successful events in the whole of the Youdunjie area, a large district that includes the two Gao villages. The person in charge of the 100th anniversary of this big

Photo 28. A local opera being performed with traditional themes and costumes. Taken by Pei Fei in 2015.

Gao Village was Gao Changyan, the man I discussed in *Gao Village* and mentioned above in relation to my getting recruited to Xiamen University in 1973. He was a member of the CCP and was transferred at the beginning of the post-Mao era from Yibaohu Commune government to be the party secretary of the leading high school in the area, the Youdunjie High School, one of the only two key rural schools[9] in the whole of Jiangxi Province. The school was first established during the Great Leap Forward and was expanded to include a high school component during the Cultural Revolution. It is not surprising, but it is interesting, that one of the vanguards of the CCP 1949 revolution in bringing modernity to the area was leading the way to enhance lineage identity, which was considered traditionally backward and "feudal" by the May Fourth Movement's discourse, which was the intellectual background for the establishment of the CCP in 1921. One outcome of

9   "Key" schools are the ones designated by the national government at various levels that have preferential treatment in terms of government funding and assignment of high-quality teachers. There are many in China's urban centers, but very few in rural China.

the anniversary celebration was a booklet that was designed, compiled, and produced by a committee headed by Gao Changyan. In the booklet, the history and accomplishments of this Gao Village was recorded, along with poems by village celebrities and important personalities, again headed by Gao Changyan himself. What is notable in the poems is that, along with a celebration of how prosperous village life has been since the reform, they praised the Mao era for the development of Gao Village, with a seemingly reasonable narrative of modernity combining the triple legacies: the legacy of traditional values of lineage identity, the legacy of the 1949 revolution, and that of post-Mao economic development (Gan 2007).

Local Governance in Villages and Lineage Politics in Democracy

Clearly, members of the CCP, a party that is supposed to be anti-"feudalist," are active in promoting lineage identity by reinventing tradition through organizing the building of lineage halls, theatrical performances and anniversaries. In this section, I will demonstrate how lineage politics influences local governance by describing how lineage politics plays a role in local elections and in the allocation of state resources.

The administration at the lowest level in rural China is the *cun xiaozu* ("village team"), which usually governs one village the size of Gao Village, with a population of around 400 people.[10] The "governor" is the village head, who really does not have much work to do, as there are no taxes or levies to be collected (except levies for few special projects, like a levy to pay rubbish collectors), and education is not in the realm of village governance. There is now even not much to do about family planning, for the reasons discussed in chapter 11. Perhaps for the very reason that there is very little work for the village head to do, there is also very little reward for being the head, with a salary of only RMB 1,500 a year as of 2015 when

---

10   It has to be remembered that to the local administration, a village population includes migrant workers who live and work in urban centers away from home.

I interviewed him. The young and able Gao villagers have almost all left as migrant workers and hardly any of the retired, elderly and women want to bother about anything beyond their own family affairs. The village head is supposed to be chosen by elections, but more often than not there is nobody who wants to be the head of the village, in which case there will be no election called and the village head will be appointed by the village committee. The village head in 2015, Gao Chaojiang, a retired local schoolteacher, was more or less coerced into the position by his *xiang* (the new name for the commune) government friend, so he told me.

Above Gao Village, the second layer of administration is the *Qinglin cun weihui* (Qinglin Village Committee), which covers several villages. Each village committee has a chairperson (*zhuren*), and four committee members, including one woman for Women's Affairs. The committee members are not appointed but must be elected. Anyone can nominate someone and there is a pre-election selection to screen the least popular candidates until eventually there are two candidates for the position of chairperson and four candidates for each member of the committee. In theory, this is genuine democracy by popular vote, and once the election campaign starts to take place, the candidates attempt to lobby for votes, mostly with gifts such as wine and cigarettes. No candidate seems to canvass on the promise of public service, since there are no resources at their disposal.

Competition or not, the final result of this seemingly genuine election is very much predetermined by the size of lineage village. Qinglin Village Committee consists of a village in which all the inhabitants are surnamed Gao, a village in which all the inhabitants are surnamed Cao, a village in which all the inhabitants are surnamed Xu, and three villages in which all the inhabitants are surnamed Jiang. The Jiang lineage has the largest number of people and the Xu lineage has the second largest number of people. It is no coincidence that the party secretary of the Qinglin Village Committee—who in theory and according to the Chinese Constitution has supreme power—was (in 2015) from the Jiang lineage and the chairperson of the Village Committee was from Xu Village. In general and in theory, the chairperson of a village committee and the CCP party secretary run the affairs together with other committee members. The division of labor in general is that the village committee head runs the day-to-day administration, while the party secretary makes sure that the CCP policies are implemented. In practice, who of the two is the more powerful depends on the personality of the position holders and their lineage power behind them. If one wants to, the person from the largest lineage village can exercise more power irrespective of whether that person is the party secretary or village committee chair.

Even though the party secretary of the Qinglin Village Committee is not elected by popular vote but rather by appointment by the *xiang* CCP committee, the appointee is most likely to be from a larger village. For the *xiang* CCP committee to appoint someone from Gao Village as the party secretary is not only "undemocratic," since Gao Village has the smallest number of party members, but also makes administration difficult in practice because a small village does not have the necessary influence. As for the Qinglin Village Committee in 2015, the Women's Affairs member was a Gao villager, but only because the elected woman from the Jiang clan declined to take up the position.

During the Mao era, when the most radical anti-traditional policies were attempted, measures were taken to break down the entrenched lineage interest and influence. For instance, even for the Guantian Production Brigade, which covered a small area of only three villages, Gao, Cao and Xu, among which Xu was about the size of Cao and Gao combined, the party secretary of the brigade was Gao Changyin and the chairperson was Wang Biaohua, the former from Gao Village and the latter from another village outside of Guantian. This was designed to counter the potential for dominating the lineage influence of Xu Village. When the Cultural Revolution broke out, Gao Changyin, as a number one power holder in Guantian, was struggled against and in the process I myself became a minor victim (Gao 1999, 2014).

Since the system of elections was introduced, such a counterbalance policy is rarely implemented. As democracy is supposed to be used to elect one of the locals, someone from outside the area should in theory not be considered. At least that is how the local government has been formed in recent years. So practically, the practice of democracy by popular vote makes lineage politics not only more prominent but also more legitimate.

Rent-Seeking and Lineage Politics in State Allocated Resources

Salaries are low for the local village committee officials, but not too bad considering how little they have to do for their work. In 2015, the party secretary and the chair of the Village Committee each earned about RMB 20,000 and a committee member earned over 10,000 RMB, paid by the state. However, apart from the salaries and any prestige vested in the positions, there are opportunities for the state agents to seek illicit benefit from their positions.

Here is an example. During the collective period, a huge dam, Qinglin Dam, was built at the bottom end of Qinglin Lake to prevent flooding to the rice fields nearby. In those days when Qinglin Dam was built, Qinglin Lake was a lake, but now it is no more. As a result of lower water levels in Poyang Lake, the water in Qinglin Lake flowed out and down quickly, so there was little water left in Qinglin Dam. Thus, the lake was turned into a fertile rice field, of which Gao Village was allocated some acres. The former head of Gao Village decided to sell the user rights of these acres to someone from another village for 10 years, with an income of RMB 200,000 a year for Gao Village. There is some rationale in the sale. If these acres were allocated to Gao villagers, they would have to be divided into many pieces for a fair and equal distribution on a per capita basis to each household, and the practical work of division and cultivating rice in so many divided pieces would have been difficult. The person who bought the user rights for 10 years certainly could make better use of the land by farming it as one piece. The problem, however, was that the head of the village did not inform the villagers of his decision until after the deal was done. The villagers had no say in the matter, not even in the price of the sale. On top of that, no villager knows how the money has been spent. There is some speculation among the villagers that the former head of Gao Village pocketed some of the income from the sale.[11]

As the state has been investing more in the rural sector, how resources are obtained and how they are allocated give rise to opportunities for "rent seeking" at every level of administration. Poyang County, where Gao Village is located, is considered one of the poorest counties in Jiangxi Province, and for that reason the county is not even open for "foreigners" to visit.[12] In such a poor county, where agriculture is the main source of income and where the central government has to subsidize agriculture, the total financial income of this county of more than 1.5 million people was recorded to be only RMB 410 million in 2010. It is indeed astonishing that in such a county, a department head of the county's Finance Bureau, Li Huabo, was able to embezzle RMB 94 million of the state agriculture subsidies without being noticed for five years, starting in 2006. This department head of a little finance bureau of a little county was discovered to have done this only when he rang up his boss from Canada to say that he was sorry for taking a lot of money out of the system. He was on the list of 100 criminals released for international notification that the Chinese police wanted to arrest (*Jiangxi ribao* 2015).

When and if some of the subsidies or investments do come to the grassroots level, lineage politics plays a role in their allocation. Some state investments in rural China are in the name of the New Socialist Rural Construction, a program that includes projects such as building roads and modern toilets with a sewage system. Of the villages that are part of the Qinglin Village Committee, to which Gao Village belongs, the two largest lineage villages seem to have had the best New Socialist

---

11   When I interviewed this former head of the village, he denied anything of that kind.

12   In the late 1990s, when a BBC documentary director approached me to make a film about Gao Village, access was denied because Poyang, as one of the poorest counties, was not on the list that could be open to foreigners.

Rural Construction results. One of them, Jiang Village, has built straight streets with a sewage system and the other, Xu Village, has proper roads crisscrossing the village plus a ring road around it. Gao Village, however, has only one road in the middle of the village, which had been built from different funding before the New Socialist Rural Construction program even started, as it is the main road through this area leading to the Poyang, Jingdezhen, Nanchang, Jiujiang and beyond. Gao villagers complained to me that they have not benefitted from any funding that was allocated from the government for New Socialist Rural Construction.

Another program is related to land and is designed to encourage rural people to move their houses away from fertile land. The stated rationale for the program, as discussed in Chapter 2, is to preserve enough arable land for growing food, in the face of the rapid increase of commercial use of land. The removal of the old houses to hillsides where land is not fertile in Gao Village actually started earlier. In 1998, when there was one of the worst floods in Jiangxi, then-Premier Zhu Rongji ordered all the houses on lower land to be moved to the higher hillsides, with state subsidies of RMB 10,000 for each household. Gao villagers were forced to move,[13] with a result that some fertile land was left open for crops. Since the real estate boom, however, Gao villagers have started to build more and more houses on lower land, which is fertile, arable land, on both sides of a public road. As a result, more fertile land has been taken up for house construction, more than the land on which the old houses were based. Without reporting the shrinkage of arable land, the Village Committee instead took photos of the opened-up land on which the old houses were based and used that to ask the state for land reclamation subsidies. However, not a cent of the subsidies for turning this piece of land into agricultural use went to Gao villagers, according to my informants.

---

13   The *xiang* government organized militia to force the villagers to move, and if anyone refused they would break through the roof and damage the house, as discussed in Chapter 9.

Conclusion

This chapter presents a case of how village lineage identity has been articulated through the reinventing of tradition by the members of the CCP, which is supposed to be anti-tradition. Furthermore, the chapter demonstrates how lineage identity politics play a role in local governance. It describes and analyses not only how grassroots democracy is played out by lineage politics, but also how the practice of village elections actually legitimizes linage politics in local governance. Furthermore, it demonstrates that lineage politics in local governance influences the allocation and distribution of state resources. In contrast to the authoritarian countermeasures against lineage influence in local governance in the Mao era, which was done by appointing local officials from outside of the area (or if local from a smaller village), the current situation of popular vote legitimizes lineage influence. Therefore, local governance by democratically elected locals not only makes lineage politics more prominent, but also morally legitimate.

Other related conclusions are, firstly, that since the beginning of the 21st century, the state has, to some extent, resumed providing public goods, which has improved local governance. The second is that state agents will use every opportunity possible to seek rent, whether or not they are democratically elected. It is the accountability that matters most, but this is lacking. Clearly, lineage activities are on the rise in the Gao Village area to the extent that even traditions are being reinvented in the absence of other ideologies. Though lineage identity is not something "feudalistic" or "backward" that needs to be wiped out, as it was officially assumed during the Mao era, it nevertheless interferes in local governance in terms of village election results and in resource allocation and distribution. Lineage identity can be a positive influence for the villagers, for it gives them a sense of identity, solidarity and belonging, which assists in social cohesion in times of difficulty (for example, when they are far away from home as migrant workers), uncertainty or even political disorder. However, lineage influence needs to be guided and channeled by the state so that it can be counterbalanced for fairer local politics, just as lineage halls can be used as a public space for cultural activities. A strong and clear message is that local governance transparency and accountability are not something that can be ensured by a simple "one person, one vote" form of popular election. This kind of formal "democracy" cannot ensure accountability and transparency, not only because of the increasingly corrupting influence of money—or, as one villager from Xunde in Guangdong complained, *dou shi youqian ren de youxi* ("everything is a game for the rich")[14] —but also because of traditionally entrenched lineage influence.

---

14   Zhou et al. 2006. In May 2006, about 100 students, with their supervisors from the Sociology Department of the Media Institute of Nanjing University, together with the Research Office of the Jiangsu Province Propaganda Bureau and the Media Center of the Jiangsu Broadcasting Station, carried out a survey of 20 villagers with 940 valid return questionnaires, plus 156 in-depth interviews. The report of that survey is in Zhou et al. (2006).

CHAPTER 13

The Future of Gao Village and Rural China[1]

Introduction

Chapter 3, "A Brief Survey of Gao Village since the Late 1990s," discussed the major themes related to what has been happening in Gao Village since the late 1990s, such as population and family planning, health care, education, migration, farming, incomes, living standards, and the environment. That chapter shows that there have been some welcome developments, such as the abolition of agricultural taxes and free schooling for up to nine years, some attempts to build up an affordable health care system, but also some other more or less ambiguous developments, such as the emergence of private schools. Environmentally speaking, it has been a mix of both good and bad. It is good to have the grass and wetlands and the trees back, as well as the birds. However, marine life has almost become extinct, though the signs of this were already apparent before 1997, where the first Gao Village book left off. As a positive sign, by 2015 there had been an improvement in environmental awareness and in attempting to deal with the issue of rubbish.

---

1   This is a revised version of Gao 2017b, 23–43.

Living standards in general have been improving since the late 1990s, along with a boom in housing construction. The chapters focusing on individuals, that is, Chapter 5, about the richest Gao Village entrepreneur Gao Wenshu; Chapter 6, on the hotel managers Gao Changxian and Gao Mingxia; Chapter 9, about the rubbish collector Gao Changqi; and Chapter 8, on the poorest person in Gao Village, Gao Lati, more or less support the above conclusions. While all of these individual Gao villagers, except Gao Lati, could be referred to as successful, most of them fall somewhere in between: not too poor but not too well-off either. For most of the Gao Village families, the realization of the three major aspirations, i.e., building the best possible house in the village, getting the males in the family married, and owning a car (this one is a more recent aspiration), rely on migrant working income. Therefore, this kind of life story has been sustained by the sweat of the young Gao villagers working away from home, a situation that was described in *Gao Village* with a note of uncertainty. Nearly 20 years later, this pattern has not changed. The village economy is still sustained by migrant workers. The young Gao villagers still don't know where their future lies, in the same way that the whole of China does not. For this reason, I will now provide a retrospective discussion of what the likely future direction of Gao Village is.

Land Ownership and Urbanization

According to a news report published in the *China Youth Daily* (2013), nearly a million villages disappeared in the ten years prior to 2013. Nankang Village, referred to in the report, which used to have 136 villagers but now has only two, is a village only 80 kilometers away from Nanchang, the capital of Jiangxi Province, where Gao Village is located.

Most of the year, Gao Village looks deserted, with many houses empty and some only occupied by the elderly, children and some women. On the other hand, as has been discussed in Chapter 9 on Gao Changqi, there has been a real estate boom in the village since the late 1990s.

During Chinese New Year each year, for a period of two weeks, Gao Village is bustling and hustling. There are cars parked along the street and in front of many houses during this time. The one and only street running through Gao Village does not look any different from an urban street, say, in Jinan, the capital of Shandong Province, only with better-looking and more spacious houses. Why do the migrant workers continue building houses in which they apparently don't live most of the year? The answer to this question is related to two important issues of contemporary China: the issue of land ownership and that of urbanization.

Land Ownership

The current land ownership system in rural China is neither strictly public nor strictly private. The land inherited by the villagers historically, a history that goes back to before the 1949 revolution, is collectively owned by the village, as it was during the Mao era, but the use of land in the post-Mao era is private, as the collective land is allocated to households on a per capita basis. The amount of land that a person is allocated depends on how much land the village collectively owns. A Xu villager might have more, or less, allocated land than that of a Gao villager, depending on the land-to-person ratio at any given time. In 2015, Gao villagers were demanding that land allocation be renewed every five years, responding to demographic changes, though different arrangements are being carried out in other places in rural China. One could argue that this system of ownership of the means of production is neither communist nor capitalist. The issue, as elaborated below, is whether this ambiguity should be terminated.

Urbanization and Rural Communities

One could argue that there is no intrinsic reason why human beings should live in urban centers, either for survival or for comfort. When asked whether Gao Village would eventually disappear, the villagers I talked to all seemed surprised by such a question. They never imagined that Gao Village might not be there anymore. They felt life in the cities was not safe, and (said Changxian) in the dynastical history of China, when there was war, the city people ran away to rural villages. They thought the cities were too noisy and polluted. When I asked a number of Gao villagers [2] if they would like to move to a city, their responses were that they might move there for the sake of their children. They felt that conditions in Gao Village were reasonable, with some inconveniences in terms of entertainment and shopping, but that this could only get better.[3] As Lu (2013) and Liang (2014) point out, Chinese rural communities are the roots of Chinese culture and civilization. Trying to modernize China by uprooting rural communities would have traumatic implications for so many people. To the east of Gao Village is Wang Village, which is four times the size of Gao Village; to the southwest, Xu village is twice as large; to the west, Jiang Village is two times larger than Xu Village; and finally, to the north there is a smaller Lai Village. All of these villages are within one or two kilometers' distance away from each other. This kind of density is not unusual in Jiangxi Province.

The Debate

In recent years, there has been a push for the wholesale privatization of land so as to put an end to the ambiguity resulting from the private ownership of land use rights and the collective ownership of land rights. Those who are pushing for privatization are in fact advocating for

---

2 The surveyed villagers were Gao Yineng, a male aged 42; Gao Fengying, a female aged 38; Gao Wengui, a male aged 40; Gao Xiying, a female aged 39; and Gao Xindan, a male aged 43.

3 In some other more prosperous areas, the rural people are even less keen on being urbanized. An Academy of Social Sciences study shows that 80 percent of farming households do not want to relinquish their rural household registration (Xie 2011).

capitalist commercialization of farming and the proletarianization of the villagers (Zhou 2014, Wen 2014). Such critics of the present system argue that if land is privately owned, land cannot be taken away by the state agent at will, and if the state has to take back the land, the owner must be compensated at market price. However, as pointed out by those who are against privatization, like He Xuefeng (2010, 2014), what is often ignored is that vast amounts of rural land have no commercial development value. Land that has commercial value consists only a small percentage, usually on the fringe of a strategically-important city or state project area. There has never been a land seizure issue in Gao Village, as it is not in such an area.

Privatization is also being pushed from another point of view, i.e. large-scale farming for the increase of productivity and efficiency. This view is of course endorsed by the capitalists who want to make farming commercial for profit, as well as by ideological liberals who think that public ownership only leads to slavery (Hayek 1944).

Any Chinese person who visits the USA, Australia, Canada or New Zealand cannot fail to be impressed by the fact that only a small percentage of the country's population, around five percent or less, are engaged in farming, but the country is able to produce not only abundant food for domestic consumption but also for export. Would it not be wonderful if China could copy this model by developing such an efficient farming system? For liberals and some economic rationalists, the first step is privatization, because only privatization could lead to large-scale commercial farming. The villagers in China would have to sell their land and resettle in urban centers in order for China to accomplish efficient farming and urbanization at the same time.

Aside from ignoring the fact that farming is hugely subsidized in affluent countries, there is another issue that the privatizers fail to address—the environmental implications of large-scale commercial farming. To achieve efficiency and productivity so as to make a profit, large-scale commercial farming tends to be monoculture. As Saunders (2015) argues, single-crop farming destroys the diversity of wild life, and has very serious environmental consequences.

As Lin Chun (2015) neatly summarizes, there are currently three schools of thought on this debate. The dominant school is the liberal market school of privatizers. The second school (He and Yi 2015; Huang 2015) argues for small-scale household farming, with support and guidance from the state to form co-ops to deal with market forces. Another school of thought has emerged in recent years, which takes up the unfashionable class theory (Yan and Chen 2015). This Marxist school would argue that the Chayanovan idea of agricultural co-ops (Chayanov 1986) cannot apply to China, since the Chinese rural economy is already in the chain of global capitalism, as there is already a disparity between farmers—commercialization and proletarianization can be seen even among the rural communities.

The Marxist school and the school that advocates co-ops have one idea in common that is against wholesale privatization. Huang (2010a, 2010b, 2014a, 2014b, and 2014c) repeatedly argues that the liberals tend to ignore what the Chinese conditions are. The arable land-to-person ratio in China is one of the lowest in the world and is quickly shrinking. One of the very important factors for the feasibility of large-scale farming in countries like the USA and Australia is their abundant arable land for food production beyond feeding the domestic population. One also has to note that much of the agricultural land in the south and southwest China is terraced and is thus unsuitable for large-scale mechanized farming. When one talks about productivity, one tends to stress on efficiency and overlook the overall production output. Unit production output in China is very high, compared with the world standard, as labor-intensive farming tends to yield higher than mechanized farming. It is quite likely that large-scale farming would lead to a reduction of total grain output, and would therefore place China at greater risk in terms of adequate food supply. Another issue is that large-scale farming would mean more labor redundancy, which in turn means that China would have to provide job opportunities for millions of people, a capacity that China does not have. Finally, family farming acts as social security for millions of migrant workers who can return home, when and if they cannot find work in urban areas (He 2010, 2014).

So the issue of whether land should be privatized is closely related to the issue of urbanization. From the point of view of the Western model of urbanization, the logic of privatization is compelling. Nonetheless, the Chinese policy makers themselves, including senior officials like Chen Xiwen (Chen 2013), know also that the reality in China is far more complex than the abstract economic rationalist logic. They are aware of the practical and conceptual problems outlined above.

To start with, the Chinese state would need to invest enormously to accommodate hundreds of millions of people in the urban centers if urbanization were going to be like in the West. Currently, the Chinese state is not doing that. Instead, it is still reluctant or afraid of relaxing the *hukou* restrictions, which have prevented even the rural Chinese who work and live in urban centers from having urban resident status. On the one hand, the so-called urban middle class buys up apartments as investments. On the other, the urban centers don't seem to have enough infrastructure to accommodate migrant workers from rural areas, and even young professionals can not afford housing at market prices.

There is a conceptual problem the liberals have to overcome, and that is that according to China's Constitution, land must be either publicly or collectively owned. This is by far the most important stipulation in the Chinese Constitution at this juncture of contemporary Chinese politics. Public ownership of land is the final and probably the only "fig leaf" for China to still claim to be a socialist country. Even Deng Xiaoping dared not take off the fig leaf, hence the arrangement of private ownership of only land use right.

As Wilmsen (2016) argues, even in areas where land acquisition makes commercial sense, which is a small percentage of the total land in the country, and even in cases in which the acquisition of land does not violate the Constitution in the name of "public" interest, as a result of undervaluation, elite capture, exploitation and the expansion of the urban underclass, China's steadfast resolve to expand capitalism in rural China is undermining its attempts to secure rural property rights.

The Future of Gao Village

The issue of land ownership is therefore closely related to the issue of urbanization, which is related to the state's restriction on genuine migration. Currently, the threshold for Gao villagers to become urban citizens is so high that migrant Gao villagers have to return to the village after they are too old to work in urban centers. The Gao Village population has been increasing slightly, in spite of the sometimes strict population control policies and practices, and in spite of the fact that some villagers have left the village. Now as the birth control policy seems to be relaxing, population growth is unlikely to decline, although it is unlikely to increase dramatically either.

But is the current model—by which generation after generation migrate to work when they are young and return home when they are old, and by which children of young parents are left behind to be looked after by grandparents—sustainable? One of the main motivations for Gao villagers to work hard and save is to build a house. It is unlikely that the real estate boom will last much longer, not because there is a bubble to burst, since these houses are not built on debt from banks or financial institutions, but because there are not enough people to live in them. Another motivation for Gao villagers to work hard and save is to pay for the cost of a wedding. The two weddings that I attended each cost around RMB 200,000–300,000. The families probably recovered a third or half of the cost from gifts, including gifts of money. Nonetheless, that is still a lot of money for a migrant worker who earns anything between 2,000 and 4,000 RMB a month.

An often-heard complaint from young Gao villagers is that life is too boring back home and there is no entertainment and no place to have fun, though working in Foxconn as a migrant worker is anything but fun. In the whole area of the Qinglin Village Committee, consisting of six villages, an administration unit that had a registered population of 3,149 in 2015, there is not one cinema or theatre, and not one sports ground, law office, post office, or proper medical clinic. (There were only a couple of doctors who worked at home, with no reception or designated office.) There are several little family run shops selling more or less the same thing, but the only supermarket is located in Youdunjie, 15 kilometers from Gao Village.

So on the one hand, the push and pull factors are such that regularly 30 percent of the Gao villagers, almost all the young and able villagers, work and live away from home as migrant workers. On the other hand, discriminatory and market factors—such as unaffordable housing, few educational opportunities for children, a lack of access to many types of jobs, and a lack of many of the skills needed in the market—mean that migrants from rural China cannot permanently settle in the urban centers where they work. Gao villagers are torn between the two, one foot in each world, their hometown of the rural world and their working destination of the urban world. It is thanks to their extraordinary resourcefulness and entrepreneurial spirit that they are not torn apart. However, there are reported stories of how migrant workers from rural China *are* torn apart: the suicides of young workers in Foxconn factories, and suicides of the elderly, women, and even young children of migrant workers' families. Household farming does not have the productivity of the economy of scale and the economy of scale requires concentration of land. But concentration of land can only take place either through the restoration of private ownership of land as in pre-1949 revolution China or the restoration of collectivism as in the era of Mao. Therefore regarding land and rural development, China is again at a crossroads: the road to privatization or the road to collectivization, and CCP does not seem to be happy with either.

The Future of Rural China

The retreat of the State from the rural sector has been halted in recent years. However, some of the new policy developments do not go far enough, while others have reached their limits. Medical care is still a huge problem. For example, the majority of Gao villagers are practically not serviced medically. While the abolition of agricultural taxes and the provision of subsidies are warmly welcomed by rural people, agricultural subsidies seem to have reached their limits. According to the authoritative account of Chen Xiwen (2014), being bound to the clauses and terms agreed to by the Chinese government under then-premier Zhu Rongji to enter the World Trade Organization (WTO), China has reached its limit for agricultural subsidies. At the same time, government protected prices of agricultural produce have, or almost have, reached the level of international market prices. China has run out of ways to boost the income of the rural sector.

During the second decade of the 21st century, China needs a new grand narrative for modernity, especially in relation to the rural community. As the school of class analysis would like to remind us, scholars like He (2010, 2014) and Huang (2015) may be too romantic about household farming and a little too idealistic about the capitalist market. Huang would like to use the East Asian societies, i.e., Japan, Taiwan, and South Korea, as a model for developing successful agriculture and modern rural communities. But it is far from clear that their agriculture sectors are a success story. As Zhang Yulin (2011) argues, the success in rural development in these societies did not last. By 2010, the average farmers in Japan had reached a shocking age of 66 years and much of the land was left unfarmed. During the 1960s, food sufficiency rates for all three of these East Asian societies was at 80 percent or more. By 2000, their reliance on imported food had increased to a staggering 70 percent. Heavy reliance on imported food is not what China can afford, nor can the world afford to provide enough food to feed 20 percent of the world population.

How is China to reconcile the logic of economic rationalism, which demands productivity, with its socialist Constitution's stipulation of public ownership of land, which has ended up being small household farming that is considered inefficient and low in productivity? The privatizers are gathering dominance and they are calling for changes to the Chinese Constitution. As has been the case since the death of Mao, the anti-socialist power-holders are most likely to privatize land in China unannounced and in a step-by-step way. Since the beginning of the 21ˢᵗ century, the concept of *liuzhuan*, referring to the practice of trading of land use rights, has been promoted for this purpose. The practice and the concept of *liuzhuan* originated in the 1990s, when the huge migration from rural areas to urban centers started, and when there were agricultural taxes and levies on land. Some villagers who were not able to work on the land would give their land to their relatives or friends to use for free, so long as the latter were willing to pay the taxes and levies imposed on the land. The Chinese government has been encouraging large-scale trading and even commercial trading of user rights under the name of *liuzhuan*. By the end of 2014, about 30 percent of all the arable land in China was under trading contracts (Yan 2015). By 2015, almost half of the rice-growing land in Gao Village had been traded off.

In Gao Village, the trading of land use rights has not yet led to much large-scale farming because the amount of land involved is still too small. In fact, all of the land that belongs to Gao Village pooled together is not enough for large-scale farming, so there has been not much of an increase in productivity. Nationally, larger trading contracts have been undertaken but the results of such a development is still ambiguous. It has been reported frequently in the Chinese official media that there are two new developments that have emerged from *liuzhuan*. One is that some entrepreneurs take advantage of the initial government funding support for such a trading contract and then don't do anything with the land once they receive the subsidies. At the same time, they either delay or avoid the payment of the rent owed to the original owners of the land. The other development that emerged is that the contracted farmers started to realize after a year or so that they could not make as much profit as they had expected, or any profit at all. Many contract farmers or specialized farming households have gone bankrupt.

Conclusion

So, what is the future for rural China? It hinges on the settlement of land ownership. State policy makers are impressed with the economic rationalist logic and with Western agricultural efficiency, but at the same time are aware of the Chinese reality of a larger population dependent on a smaller percentage of arable land. So the Chinese state is ambiguous towards the ambiguity of land ownership. On the one hand, it encourages larger scale and more efficient farming by promoting farming capitalists and by subsidizing specialized farming households. On the other hand, it doesn't seem to want to take the plunge of privatizing land.

The state's ambiguity can be seen by two events that occurred in 2015. On the May 24, 2015, Finance Minister Lou Jiwei, in his public speech at Tsinghua University, declared that unless his suggestions for reform were taken, there was at least a 50 percent possibility that China would fall into what is called "the middle income trap." Lou's suggestion regarding rural China was to reduce agricultural subsidies (SCMP 2015).[4] The other event was on December 12, 2015, when the Finance Ministry headed by the very same Lou Jiwei issued a circular announcing the state's support to promote the experiment of a village-level collective economy. The experiment started in some provinces in 2012 and the Finance Ministry stated that the experiment should be enlarged to include 11 provinces. (Chinese Finance Ministry 2016). The year of 2016, when this book was completed, was still a year of uncertainty and the question about the future of rural China was still hanging in the balance. China, like the rest of the world, is crying out for a grand narrative.

---

4   Lou's suggested recipe is based on not only the logic of economic rationalism and the Western model of development, but also the current status quo of geopolitics and the Western dominance of global politico-economic organizations. The term "middle income trap" itself is a loaded term premised on not only economic rationalism but also the current global structure in which the peripheral South transfers its labor value to the core North (Wen 2013; Lauesen and Cope 2015).

Appendix

Below is the author's transcribed interview with the *Wall Street Journal* in 2016, which has until now remained unpublished. It is published here not only because it refers to *Gao Village* and its surrounding issues, but also because it touches on many of the themes and arguments either overtly or implicitly in the present book. The interview questions were put to the author in Chinese and were kept intact here, with translation. His answers were all in English.

我是《華爾街日報》北京分社的研究員林奕谷。我們的一位專欄作家班安祖（Andrew Browne）先生在寫一篇有關中國產業升級的文章，其中希望能夠探討「新左派」思想和政策在轉型過程中的影響。希望能夠請教您以下問題。

Question (Lin): I am Lin Yigu, a researcher for the *Wall Street Journal*. Our columnist, Mr. Andrew Browne, is writing about industry upgrading in China, and wishes to examine the influence of the New Left on China's policies on its industrial transformation. We would like to interview you regarding the following questions.

Answer (Gao): I notice that these questions are not really directly related to the topic of China's upgrading of manufacturing industries. But I will still answer them.

1）新左派學者怎麼評價當代中國社會？

Question 1): How do the New Left evaluate current Chinese society?

Answer: About the current state of affairs in China, we believe the model of development since Deng's dictate, *fazhan shi ying daoli* ("development is the absolute principle"), is not sustainable for its increasing disparity and for its environmental destruction. This is not a radical position, and the right wing side of the political persuasion would agree with this assessment, and even the Chinese authorities themselves would admit this. The differences lie only in what the solutions are.

We believe corruption is not only consequences but also symptoms of such a development model. The current anti-corruption campaign is popular, but it is only addressing the symptom rather than the root of the problem, and that is why most sectors of Chinese society are still waiting for further development while some sectors have become cynical.

Post-Mao China for many years has had the worst of both worlds: the worst world of one party rule and the worst world of naked capitalism. The root of the problem for this model of development is that it ignores the governing principle that any and all development must be for the improvement of conditions for society as a whole, not for just a few. That is why we think it is morally bankrupt for a government to advocate the philosophy of "let some get rich first."

How to achieve the goal for which governance is to serve the people and not for which governance serves few? Some accountability of the privileged, the capitalist class and the political and intellectual elite is required. One of the measures in doing so is to maintain public and collective ownership of the means of production. Therefore we don't advocate privatization of land. We are also against further privatization of large SOEs, and certainly not privatization of rivers, mountains, roads, banks, telecommunications and national defense. However, the right and so-called liberals would like a total and wholesale privatization of everything. For them all problems derive from collective and public ownership of means of production. They are true Thatcherites and Reaganites who were huge fans of Hayek, or so they were credited to be.

We don't believe private ownership in and by itself can check the abuse of power by the power holders. How do we hold the party officials accountable then?

2）如何解決目前中國社會在改革進程中出現的貧富差異問題以及其他社會問題？

Question 2): How do we solve the problem of disparity between the rich and the poor and other social problems in the process of reform?

Answer: How do we scrutinize state agents, not only the CCP party and government officials but also managers of SOEs? We are genuine liberals in that we want genuine political reform and more liberty in society. We would welcome "universal suffrage" and "public service" earning "workman's wages" by state agents (two principles suggestions by Marx, drawing lessons from the failure of the Paris Commune). This may sound too idealistic, but can be a normative philosophy for political pursuits. Good politics is the art of the seemingly impossible.

We would like to have press freedom and freedom of expression. It has to be remembered that the so-called Four Freedoms (*si da ziyou: da ming, da fang, da bianlun, da zibao*), speaking up and loudly, holding big debates and putting up big posters) were written into the Chinese Constitution in 1975 but abolished in 1980 by the post-Mao leadership. Freedom of expression helps transparency and therefore not only functions as a means to hold those responsible accountable, but also an end in and by itself for being fulfilled human beings.

3）這些解決方法和西方社會中部分政治家提倡的反貿易、反全球化有何區別／相似？

Question 3): What are the differences between these solutions and the anti-trade and anti-globalism suggested by some politicians in the West?

Answer: Given the current systems of the world, solving the issue of disparity and inequality by globalism and trade is a contradiction in terms. Trade, by definition, should be self-willing and mutually beneficial in an ideal world; but no world is ideal. Currently, China and other developing countries can trade only with labor (or primary resources). Because of the existing disparity of living standards, Chinese labor has been and still is cheap. Due to the fact that the Chinese governments, both central and local, and especially local, guided by Deng Xiaoping's "development is the absolute principle," have been willing to overlook labor conditions and environmental responsibilities, and global capitalists have been only too happy to move manufacturing industries and assembly lines to China. It looks like a win-win situation: the migrant workers from rural China earn a living by getting paid a wage; the consumers in the West enjoy unprecedented affordable consumer goods; and the capitalists make huge amounts of profits. But of course global capitalists would like to and did try to maximize their profits by paying as little as possible. If and when the Chinese authorities don't protect the Chinese migrant workers, who have long been treated with contempt by the mainstream Chinese political and intellectual elite, the logical outcome is increasing disparity. Therefore, it is difficult to be concerned about the disparity on the one hand and to support the current global trade arrangements on the other, when the West enjoys hegemony in almost everything.

This is why Western politicians are caught in a dilemma: On the one hand they want to increase exports and decrease imports so as to maintain not only a trade balance but also, and better, a trade surplus. They therefore want to maintain, if not to develop, domestic manufacturing industries, like what the American President Donald Trump claims. And yet at the same time, they want to protect the interest of the capitalists. After all, that is why these societies are called capitalist. How can you stop global capitalists from basing their manufacturing industries in China and other developing countries given the profits that can be made on the basis of this enormous disparity of living standards? Furthermore, when capitalists become global it is hard to tax them, when they can legally, for instance, do transfer pricing, and without increasing taxes it is hard to meet the increasing demand of welfarism in the affluent societies where more and more people are not working or if they do work, are not engaged in manufacturing industries. Hence Western politicians are caught in a triple-sided trap: the unaccountability of the global capitalists, especially in financial capitals, the despair of the working or non-working poor, and the decline of manufacturing capacities. Hence we have a very weird phenomenon: materially, Western societies have never been so abundant, and yet the electorate has never been so discontent.

Mao then, and the so-called New Left now, have never been anti-trade. Mao called for self-reliance not because he was anti-trade but because the first world placed trade, economic, technological and even scientific sanctions against China. I think one thing Marx got wrong, at least according to the slogan in the Communist Manifesto, was that he thought that the working class of the world could unite because they would have nothing to lose but chains. That is really an intellectual fiction. Working classes can be very nationalistic and even racist (witness how the working class and the Trade Unions pushed for the infamous White Australia Policy during the second half of the 19th century). Working classes in the first world enjoy the benefits not only from colonialism but also from the leftover profits of the global trade, and yet they tend to blame the developing countries for their insecurity. Of course, this is largely, or at least partly, a result of the mainstream media brainwashing, or "false consciousness." In fact, only the capitalists are truly international. They are global and far-sighted.

To upgrade China's industrial capacities from those based on cheap labor to those based on value-added technology and innovations requires sustained long-term efforts for developing countries because they have to fight against sanctions, protectionism and bullying. That is why there are so many intellectual and copyright and trade dispute issues. To achieve results, private initiatives should be encouraged and therefore there should be more freedom of ideas. At the same time, the state has to intervene so as to plan, invest and protect its vital interests. I think China is still a third world country, and like all third world countries, China should be more open to trade and change but at the same time be guarded with a policy of self-reliance. This is not just to fight against hegemony but also to develop a more sustainable and environmentally more sophisticated upgrade of China's industries that suit its cultural, historical, and socio-economic conditions. China is a big enough market for any industry to succeed internally and therefore does not necessarily need to reach the international market for success.

By being locally specific and innovative, China not only develops itself but also contributes to mankind universally. China should define and design its own narrative of what happiness is and what is modern and developed. A Chinese woman does not have to carry a Louis Vitton bag to walk the talk. A Chinese man does not have to drive a Porsche to demonstrate his existence. For us to advocate these kinds of ideas is not Chinese nationalism, but arguments for common sense decency of human existence.

4）習主席曾表示要警惕歷史虛無主義並肯定了毛主席在現代史的地位和作用。這一表態是否能夠激勵國內新左派的發展？是否表明了領導層對於民怨的一種回應？

Question 4): Chairman Xi wants to be on guard against historical nihilism and affirms Mao's positive role in contemporary Chinese history. Does this mean encouragement of growth in the New Left? Is that a response to the grievances of the people by the Chinese leadership?

Answer: First of all, I have to point out that Chinese society is now so multifaceted and vested interests are so diversified that whatever Xi pronounces does not necessarily mean a taken-for-granted Chinese official position, even less a policy to be implemented. This is hard for many Westerners to understand because to understand current Chinese society requires not only hard work, like research through reading and speaking Chinese to stay updated on the fast-changing China, but also emptying their brains of a lot of assumptions and presumptions about China, past and present.

We welcome Xi's pronounced long overdue correction of the distortion of the first 30 years of history of the PRC by the post-Mao political and intellectual elite. But that does not necessarily mean any encouragement for the Left, who have been marginalized in China. In Western media, Chinese political censorship and oppression of the Western-connected, Western-orientated or Western-cultivated Chinese dissent is often highlighted. In fact, political censorship and oppression on the Left is even more pervasive. Xi's embarking of the leadership has not changed that.

I will just list two examples that are related to myself. In 2003, the then influential journal *Dushu*, of which Wang Hui, a prominent scholar of the left, was still the chief editor, published a piece by me that introduced my Gao Village book. In that short article I was, in a very indirect way, addressing what is now called "historical nihilism." I tried to summarize one of the points supported with empirical evidence in the book that education and health care in rural China had improved dramatically during the Mao era in general and the Cultural Revolution in particular. That was enough to have offended the Right: the newspaper *Nanfang Zhoumo* immediately organized a panel of the then much-admired *gongzhi* ("public intellectuals") to attack my *Dushu* article.

As another example, let me fast track to 2014, ten years later, when my *Gao Village* book was translated into Chinese, with a plan that the Chinese University of Hong Kong Press would publish a traditional Chinese character version and the mainland publisher Sanlian Shudian would publish a simplified character version, so as to cater for the different markets. But Sanlian Shudian was eventually not allowed to publish the Chinese version of *Gao Village*, even though the book does not say anything about elite politics. Further evidence of censorship is that copies of the book sent from Hong Kong to its translators in the mainland could not reach their destination.

I don't think Xi's pronouncement is a reaction to the expressed grievances of the people. Rather, it shows Xi's genuine conviction. Of the three leaderships after Deng Xiaoping, Jiang Zemin and Zhu Rongji, Hu Jintao and Wen Jiabao and Xi Jinping and Li Keqiang, only the last one is really the Cultural Revolution generation leadership. Though Xi's father is in many ways a victim of the politics of the Mao era, Xi himself does not seem to complain about his experience as an educated youth sent down to a poor village during the Cultural Revolution. From anecdotal evidence (I have not made a study of Xi), his work and life with the poor villagers not only toughened his personal character but also consolidated his belief in the original Maoist CCP mission of serving the people. Though the jury is still out, much of Xi's leadership style and policy content reminds one of Mao: anti-corruption, stress on moral education, the mass line, constraint on bureaucracy, and restriction on official privilege.

5）是否能夠把新左派學者稱為毛派學者？如果不可以的話，為什麼？

Question 5): Can the New Left scholars be called Maoist scholars? If not, why?

Answer: I don't think we can put the small groups of scholars into a category of New Left, though the label has its function of reference. Some of these scholars, without the need to name them, would not even admit themselves as the Left. I would refer to myself as a post-modern libertarian. I genuinely enjoy the tradition of liberty that is credited to the West and therefore would not like to live and work permanently in current China. But I don't believe in a transcendental and reductionist philosophy of truth. There are truths, rights and wrongs, but these are all historical, and have to be contextualized in specific time and space. In that sense I am also a post-modern deconstructionist.

I do believe in the usefulness and realist grounding of class theory but I don't accept the totalitarian and fundamentalist theory of class struggle. I find the violent practice of class struggle that humiliates individual persons and violates personal dignity distasteful and unacceptable, to say the least. I think the Maoist idea and practice of land reform have been basically positive; but violence against individual landlords was not only too cruel but also unnecessary. Once the 1949 Revolution had enough momentum to overthrow the old system of land ownership, the individual landlords should have been spared personal indignity. Therefore, I have sympathy with the "landlord" and "rich peasant" in Gao Village, as expressed in *Gao Village*. On the other hand, I do find many of the ideas, some of which were advocated and some practiced during the Cultural Revolution, are not just Maoist, but actually post-modern, and not only Chinese but also universal. This is something that is very hard to understand not only for the hard core anti-communist Cold Warriors, but also the Eurocentric Humanists of the Enlightenment tradition.

I do believe that Maoist China needed reform, just as post-Mao China needs reform. Some of the post-Mao reforms are good, such as stopping labeling of some rural Chinese as belonging to the landlord or the rich peasant class, or urban Chinese Rightists for that matter, who are more open to Western (and should also be non-Western) ideas and technology, more personal liberty and less bureaucratic control of movement. I especially welcome the abolition of all agricultural taxes, for the first time in 2,500 years of China's history.

When we want, as we have been trying to do, to deconstruct the manufactured truths of the history of the Mao era, we are not calling for the return to the era of Mao, whatever that means. We are trying to argue that there is no such thing as an economic miracle in the post-Mao period. The fact that the Chinese economy took off dramatically in the past three decades or so is a result of the hard work, resourcefulness and resilience of the Chinese people, especially the Chinese rural people, as I have described in this second book on Gao Village. More important to be pointed out by us is that the Chinese economy has developed along the path laid down by the Mao era, when the industrial, educated and healthy migrant working population and infrastructure bases were developed.

One controversial area about the Mao era concerns the Great Leap Forward, especially the number of those who died from famine. We, the so-called New Left, are not directly involved in this controversy but are keen observers of the debates because it is relevant to the Maoist legacy and socialist China. In the West and among the right wing circles in China, Yang Jisheng, Frank Dikotter and Jung Chang are taken as experts who estimated that the famine death toll is something like 40 to 50 million.

As we know, anyone can claim to be an expert on something so long as one does some research on the topic. What matters are three points. The first point is whether the research methodology is rigorous and whether it can stand up to critical examination. The second point is whether the results can get published. The third point is whether the published work is taken seriously. The three may be related but are not necessarily so. Not everyone can get published. Not every publication is taken seriously. When something published is about human society, which is different from physical and chemical sciences or astronomy, the results have to be treated with extreme skepticism. Research results on human society cannot always be proved or disproved by repeated lab experiments. Furthermore, matters about human society involve political positions and ideology. For example, Yang, Dikotter and Chang have been repudiated by serious scholars not only for their dubious methodology but also for their deliberate distortion of evidence documented, for instance, in *Constructing China: Clashing Views of the People's Republic* (Gao 2018). However, Yang and Dikotter are taken seriously and are widely accepted in the West because their work fits the unchallenged assumptions about Mao, fits the political position of anti-communism and liberal capitalist triumph and the geopolitical agenda of the China threat anxiety.

6）您怎麼看大眾對於新左派思想和政策的？

Question 6): How do you see the attitudes of the masses towards the ideas and policies of the New Left?

Answer: Two points about this question itself seems warranted. First, we need to define what *dazhong* (masses) is. Does it mean the lower classes of people like the workers and farmers? Or does it mean the political, intellectual and increasingly the business elite? The latter category of people have the resources to make their voices heard and there are a lot of them. Secondly, the New Left has never been in a position to articulate policies. They are marginalized and they are not sought for advice. It is hard to know what the masses think of the New Left, as no study has been conducted, though I have collected some evidence in *The Battle for China's Past: Mao and the Cultural Revolution* (Gao 2008). For most of human history so far the masses have no history, because they are not articulate enough and do not have the resources to write history. The post-Mao political and intellectual elite keep on telling us that the

Cultural Revolution was a ten-year disaster for the Chinese people. It is hard to think of any grounds to justify their assumption that they can always speak on behalf of the Chinese people.

Recently however, the development of technology does provide some opening for the lower classes of people to express themselves. If you look at Chinese social media, you will see that the masses are actually more sophisticated than the highly educated historians and scholars, in that the former could see the connection between the era of Mao and the post-Mao economic development. They could see both the positive and negative sides of both the Mao period and the era of post-Mao. It is reported in social media, though I have not seen it reported in the Chinese official media, nor the free Western media as far as I know, that when a Deng Xiaoping website was set up, the condemnation and negative comments of Deng were so great that the Chinese authorities had to close it down.

Glossary

baitang	拜堂	a traditional marriage ceremony in which the couple kowtow first to Heaven and Earth, then to the ancestry, and finally to the grand-parents and parents
baogong tou	包工頭	subcontractor
baohu jia	保護價	a state guaranteed floor price of grains in the market so as to subsidize food production
buxing jie	步行街	a street where no motor traffic is allowed, or sometimes called a Walking Street
chengguan	城管	"city management" literally, administration and police management of urban residents normally outside the duty of the police
chujia	出嫁	a female getting married into the male's family
citang	祠堂	ancestral hall, clan hall, or ancestral temple
cun	村	usually a clan village, in this book Gao Village is *Gaojia cun*, the Gao Family Village
danwei	單位	a unit of administrative institution with budgetary responsibilities, like salaries and welfare. A school or a hospital or a factory is a *danwei*. In the era of Mao many *danwei* had their own nurseries, schools, hospitals, and even houses for the staff members. Some of these *danwei* still exist in China, especially state owned enterprises
dibao	低保	government cash support of a family that has a below locally specific-defined poverty line
fanshen	翻身	meaning "turn over a new leaf in life"
hongbao	紅包	cash in a red envelope given to friends and relatives as a gift

huaqiao	華僑	a general term for overseas Chinese
hukou	戶口	household registration system established since the mid-1950s by which movements are restricted so as to control the allocation of resources and consumer good rations
jiaoche	轎車	sedan car
jiaxiang qing	家鄉情	a sense of affiliation with someone from the same hometown
laoban	老闆	boss
liang	兩	Chinese weight unit, one *liang* is about 50 gram
liushou ertong	留守兒童	left-behind children, referring to the children of young rural migrant workers who could not bring their children to the city they work; these children have to stay at their hometown villages on their own
liuzhuan	流轉	trading of land use rights
meiche dian	美車店	garage
mianzi	面子	literally "face," in usages such as "to lose face"
nongmin	農民	usually translated as "peasants," but a more neutral term would be a "farming person"
RMB	人民幣	unit of Chinese currency
shangfang	上訪	to appeal to upper authorities for injustice suffered at hands of local authorities, and those who do this, usually rural residents, are called *fangmin* (appealing person). The phenomenon was widely spread during the 1990s
shanglou	上樓	referring to the campaign to uproot rural residents from their traditional dwellings to storeyed houses so as to have modern facilities such as running water and toilet but at the same time to make more land for commercialization
tianjing	天井	an opening in the middle of the house to obtain light in traditional houses in the Gao Village area
tongxiang ren	同鄉人	a person from the same hometown
xiahai	下海	to leave a secure job to find better opportunities in the market
zao	灶	traditional cooker made of mud and bricks in which heat is created by burning wood
zongpu	宗譜	lineage or clan records of a lineage village
xiang	鄉	township
yiqi	義氣	brotherhood loyalty

zhaozhui	招贅	a marriage practice by which a man marries into the female's family. This happens usually for three reasons: the male's family is too poor to get married, or the male family has more than one male offspring, or the female is very attractive either in terms of looks or wealth. Usually the female family wants to get a man in the family to continue the family line, for instance, if the family does not have a male offspring.

Bibliography

Baidudbaike. "Panyu qu" [Panyu Region]. https://baike.baidu.com/item/%E7
%95%AA%E7%A6%BA%E5%8C%BA/246947?fromtitle=%E7%95%AA%E
7%A6%BA&fromid=1406230&fr=aladdin, accessed 2nd May 2018.

Bakken, Borge. 2000. *The Exemplary Society: Human Improvement, Social Control, and the Dangers of Modernity in China.* Oxford: Clarendon Press.

Beckett, Lois. 2012. "By the Numbers: Life and Death at Foxconn." *ProPublica*, January 27, 2012. http://www.propublica.org/article/by-the-numbers-life-and-death-at-foxconn, accessed on 13th May 2015.

Blumenthal, David, and William Hsiao. 2015. "Lessons from the East: China's Rapidly Evolving Health Care System." *New England Journal of Medicine* 372, no. 14 (April 2, 2015): 1281–1285.

Bo Yang. 1986. *Chouloude Zhongguo ren* [The Ugly Chinese]. Changsha: Hunan wenyi chubanshe.

Branigan, Tania. 2010. "Chinese Workers Link Sickness to N-hexane and Apple iPhone Screens." *The Guardian*, May 7, 2010.

Cai Yongshun. 2015. *State and Agents in China: Disciplining Government Officials.* Stanford: Stanford University Press.

Chan, Anita. 2001. *China's Workers Under Assault: The Exploitation of Labor in a Globalizing Economy.* Armonk and London: M.E. Sharpe.

Chan, Anita. 2002. "Culture of Survival: Lives of Migrant Workers through the Prism of Private Letters." In *Popular China*, edited by Perry Link, Richard Madsen and Paul Pickowicz, 163–188. Boulder: Rowman and Littlefield.

Chan, Anita. n.d. "Exploitation of Migrant Workers in China's Export Manufacturing Sector." *The Magazine of the LERA: Online Companion.* https://web.archive.org/web/20120430032907/http://www.lera.uiuc.edu:80/Pubs/Perspectives/onlinecompanion/fall04-chan.html, accessed on 15th May, 2015.

Chan, Jenny, and Pun Ngai. 2010. "Suicide as Protest for the New Generation of Chinese Migrant Workers: Foxconn, Global Capital, and the State." *The Asia-Pacific Journal* 8, no. 37, September 13, 2010. https://apjjf.org/-Jenny-Chan/3408/article.html.

Chang, Gordon G. 2001. *The Coming Collapse of China*. New York: Random House.

Chang, Leslie T. 2008. *Factory Girls: From Village to City in a Changing China*. New York: Spiegel and Grau.

Chayanov, A. V. 1986. *The Theory of Peasant Economy*. Edited by Daniel Thorner, Basiel Kerblay, and R. E. F. Smith. Manchester: Manchester University Press.

Chen Jia. 2010. "Country's Wealth Divide Past Warning Level." *China Daily*, May 12, 2010.

Chen Jian. 2015. *Zhongguo shengyu geming jishi 1978–1991* [Documentation of China's fertility revolution]. Beijing: shehui kexue wenxian chubanshe.

Chen Jiandong, Fang Fuqian, Hou Wenxuan, et al. 2015. "Chinese Gini Coefficient from 2005 to 2012, Based on 20 Grouped Income Data Sets of Urban and Rural Residents." *Journal of Applied Mathematics* 2015: 939020. https://dx.doi.org/10.1155/2015/939020.

Chen Jing. 2013. "Jinru yu tuichu: 'Ziben xiaxiang' weihe taoli zhongzhi huanjie — Jiyu wanbei huang cun de kaocha" [Enter or withdraw: Why isn't capital in rural China used for growing crops — Research based on the north of Anhui]. *Huazhong nongye daxue xuebao*, August 2, 2013.

Chen Qingqing. 2015. "China May Hit Middle-Income Trap: Minister." *Global Times*, April 26, 2015.

Chen Xiwen. 2013. "Nongcun tudi zhidu gaige, san tiao dixian buneng tupo" [Rural land reform, three bottom lines that must not be crossed]. *Renmin ribao*, June 9, 2013.

Chen, Xiwen. 2015. "Zhongguo nongye fazhan xingshi ji mianlin de tiaozhan" [The current state of China's agricultural development and its challenges]. Speech given at the Second Yuan Longping Forum, http://www.zgxcfx.com/Article/78082.html, accessed 4th May 2018.

Chen Yiming. 2011. "Renqiong zhi buduan" [Poor in money but not in will]. *Nanfang zhoumo*, July 28, 2011: E21–22.

Cheng Biancun. 2011. "Nongmingong jiuye zhuangkuang: Pubian quefa anquan gan" [Employment conditions of migrant workers: A widespread lack of security]. *Wuyou zhixiang Utopia*, April 7, 2011. Available at https://web.archive.org/web/20110412005821/http://www.wyzxsx.com:80/Article/Class4/201104/225758.html.

China Labour Bulletin. 2011. "Pepsi's Offer Fails to Satisfy Angry Workers." December 6, 2011. http://www.clb.org.hk/content/pepsi%E2%80%99s-offer-fails-satisfy-angry-workers-1.

China Youth Daily. 2013. "Hui bu qu de jia: Zhongguo guoqu 10 nian jin baiwan ge ziran cun xiaoshi" [A home that you cannot go back to: Nearly a million natural villages have disappeared in the past decade]. January 8, 2013.

Chinese Finance Ministry. 2016, "guanyu yinfa *fuchi cunji jiti jingjifazhan shidian de zhidao yijian* de tongzhi" [On printing *Guidance opinion on supporting collective economic development point on village level*]. http://www.prcfe.com/web/2016/01-02/87520.html accessed on the 10th January 2016.

Clem, Will. 2011. "Shanghai Strike Enters 7th Day." *South China Morning Post*, December 6, 2011.

Clifford, Geertz. 1968. *Islam Observed: Religious Development in Morocco and Indonesia*. New Haven and London: Yale University Press.

Clifford, Geertz. 1973. *The Interpretation of Cultures: Selected Essays*. New York: Basic Books.

Creaders.net, "Hongse tongqiling erhao taofan huiguo: zongshi mengjian beizhua" [Number two on Red Notice returned to China: Always dreamt of getting caught]. http://news.creaders.net/china/2015/05/09/big5/1527492.html, accessed 2nd May 2018.

Crook, Isabel. n.d. "Land Reform 1947 十里店 ." http://www.isabelcrook.com/pursuits/10mileinn/, accessed December 8, 2016.

Davies, Gloria. 1991. "The Problematic Modernity of Ah Q." *Chinese Literature: Essays, Articles, Reviews (CLEAR)* 13 (December 1991): 57–76.

Ding Jun, Li Xiaoxia, Xie Yiguan, et al. 2016. "Xinxing chengzhenhua zhiwen: weihe nongmin gong shiminhua yiyuan bu gao?" [A question on new urbanization: Why are migrant workers not keen on becoming urban residents?], 21 shiji jingji baodao, 23 November, http://nb.house.sina.com.cn/news/2016-11-23/07516206977170234206503.shtml?wt_source=news_dbxw_xx02, accessed 2nd May 2018.

Dreyfuss, Robert. 2010. "China in the Driver's Seat." *The Nation*, September 22, 2010.

Du Runsheng. 2005. *Du Runsheng zishu: Zhongguo nongcun tizhi biange zhongda juece jishi* [Told by Du Runsheng himself: A record of truth of important policy decisions in China's rural reform]. Beijing: Renmin chuban she.

Dyer, Geoff, David Pilling, and Henry Sender. 2011. "A Strategy to Straddle the Planet." *Financial Times*, January 17, 2011.

Easterlin, Richard A., Robson Morgan, Malgorzata Switek, et al. 2012. "China's Life Satisfaction, 1990–2010." *PNAS* 109, no. 25 (June 2012): 9775–9780.

The Economist. 2011a. "Beware the Middle-Income Trap." June 25, 2011.

The Economist. 2011b. "Getting On." June 25, 2011.

The Economist. 2014. "Poverty Elucidation Day." October 20, 2014.

Evans-Pritchard, Ambrose. 2011. "Age-Old Problem Threatens Eastern Rising." *Sydney Morning Herald*, March 5, 2011.

Fauna, 2011, January 6, "Female Chinese Soldiers Traveling with Louis Vuitton Bags." ChinaSMACK, https://www.chinasmack.com/female-chinese-soldiers-traveling-with-louis-vuitton-bags, accessed 2nd May 2018.

Feng Wang, Cai Yong, and Gu Baochang. 2012. "Population, Policy, and Politics: How Will History Judge China's One-Child Policy?" *Population and Development Review* 38 (February 2012): 115–129.

Foster, Paul B. 2006. Ah Q Archaeology: Lu Xun, *Ah Q, Ah Q Progeny, and the National Character Discourse in Twentieth Century China*. Lanham: Lexington Books.

Fukuyama, Francis. 2014. *Political Order and Political Decay: From the Industrial Revolution to the Globalization of Democracy*. London: Profile Books.

Gadamer, H.-G. 1976. *Philosophical Hermeneutics*. Berkeley: University of California.

Gan Yang, ed. 2007. *Wenhua: zhongguo yu shijie xinlun—tong san tong* [Culture: A new comment on China and the world—A unification of three traditions]. Beijing: Sanlian chubanshe.

Gao, Mobo. 1994. "Migrant Workers from Rural China: Their Conditions and Some Social Implications for Economic Development in South China." In *Entrepreneurship, Economic Growth and Social Change: The Transformation of Southern China*, edited by David Schak, 21–38. Brisbane: Centre for the Study of Australia-Asia Relations.

Gao, Mobo. 1997. "Welfare Problems and Needs for Migrant Workers in South China." In *Social Welfare Development in China: Constraints and Challenges*, edited by Wing Lo and Joseph Cheng, 101–120. Chicago: Imprint Publications.

Gao, Mobo. 1998. "Rural Situation in Post-Mao China and the Conditions of Migrant Workers: The Case of Gao Village." *Bulletin of Concerned Asian Scholars* 30, no. 4 (October-December 1998): 70–76.

Gao, Mobo. 1999. *Gao Village: Rural Life in Modern China*. London: C. Hurst and Co.; Honolulu: University of Hawaii Press; Hong Kong: Hong Kong University Press; Bathurst: Crawford House Publishing. Reprint, Honolulu: University of Hawaii Press, 2007.

Gao, Mobo. 2000. *Mandarin: An Introduction*. Melbourne: Oxford University Press. Reprint, 2007.

Gao, Mobo. 2008a. *The Battle for China's Past: Mao and the Cultural Revolution*. London: Pluto.

Gao, Mobo. 2008b. "Chinese, what Chinese: The Politics of Authenticity and Ethnic Identity." In *National Boundaries and Cultural Configurations*, edited by Lee Guan Kin, 257–287. Singapore: Centre for Chinese Language and Culture, Global Publishing, and Nanyang University of Technology.

Gao, Mobo. 2012. "The Transitional Role of the Hu-Wen Leadership in China: A Case Study of Liu Xiaobo." In *China: A New Stage of Development for an Emerging Superpower*, edited by Joseph Cheng, 175–192. Hong Kong: City University of Hong Kong Press.

Gao, Mobo. 2014. *Gaojia cun: Gonghueguo nongcun shenghuo sumiao [Gao Village: Rural Life in Modern China]*. Translated by Zhang Shaoquan et al. Hong Kong: The Chinese University Press.

Gao, Mobo. 2017a. "Vital Factors for Chinese Rural Development: The Reach of the State and Lineage Identity in Villages." *Journal of the Asia-Pacific Economy* 22, no. 4 (2017): 547–559.

Gao, Mobo. 2017b. "Whither Rural China? A Case Study of Gao Village." *The China Quarterly* 229 (March 2017): 23–43.

Gao, Mobo. 2017c. "Sojourners or Settlers: A Critique of the Cultural Perspective on 19th Century Chinese Migrants to the British Colonies." *Asian Studies Review*. Vol 41, No 3, pp 389-404.

Garnaut, John. 2011. "China Investors Need Nerves of Steel." *Sydney Morning Herald*, May 28, 2011.

Gittins, Ross. 2011. "East Moves West—And It's Not Just a Miner Miracle." *Sydney Morning Herald*, May 28, 2011.

Gracie, Carrie. 2015. "The Village and the Girl." *BBC News*, July 2, 2015. http://www.bbc.co.uk/news/resources/idt-dd0e6fd5-12fc-4a4a-a0eb-4ef064900f92.

Gu Hongming (Ku Hung-Ming). 1915. *The Spirit of Chinese People: With an Essay on "The War and the Way Out."* Peking: The Peking Daily News.

Guo Hengpeng, and Huang Hui. 2011. "Poyang jin yi caizheng zijin bei zhuan zou: Caizhengju wei an guiding jizhong guanli zhuanhu zijin" [Nearly one hundred million dollars of an economic project fraudulently transferred in Poyang: Finance bureau failed to manage special funds]. http://china.huanqiu.com/roll/2011-02/1511716.html, accessed 4th May 2018.

Guo Yingjie, and Sun Wanning. 2012. *Unequal China: The Political Economy and Cultural Politics of Inequality*. London: Routledge.

Han Chunping. 2012. "Satisfaction with the Standard of Living in Reform-Era China." *The China Quarterly* 212 (December 2012): 919–940.

Han Shurong. 2014. "Migrant Workers' Old-Age Insurance Policies in China: Beyond an Economic Development Perspective." PhD thesis, University of Adelaide. http://hdl.handle.net/2440/92607.

Hart-Landsberg, Martin. 2011. "The Chinese Reform Experience: A Critical Assessment." *Review of Radical Political Economics* 43, no. 1 (March 2011): 56–76.

Hartcher, Peter. 2011. "Battle of Pacific Rim Reshapes the World." *Sydney Morning Herald*, March 15, 2011.

Hayek, Friedrich. 1944. *The Road to Serfdom*. Chicago: University of Chicago Press.

He Baogang, and Lang Youxing. 2002. *xunzhao minzhu yu quanwei zhijian de pingheng: Zhejiang cunmin xuanju zhi jingyan yanjiu* [Balancing democracy and authority: An empirical study of village elections in Zhejiang]. Wuhan: Central China Normal University Press.

He Baogang. 2007. *Rural Democracy in China: The Role of Village Elections*. New York: Palgrave Macmillan.

He Dan, Su Jiangyuan, and Jin Huiyu. 2011. "China Takes a Tough Line on Poverty." *China Daily*, November 30, 2011.

He Xuefeng. 2010. *Diquan de luoji: Zhongguo nongcun tudi zhidu xiang hechu qu* [The logic of land ownership: Whither China's rural land system?]. Beijing: Zhongguo zhengfa daxue chubanshe.

He Xuefeng. 2013. "Guanyu zhongguo shi xiaonong jingji de jidian renshi." [Several points on China's "household economy"]. *Nanjing nongye daxue xuebao* (social sciences edition), no. 6 (November 2013).

He Xuefeng. 2014. *Chengshihua de zhongguo daolu* [China's road to urbanization]. Beijing: Dongfang chubanshe.

He Xuefeng, and Yi Zi. 2015. "Xiaonong jingji yu nongye xiandaihua de lujing xuanze: Jian ping nongye xiandaihua de jijin zhuyi" [Small household agriculture and the choice of approaches to rural modernization: A further commentary on radicalism in rural modernization]. Originally *Wuyou zhixiang Utopia*, April 28, 2015. Accessible at the website https://web.archive.org/web/20160829161100/http://www.wyzxwk.com/Article/sannong/2015/04/343022.html, or https://wenku.baidu.com/view/ac18ea01b5daa58da0116c175f0e7cd184251838.html, accessed 4th May 2018.

Heilmann, Sebastian, and Elizabeth J. Perry, eds. 2011. *Mao's Invisible Hand: The Political Foundations of Adaptive Governance in China*. Cambridge: Harvard University Press.

Hinton, William. 1966. *Fanshen: A Documentary of Revolution in a Chinese Village*. New York: Monthly Review Press.

Hinton, William. 1990. *The Great Reversal: The Privatization of China, 1978–1989*. New York: Monthly Review Press.

Huang, Philip C. C. 2010a. "Zhongguo de xinshidai xiao nongchang jiqi zongxiang yitihua: Longtou qiye haishi hezuo zuzhi" [China's small farms of the new era and vertical integration: Leading enterprises or cooperative groups?]. In *Zhongguo xiangcun yanjiu*, edited by Philip C. C. Huang, 11–30. Fuzhou: Fujian jiaoyu chubanshe.

Huang, Philip C. C. 2010b. "Zhongguo fazhan jingyan de lilun yu shiyong hanyi: Feizhenggui jingji shijian" [Theoretical and practical implications of China's development experience: Irregular economic practices]. *Kaifang shidai* 10 (2010): 134–158.

Huang, Philip C. C. 2014a. *Ming Qing yilai de xiangcun shehui jingji bianqian: Lishi, lilun yu xianshi (di san juan): Chaoyue zuoyou: Cong shijian lishi tanxun Zhongguo nongcun fazhan chulu* [Socio-economic changes in the countryside since the Ming and Qing: History, theory, and reality (Vol. 3): Transcending left and right: Finding a path for China's rural development by exploring past practices]. Beijing: Falü chubanshe.

Huang, Philip C. C. 2014b. " 'Jiating nongchang' shi Zhongguo nongye de fazhan chulu ma" [Is the "family farm" the way forward for the development of Chinese agriculture?]. *Kaifang shidai* 2 (2014): 76–194.

Huang, Philip C. C. 2014c. *Ming qing yilai de xiangcun shehui jingji bianqian: Lishi, lilun yu xianshi (di yi juan): Huabei de xiao nong jingji yu shehui bianqian* [Socio-economic changes in the countryside since the Ming and Qing: History, theory, and reality (Vol. 1): Economic and social changes in northern China's small farms]. Beijing: Falü chubanshe.

Huang, Philip C. C. 2015. "Nongye hezuohua lujing xuanze de liang da mangdian: Dongya nongye hezuohua lishi jingyan de qishi" [Two big blind spots on the road to rural cooperatization: Revelations from East Asia's historical experience of rural cooperatization]. https://wenku.baidu.com/view/2dc4e528 bb1aa8114431b90d6c85ec3a87c28b67.html, accessed 4th May 2018.

Iser, W. 1987. *The Act of Reading: A Theory of Aesthetic Responses.* London and New York: Routledge and Kegan Paul.

Jiang Gaoming. 2016. "Zhongguo ren jun mei nian 'chi' huafei 40 jin" [Chinese people "eat" 20 kilograms of chemical fertilizer a year per person]. *Renmin shiwu zhuquan* [Food sovereignty of the people] , October 7, 2016. https://web.archive.org/web/20170114095418/http://shiwuzq.com/food/ knowledge/guard/20161007/3562.html, accessed 5th May 2018.

Jiangxi ribao. 2015. "Guoji xingjing zuzhi fabu 'hongse tongji ling,' Poyang yi wai tao renyuan zai lie tanwu 9400 wanyuan waitao Xinjiapo" [International police issues "red alert" of the wanted list: A runaway person hiding in Singapore is included for a corruption charge of 94 million RMB]. April 23, 2015.

Johnson, Ian. 2015. "An American Hero in China." *The New York Review of Books*, May 7, 2015.

Koopman, Robert, Wang Zhi, and Wei Shang-Jin. 2008. "How Much of Chinese Exports is Really Made in China? Assessing Domestic Value-Added When Processing Trade is Pervasive." Working Paper No. 14109, National Bureau of Economic Research, Cambridge, June 2008. http://www. nber.org/papers/w14109.

Krishnan, Ananth. 2011. "China's Rural Poverty Falls but Inequality Rises, Says White Paper." *The Hindu*, November 20, 2011.

Lauesen, Torkil, and Zak Cope. 2015. "Imperialism and the Transfer of Value in Prices." *Monthly Review* 67, No. 3 (July 2015).

Li Changping. 2011. "Liangshi anquan yu nongye zhidu" [Food security and the agricultural system]. *Li Changping Boke* (blog), March 14, 2011. http://www.caogen.com/blog/Infor_detail/25729.html.

Li Changping. 2013a. "Zhongguo tudi zhidu xiang hechu qu" [Whither China's rural land system]. *Li Changping Boke* (blog), September 20, 2013. http://www.caogen.com/blog/infor_detail.aspx?id=38&articleId=53033.

Li Changping. 2013b. "Diquan gaige de zhidu luoji" [The institutional logic of rural land ownership reform]. *Li Changping Boke* (blog), December 5, 2013. http://www.caogen.com/blog/infor_detail.aspx?id=38&articleId=55397.

Li Ling. 2011. *Jiankang qiangguo: Li Ling hua yigai* [A healthier, stronger country: Li Ling on medical reform]. Beijing: Beijing daxue chubanshe.

Li Mingqi. 2011. "The Rise of the Working Class and the Future of the Chinese Revolution." *Monthly Review* 63, no. 2 (June 2011).

Li Yongfeng, and Zhang Jieping. 2011. "Zhongguo xinyidai mingong" [The new generation of migrant workers in China]. *Wenhua zongheng*, January 26, 2011. http://www.21bcr.com/a/shiye/guancha/2011/0126/2284.html.

Liang Shuming. 1949. *Zhongguo wenhua yaoyi* [Outline of Chinese culture]. Shanghai: Shanghai renmin chubanshe.

Liang Shuming. 2014. *Liang Shuming riji* [The Diary of Liang Shuming]. Shanghai: Shanghai renmin chubanshe.

Liang Zhongtang. 2012. "Ma yingchu shijian shimo" [The ins and outs of the Ma Yingchu Incident]. *Gongshiwang*, May 30, 2012. https://web.archive.org/web/20160519113021/http://www.21ccom.net/articles/lsjd/lsjj/article_2012053060762.html, accessed 4th May 2018.

Lin Chun. 2015. "Xiaonong jingji pai yu jieji fenxi pai de fenqi ji gong shi: 'Zhongguo nongye de fazhan daolu' zhuanti pinglun" [The disagreements and consensus of the small rural economy school of thought and the class analysis school: A commentary on the special subject of "China's agricultural development path"]. Online version: http://www.360doc.com/content/15/1004/07/6847150_503148661.shtml, accessed 4th May 2018.

Lin Yutang. 1935. *My Country and My People*. New York: Reynal and Hitchcock.

Linden, Greg, Kenneth L. Kraemer, and Jason Dedrick. 2007. "Who Captures Value in a Global Innovation System? The Case of Apple's iPod." Working paper, The Paul Merage School of Business, University of California Irvine.

Little, Daniel. 1989. *Understanding Peasant China: Case Studies in the Philosophy of Social Science*. New Haven: Yale University Press.

Litzinger, Ralph. 2013. "The Labor Question in China: Apple and Beyond." *South Atlantic Quarterly* 112, no. 1 (Winter 2013): 172–178.

Liu et al., eds., 1989. Boyang Xianzhi (Boyang County Gazette). Nanchang: Jiangxi renmin chubanshe.

Liu Feng. 2008. "Pingan baoxian dongshi zhang Ma Mingzhe nian xin weihe 6600 wan" [Why does the board director of Pingan Insurance, Ma Mingzhe, have a salary of 66 million?] *Zhongguo baoxian wang*, March 24, 2008. http://www.china-insurance.com/news/newslist.asp?id=110940.

Liu Sha. 2012. "Sexual Abuse of Children 'Left Behind' by Migrant Worker Parents on Rise." *Global Times*, June 19, 2012. http://www.globaltimes.cn/content/715754.shtml, accessed 2nd May 2018.

Liu Shaoqi. 2004. *Liu Shaoqi xuanji [Selected Works of Liu Shaoqi] Vol. II.* Beijing: Renmin chubanshe.

Lu Jie. 2015. *Varieties of Governance in China: Migration and Institutional Change in Chinese Villages.* New York: Oxford University Press.

Lu Xinyu. 2013. *Xiangcun yu geming (Zhongguo xin ziyouzhuyi pipan sanshu)* [Countryside and revolution (A three-volume critique of China's new liberalization)]. Shanghai: Huadong shifan daxue chubanshe.

Lu Xun. 1921. *Ah Q Zhengzhuan [The True Story of Ah Q].* It was first published as a serial between December 4, 1921 and February 12, 1922 in *Chenbao* [The morning post]. Online version in English: https://www.marxists.org/archive/lu-xun/1921/12/ah-q/index.htm, accessed 4th May 2018.

Mao Zedong. 1939. "The Chinese revolution and the Communist Party of China" . In *Selected Works of Mao Tse-tung Vol. II.* Peking: Foreign Languages Press.

Marks, Robert. 1984. *Rural Revolution in South China: Peasants and the Making of History in Haifeng County, 1570–1930.* Madison: University of Wisconsin Press.

Meisner, Maurice. 1999. *Mao's China and After: A History of the People's Republic.* New York, NY: Free Press.

Moore, Malcolm. 2013. "The Great China Corruption Fire Sale." *The Sydney Morning Herald*, January 22, 2013.

Murphy, Rachael. 2002. *How Migrant Labor Is Changing Rural China.* Cambridge: Cambridge University Press.

Naquin, Susan. 1976. *Millenarian Rebellion in China: The Eight Trigrams Uprising of 1813.* New Haven and London: Yale University Press.

Naughton, Barry. 1988. "The Third Front: Defence Industrialization in the Chinese Interior." *The China Quarterly* 115 (September 1988): 351–386.

O'Brien, Kevin, and Li Lianjiang. 1999. "Selective Policy Implementation in Rural China." *Comparative Politics* 31, no. 2 (January 1999): 154–157.

OECD. 2009. OECD Rural Policy Reviews *OECD Rural Policy Reviews: China 2009*. https://www.oecd.org/gov/oecdruralpolicyreviewchina.htm, accessed on 3rd May 2-18.

Oi, Jean C., and Scott Rozelle. 2000. "Elections and Power: The Locus of Decision-Making in Chinese Villages." *The China Quarterly* 162 (June 2000): 513–539.

Pepper, Suzanne. 2000. *Radicalism and Education Reform in 20th-Century China: The Search for an Ideal Development Model.* Cambridge and New York: Cambridge University Press.

Perry, Elizabeth. 1980. *Rebels and Revolutionaries in North China, 1845–1945.* Stanford: Stanford University Press.

Petty, Adrienne, 2009. *Deconstructing the Chinese Sojourner: Case Studies of Early Chinese Migrants to Tasmania*, The University of Tasmania PhD thesis.

Piketty, Thomas, Li Yang, and Gabriel Zucman. 2017. "Capital Accumulation, Private Property and Rising Inequality in China, 1978–2015." Working Paper 23368, National Bureau of Economic Research, Cambridge, April 2017. http://papers.nber.org/tmp/27759-w23368.pdf.

Poznanski, Kazimierz. 2017. "Chinese Economics as a Form of Ethics." *Real-World Economics Review* 80 (June 26, 2017): 148–170.

Pun Ngai. 2005. *Made in China: Women Factory Workers in a Global Workplace.* Durham and Hong Kong: Duke University Press and Hong Kong University Press.

Pun Ngai, and Jenny Chan. 2012. "Global Capital, the State and Chinese Workers: The Foxconn Experience." *Modern China* 38, no. 4 (July 1, 2012): 383–410.

Qian Changming. 2008. "Shui shi xin zhongguo 'jihua shengyu' chuangshire" [Who is the initiator of new China's "family planning"?]. In *Lishi xingkong tanmi: zhongguo lishi 40 ge huati pingshuo* [Secrets of the galaxy of history: On the 40 topics of Chinese history], pp. 359–363. Shanghai: Shanghai renmin chubanshe.

Rittenberg, Sydney, and Amanda Bennett. 2001. *The Man Who Stayed Behind.* Durham: Duke University Press.

Sacom. 2010. "Disney, Walmart and ICTI Together Make Workers Rights Violations Normal and Sustainable." Report, October 22, 2010. http://sacom.hk/report-disney-walmart-and-icti-together-make-workers-rights-violations-normal-and-sustainable/, accessed 4th May 2018.

Sacom 2011. "Making Toys without Joy: ICTI CARE Covers Labour Rights Violations for Global Toy Brands like Disney, Walmart & Mattel." December 5, 2011.

https://www.scribd.com/document/74886533/2011-12-05-Making-Toys-Without-Joy, accessed 4th may 2018.

Saich, Anthony. 2007. "Citizens' Perceptions of Governance in Rural and Urban China." *Journal of Chinese Political Science*, 12, no. 1 (April 2007): 1–28.

Saunders, Manu. 2015. "Single-Crop Farming Is Leaving Wildlife with No Room to Turn." *The Conversation*, May 13, 2015. https://theconversation.com/single-crop-farming-is-leaving-wildlife-with-no-room-to-turn-38991.

Sautman, Barry. 2001. "Is Tibet China's Colony: The Claim of Demographic Catastrophe." *Columbia Journal of Asian Law* 15, no.1 (Fall 2001): 81–131.

SCMP (South China Morning Post). 2011. "40 children rescued from Shenzhen plant" . March 2011, http://www.scmp.com/article/742027/40-children-rescued-shenzhen-plant, accessed 3rd May 2018.

SCMP. 2015. "Top China official's criticism of labour policy sparks controversy" . 3rd May. http://www.scmp.com/news/china/policies-politics/article/1784530/top-china-officials-criticism-labour-policy-sparks, accessed 3rd May 2018.

Shambaugh, David. 2015. "The Coming Chinese Crackup." *The Wall Street Journal*, March 6, 2015.

Skinner, William, ed. 1977. *The City in Late Imperial China*. Stanford: Stanford University Press.

Smith, Arthur. 1894. *Chinese Characteristics*. Norwalk: EastBridge. Reprinted 2003.

Solinger, Dorothy. 1999. *Contesting Citizenship in Urban China: Peasant Migrants, the State, and the Logic of the Market*. Berkeley: University of California Press.

Solinger, Dorothy. 2015. "China's New Urban Poverty." *China Policy Institute: Analysis* (blog), April 17, 2015. https://cpianalysis.org/2015/04/17/chinas-new-urban-poverty/.

Sun Xin, Travis J. Warner, Dali L. Yang, et al. 2013. "Patterns of Authority and Governance in Rural China: Who's in Charge? Why?" *Journal of Contemporary China* 22, no. 83 (May 15, 2013): 733–754.

Teets, Jessica C., and William Hurst, eds. 2014. *Local Governance Innovation in China: Experimentation, Diffusion, and Defiance*. London: Routledge.

Thibault, Harold. 2012. "China's Largest Freshwater Lake Dries Up." *The Guardian*, January 31, 2012.

Tsai, Lily Lee. 2002. "Cadres, Temple and Lineage Institutions, and Governance in Rural China." *The China Journal* no. 48 (July 2002): 1–27.

Vogel, F. Ezra. 2011. *Deng Xiaoping and the Transformation of China*, Cambridge, Massachusetts, and London, England: The Belknap Press of Harvard University Press.

Wade, Matt. 2011. "Slow Rise of India Will Be to Australia's Benefit." *Sydney Morning Herald*, April 11, 2011.

Wang Dan. 2013. *The Demoralization of Teachers: Crisis in a Rural School in China.* Lanham: Rowman and Littlefield.

Wang Hui. 2011. "Ah Q shengming zhong de liuge shunjian: Jinian zuowei kaiduan de xinhai geming" [The six moments of Ah Q's life: In memory of the beginning of the 1911 Xinhai Revolution]. *Xiandai zhongwen xuekan* no. 3 (June 20, 2011): 25–29.

Wang Jianxun. 2006. "Village Governance in Chinese History." Mini-Conference Paper, Indiana University, Spring 2006. http://www.indiana.edu/~workshop/publications/materials/ conference papers/wang.pdf.

Wang Su. 2011. "Chusheng renkou nan duo nv shao: 118:100 ling ren xinjing" [More male births than female birth: shocking ratio of 118:100]. *Caixin wang*, April 28, 2011. http://china.caixin.com/2011-04-28/100253520.html, accessed 5th May 2018.

Wang Zhongyu. 2015. "Zhongguo zai quanqiu jingji zhong de diwei" [China's position in the global economy]. *Geren tushu guan*, April 13, 2015. http://www.360doc.com/content/15/0413/08/4705243_462806107.shtml.

Wang Zhongyuan. 2011. "Xin shengdai nongmin gong yu zhongguo chengshi de kongzheng zhengzhi" [Contesting politics between the new generation of rural migrant workers and the urban centers]. *Wenhua zongheng*, May 19, 2011. http://www.21bcr.com/a/shiye/guancha/2011/0519/2787.html.

Watts, Jonathan. 2010. *When a Billion Chinese Jump: How China Will Save Mankind—Or Destroy It.* London: Faber and Faber.

Watts, Jonathan. 2011. "Rich List Fuels Thirst for Speed and Status." *Sydney Morning Herald*, July 23, 2011.

Webster, Norman. 2013. "Recollections of a China Correspondent." *Journal of American-East Asian Relations* 20, no. 2–3: 301–306.

Wei Ran. 2010. *Liangmin: Zhongguo nongcun shehui hui xiaoshi ma* [Grain citizens: Will rural China disappear?]. Shanghai: Fudan daxue chubanshe.

Wen Guanzhong. 2014. *Wu min wu di* [Our people without land]. Beijing: Dongfang chubanshe.

Wen, Philip. 2011. "Invest in China's Success, Says Hong Kong Banker." *Sydney Morning Herald*, March 18, 2011.

Wen Tiejun. 2013. *Ba ci weiji: Zhongguo de zhenshi jingyan, 1949–2009* [Eight crises: Lessons from China, 1949–2009]. Beijing: Dongfang chubanshe.

White, Chris. 2011. "Hot Labor Relations in Guangzhou." *Chris White Online* (blog), November 16, 2011. http://chriswhiteonline.org/2011/11/hot-labor-relations-in-guangzhou/.

Whitehouse, David. 2011. "A Rebellion Against Second-Class Status." SocialistWorker.org, June 28, 2011. https://socialistworker.org/2011/06/28/against-second-class-status.

Whyte, Martin King, Wang Feng, and Yong Cai. 2015. "Challenging Myths About China's One-Child Policy." *The China Journal* no. 74 (July 2015): 144–159.

Wilmsen, Brooke. 2016. "Expanding Capitalism in Rural China Through Land Acquisition and Land Reforms." *Journal of Contemporary China* 25, no. 101: 701–717.

Wines, Michael. 2011. "Once Banned, Dogs Reflect China's Rise." *The New York Times*, October 25, 2011.

Wong, Christine P. 2003. "Legacies of the Maoist Development Strategy: Rural Industrialization in China from the 1970s to the 1990s." In *The Chinese Cultural Revolution Reconsidered: Beyond Purge and Holocaust*, edited by Law Kam-Yee, 203–217. New York: Palgrave Macmillan.

Wu San. 2011. "Yige xianwei shuji de guiquan shiyan" [An experiment of land rights by a county party secretary]. *Wenhua zongheng*, January 10, 2011. http://www.21bcr.com/a/shiye/zaiminjian/2011/0110/2197.html.

Xie Tihong. 2011. "Bu yuan 'nong zhuan fei' yunhan zhengshi hua wenti" [Unwillingness to change from rural to urban implies problems for urbanization]. *Renmin wang*, August 19, 2008. http://finance.people.com.cn/15460133 html.

Xin Zilin. 2007. *Hong taiyang de yunluo: Qianqiu gongzui Mao Zedong* [The fall of the red sun: Merits and crimes of Mao Zedong]. Hong Kong: Shuzuofang.

Xu Hailiang. 2012. "1959–1961 'san nian ziran zaihai' gaishu" [A general description of three years of natural disasters, 1959–1961]. *Zhongguo jingji shilun*, March 15, 2012. https://web.archive.org/web/20130122185035/http://economy.guoxue.com/?p=5552.

Xu Youwei, and Chen Donglin, eds. 2015. *Xiao sanxian jianshe yanjiu luncong* [Research on building secondary three line industries]. Shanghai: Shanghai chubanshe.

Xu Youwei, and Chen Donglin, eds. 2016. *Xiao sanxian jianshe yanjiu lucong II* [Research on building secondary three line industries, Vol. II). Shanghai: Shanghai chubanshe.

Xu Qinghong, et al. 2011. *2011 nian zhongguo gongzhong pingjia ji zhongfu gonggong fuwu yanjiu baogao* [A report on the public evaluation of China's government and public service]. Beijing: Beijing Zero Index Information Consultancy Propriety Limited Company.

Yan Hairong. 2008. *New Masters, New Servants: Migration, Development, and Women Workers in China*. Durham, Duke University Press.

Yan Hairong. 2015. "Shijie dou zai fan mengshandou youxing, zhongguo nongye chulu zai hefang?" [Global Protest against Monsanto, what is the prospect of China's agriculture?]. Honggehui,http://www.szhgh.com/Article/health/zjy/201505/84820.html, accessed 15th August 2017.

Yan Hairong, and ChenYiyuan. 2013. "Huhuan renmin shiwu zhuquan: Cong dadou tanqi" [Call for food sovereignty: Start from soya beens]. http://wen. org.cn/modules/article/view. article.php?4000/c6, accessed 17th September 2017.

Yan Hairong, and Chen Yiyuan. 2015. "Zhongguo nongye zibenhua de tezheng he fangxiang: zixia ershang he zishang erxia de zibenhua dongli" [The special characteristics and direction of China's agricultural capitalization: The bottom-up and top-down driving forces of capitalization]. Opentimes, http://www.opentimes.cn/bencandy.php?fid=399&aid=1917, accessed 8 January 2016.

Ye Jingzhong, James Murray, and Wang Yihuan. 2005. *Left-Behind Children in Rural China*. Beijing: Social Sciences Academic Press.

Ye Jinzhong, and Pan Lun. 2008. *Bieyang tongnian: Zhongguo liushou ertong* [Differentiated childhoods: Children left behind in rural China]. Beijing: Shehukexue wenxian chubanshe.

Ye Yu. 2011a. "Xin shengdai nongmin gong, wu gen de yidai" [New generation of migrant workers, a generation without roots]. Originally published in *Nanfang zhoumo*, June 2011, archived on. http://blog.renren.com/ share/235777468/6928967275, accessed on 5th May 2018.

Ye Yu. 2011b. "Liushou ertong de weilai" [The future for left-behind children]. *Nanfang zhoumo*, June 16, 2011.

Yeates, Clancy. 2011. "Commodity prices 'unsustainable': S&P." *Sydney Morning Herald*, June 4, 2011.

Zhang Xiaobo, Fan Shenggen, Zhang Linxiu, et al. 2002. "Local Governance and Public Goods Provision in Rural China." Discussion paper no. 93, Environment and Production Technology Division, International Food Policy Research Institute, July 2002. http://ebrary.ifpri.org/cdm/ref/ collection/p15738coll2/id/57712.

Zhang Yanshuang, and John Harrison. 2013. "Pigs and pollution: China can't keep ignoring the environment." *The Conversation*, March 17, 2013. http:// theconversation.edu.au/pigs-and-pollution-china-cant-keep-ignoring-the-environment-12842.

Zhang Yulin. 2011. " 'Xiandaihua' zhihou de dongya nongye yu nongcun shehui: Riben, Hanguo, Taiwan de anli jiqi lishi yiwen." [Agriculture and rural society in post "modernized" East Asia: The historical implications of the cases of Japan, South Korea and Taiwan]. *Nanjing nongye daxue xuebao* no. 3 (2011): 1–8.

Zhao Hongxia. 2003. "Jinbao lianxian Guangdong Zhuhai — Jiudian mimou tuifan shishi" [*Jinbao live coverage from Guangdong and Zhuhai: The facts behind the hotel conspiracy*]. *Tianya shequ*, September 29, 2003. http://bbs. tianya.cn/post-funinfo-5380114-1.shtml.

Zheng Lijian et al. 2016. "Zhejiang sheng 18 wei xiangcun ganbu lianming zhi quanguo nongcun ganbu qunzhong de changyi" [An open letter proposal put forward to all of rural China jointly signed by 18 rural government officials from Zhejiang Province]. *Renmin shiwu zhuquan*, November 8, 2016. http://www.shiwuzq.com/portal.php?mod=view&aid=941.

Zhou Mian, and Zhang Zhilong. 2015. "Lirun quankao butie jiangli, nongye guimohua zhongzhi cheng xianjing" [Profit relies on subsidies and large scale farming is a trap]. Originally published in *Banyue tan*, August 3, 2015. http://www.wyzxwk.com/Article/sannong/2015/08/349038.html, accessed 5th May 2018.

Zhou Qiren. 2014. *Chengxiang zhongguo* [Urban-rural China]. Beijing: Zhongxin chubanshe.

Zhou Yingjing, Liang Jingwen, Huang Xian, et al. 2006. "Ershi ge xiangxun xingzou jilu: Jingti xin nongcun jianshe zhong san zhong qingxiang" [A travelogue of 20 villages: The risk of three tendencies in the New Countryside Construction Project]. *Sina*, August 22, 2006. http://news.sina.com.cn/c/2006-08-22/111310794920.shtml, accessed 5th May 2018.

Zhu Andong, and David M. Kotz. 2010. "The Dependence of China's Economic Growth on Exports and Investment." *Review of Radical Political Economics* 43, no. 1 (January 2010): 9–32.

Index